D1499293

SCHOOL SHOOTERS

To Katherine,

Best wishes,

Peter

Other Works by Peter Langman

NONFICTION

Why Kids Kill: Inside the Minds of School Shooters (2009)

Jewish Issues in Multiculturalism: A Handbook for Educators and Clinicians (1999)

THEATER

Monologues from the play *Hunger*

"Anorexia" and "Obesity Talks Back" in *Young Women's Monologues from Contemporary Plays #2* (ed. Gerald Lee Ratliff) (2008)

"My Battle with Bulimia" in *Audition Monologues for Young Women #2* (ed. Gerald Lee Ratliff) (2013)

POETRY

The Last Days of John Keats and Other Poems (2009)

SCHOOL SHOOTERS

Understanding High School, College, and Adult Perpetrators

Peter Langman, PhD

ROWMAN & LITTLEFIELD
Lanham • Boulder • New York • London

Published by Rowman & Littlefield
A wholly owned subsidiary of The Rowman & Littlefield Publishing Group,
Inc.
4501 Forbes Boulevard, Suite 200, Lanham, Maryland 20706
www.rowman.com

Unit A, Whitacre Mews, 26–34 Stannary Street, London SE11 4AB, United
Kingdom

British Library Cataloguing in Publication Information Available

Library of Congress Cataloging-in-Publication Data

Library of Congress Cataloging-in-Publication Data Available

ISBN 978-1-4422-3356-0 (cloth : alk. paper)—ISBN 978-1-4422-3357-7 (electronic)

∞ ™ The paper used in this publication meets the minimum requirements of
American National Standard for Information Sciences Permanence of Paper
for Printed Library Materials, ANSI/NISO Z39.48-1992.

Printed in the United States of America

CONTENTS

LIST OF FIGURES

LIST OF TABLES

ACKNOWLEDGMENTS

The place of honor in my acknowledgments goes to my late agent, John Ware. John represented my previous book and was in the midst of promoting this book when he became ill and died. This was a profound loss.

In the wake of John's death, a friend and colleague of his, Leah Spiro, came to my rescue. She believed in this project, worked hard to help me refine the proposal, and was tireless in pursuing and obtaining a publisher. She has my deepest gratitude.

Thanks also to my editor at Rowman & Littlefield, Suzanne Staszak-Silva, for seeing the value in this book and shepherding me through the process from manuscript drafts to publication.

A special thanks to Birgit Laramie for translating German articles and documents on Robert Steinhäuser and Tim Kretschmer and to Iury Roger Painelli and Danilo Françoso Tedeschi for translating Portuguese articles on Wellington de Oliveira.

Thanks to Dr. Brian Van Brunt for serving as a sounding board regarding issues of campus safety.

Thanks also to Dr. Dian Williams and *Forensic Digest* for allowing me to adapt my article "School Shootings: The Warning Signs" for use within chapter 9. The article appeared in the 2012 Winter/Spring issue of *Forensic Digest* and is reprinted with permission of *Forensic Digest*.

I have also adapted material from several of my own articles that are available on my website, including "Luke Woodham: The Search for Justification," "Adult School Shooters," "Expanding the Sample: Five School Shooters," "Two Finnish School Shooters," and "School Shooters: Nine Brief Sketches."

Thanks to Dr. Mary Ann Swiatek, who read drafts of several chapters and provided feedback.

Thanks to my daughter, Anna Langman, for her reviewing and editing of the manuscript.

Thanks to my son, Joshua Langman, as well as Dan W. Barron for their work on my website, www.schoolshooters.info, which is something of a companion to this book and the repository of many of the documents I used in my research.

Finally, my utmost gratitude to my wife, Dr. Madeleine Langman, who provided in-depth proofreading and editorial feedback, as well as ongoing support and encouragement.

INTRODUCTION

In December of 2012, while I was deep in the writing of this book, there was another shooting, more horrific than most, due to its magnitude and the fact that the killer was an adult gunning down six- and seven-year-old children. On December 14, 2012, Adam Lanza killed his mother at home and then massacred twenty-six staff and students at Sandy Hook Elementary School in Newtown, Connecticut. Even after years of studying such attacks, I find that I have not become hardened to the horror. Instead, I seem more vulnerable to the suffering of others, my heart sinking with the heaviness of "No, not again," as we as a nation and a world community one more time are left to ponder the causes of rampage attacks and what can be done to prevent large-scale violence in our schools.

I have grappled with these issues since April 30, 1999, just ten days after Eric Harris and Dylan Klebold attacked Columbine High School, when a sixteen-year-old boy was admitted to the psychiatric hospital where I worked. He was considered a potential school shooter, and it was my job to assess his risk for mass murder. Not long after this, another potential school shooter came through the hospital, and then another, and so on for more than ten years. There wasn't a flood, but a steady, disturbing trickle of these cases.

I kept a file of these potential school shooters, studied what they had in common and how they differed, and compared them to the cases I read about in the news. Over the years, I have studied dozens of school shooters, compiled charts and graphs, and looked for patterns among the data. Out of necessity, I became a reluctant researcher of mass murderers in order to do the best job I could in working with patients, recommending appropriate treatment, and keeping them—and their communities—safe.

Preventing rampage attacks, however, is a complex task. Despite the facts that schools are more safety-conscious now than ever before, and that the perpetrators often leave a trail of warning signs, school shootings continue to occur. If we are to be more successful in preventing these attacks, we need to understand who these shooters are, what drives them to kill, and how we can spot them before it's too late. This book is the culmination of many years of research and is my attempt to answer these urgent questions.

COMMENTS ON THE CASES

In this book I present forty-eight school shooters in depth and briefly reference others. There are some perpetrators I do not mention at all. I only included shooters in my sample if there was sufficient information available to gain insight into their minds and motives.

The purpose of the case descriptions is to provide enough information to classify the shooters within my typology, shed some light on the factors leading to the attacks, and allow for comparisons with other shooters. The amount of available information varied greatly from case to case; some attacks were very well documented, while others received scant news coverage after the incident.

I provide more background information for cases that are less well known and for which information is harder to find. In more well-known cases, such as the Columbine killers, I concentrate primarily on their personality dynamics, with less attention to their life circumstances. More in-depth information about their lives is available in my previous book, *Why Kids Kill: Inside the Minds of School Shooters*, my other writings, and through other resources.

Despite the attention many of these cases have received, there are still questions that remain unanswered. How badly was a shooter abused at home or bullied at school? Which of his many statements can be believed? Is there corroboration from other sources? I have worked hard to sort out these issues, but the conclusions are often tentative.

In some cases, basic information cannot be established. In the attack at Columbine High School, it is not possible to say with certainty whether Eric Harris or Dylan Klebold killed certain people, particularly when both shot the same person. This makes it impossible to definitively report the number of victims killed and wounded by each perpetrator. A similar problem exists for the Jonesboro shooting, where it is not known for certain which of the two shooters—Andrew Golden or Mitchell Johnson—shot which victims.

Even tallying the wounded can be problematic. Different sources sometimes have different figures, depending on how they count the victims. Also, in some instances the identities of the wounded were not made public, limiting the completeness of the data. For example, Wellington de Oliveira reportedly targeted girls, who constituted the majority of the fatalities. Not knowing if those who were wounded were male or female means that any attempt to tally the number of victims who were targeted because of their gender is incomplete.

For the sake of continuity, within each chapter, or section within a chapter, I present the shootings in chronological order.

COMMENTS ON DIAGNOSIS

Psychiatric diagnosis is highly subjective. Despite medical advances, there are no biological tests to determine if someone is schizophrenic, psychopathic, traumatized, or depressed. Brain scans can't do it, and neither can blood tests, DNA analysis, or anything else. The same individual could be evaluated by multiple mental health professionals and receive different diagnoses from each.

I have not personally evaluated any of the shooters presented in this book. My classifications are based on the available information, which sometimes includes mental health evaluations conducted either before or after the perpetrators committed their attacks. For some shooters, the evidence very clearly suggests a particular diagnosis, but in other cases this is less clear. The conclusions presented here are open to debate, and the release of any new information may necessitate a reconsideration of my conclusions.

COMMENTS ON SYMPTOMS AND PATTERNS

I explore many possible factors that may contribute to rampage attacks. Many of these factors are true of millions of people who never commit violence. For example, having family members in the military was a common factor for many shooters. This does not mean that having relatives who served their country causes school shootings. It is, however, a factor that shows up repeatedly in the lives of the shooters and thus may be significant, particularly for those shooters who sought military careers but failed in their aspirations.

Similarly, a particular diagnosis, mental health problem, or behavior may be common among school shooters. This does not imply that anyone with these diagnoses, problems, or behaviors is at risk for committing a rampage attack. The vast majority of people who are psychotic, psychopathic, or traumatized do not commit murder.

In addition, some perpetrators reported paranormal experiences, which can be a symptom of schizotypal personality disorder. This does not mean that everyone who has paranormal experiences is schizotypal or that they are potential killers. In the context of other facts about these individuals, however, this may indicate a tenuous connection with reality and may be important in understanding the psychology of the shooters.

I

LAYING THE FOUNDATION

This is not a simple topic. Many people seek to reduce school shootings to a bite-sized explanatory chunk, but the phenomenon defies easy analysis. There is no one cause of school shootings, there is no one intervention that will prevent school shootings, and there is no one profile of a school shooter. Apart from stating the obvious—that school shooters are people who use guns to shoot other people in educational settings—it is hard to make a statement that is true of all school shooters. Despite the frequent use of sound bites and simplifications, school shooters cannot be reduced to a stereotype.

The most common error in discussing school shooters is the assumption that they are a homogeneous group of people—that they can be lumped together and discussed as if they were essentially the same. This assumption simply doesn't hold up to scrutiny. There have been targeted attacks against specific individuals, random attacks against strangers, and attacks that included targeted as well as random victims. There have been narcissistic shooters who sought fame and a sadistic thrill, and there have been desperate, depressed youths lashing out against the world. Some shooters sought vengeance for real or perceived wrongs, and some believed their attacks were justified by political ideology or paranoid delusions.

The perpetrators presented in this book range from eleven-year-old Andrew Golden, who attacked his middle school, to sixty-two-year-old Biswanath Halder, who stormed a building at his former university; from isolated, barely functioning Adam Lanza to Harvard graduate and mother of four, Professor Amy Bishop; from sixteen-year-old, thrill-seeking Brenda Spencer to thirty-year-old, bitterly disappointed and ruthless Laurie Dann; from grandiose and sadistic Eric Harris to his depressed and desperately lonely partner in crime, Dylan Klebold.

All of these people committed school shootings, but their personalities, family dynamics, life histories, and motivations were dramatically diverse. Despite these variations, there are two things that all these attacks had in common. First, they occurred in schools or school-related settings. Second, the perpetrators intended to kill multiple people, though they did not always accomplish this.

There are many widespread misconceptions about school shooters. It is often said that they are middle class, white males, and loners. Rampages have been blamed on media violence, peer harassment, psychiatric medications, poor parenting, and easy gun access. Even when there is some truth to these ideas, it is never the whole truth. Yes, some shooters were loners and some were bullied, but so are millions of students who never go on rampages. Yes, some shooters had dysfunctional parents, but so do many other youngsters. Simplistic statements about the identity of rampage shooters and the causes of their attacks fail to capture the complicated reality of the phenomenon. It is necessary to explore the lives of each shooter to see the complexity of factors that contributed to their violence.

Attempting to make sense of the lives of forty-eight school shooters without any guiding principles or structure, however, is overwhelming. There are so many differences among them that it might seem impossible to draw meaningful conclusions. Interestingly, dividing them into various groupings allows remarkable patterns to emerge.

THREE POPULATIONS OF SCHOOL SHOOTERS

There is no reason to assume that the motivations of teenage shooters are the same as those who commit rampage attacks in their twenties, thirties, forties, fifties, or sixties. Nor should it be assumed that the same factors cause some people to attack their own schools and others to attack schools with which they have no connection. These distinctions are useful in dividing shooters into three populations.

One population consists of *secondary school shooters*. They were either secondary school students at the time of their rampage or they carried out their attack at a secondary school they had attended within the last three years. Another population, *college shooters*, committed their attacks at colleges or universities. Most of these perpetrators were current or recent undergraduate or graduate students. Three, however, were university employees. Their attacks could be viewed as workplace violence rather than school shootings; because they occurred on campuses, however, they are relevant to violence prevention in higher education. I call the last group *aberrant adult shooters*. These perpetrators were at least nineteen years old and had no current or recent connection, as either students or employees, to the schools they attacked.

THREE PSYCHOLOGICAL TYPES OF SCHOOL SHOOTERS

In addition to dividing the sample into three populations, I also discuss them in terms of the typology I established in my last book, *Why Kids Kill: Inside the Minds of School Shooters*. The typology is based on psychological characteristics, categorizing the perpetrators as psychopathic, psychotic, or traumatized. Though the three types are explained in detail in the following chapters, a brief statement about each is in order.

Psychopathic shooters were profoundly narcissistic, arrogant, and entitled; they lacked empathy and met their needs at others' expense. In contrast, *psychotic shooters* suffered from schizophrenia or a related disorder. They were out of touch with reality to varying degrees, experiencing hallucinations or delusions. Unlike the psychopathic and psychotic shooters, who generally came from well-functioning, intact families, *traumatized shooters* endured chronic abuse as children. They grew up in violent, severely dysfunctional homes.

These three categories do not, by themselves, explain school shootings, because the vast majority of people in these categories do not commit rampage attacks. By recognizing the differences between these types, however, we can begin to understand the perpetrators and why they might be particularly vulnerable to stresses such as bullying, romantic rejections, and academic failures.

For instance, although most students handle rejections and failures without becoming killers, a student with a psychopathic personality may react with fury to anything that seems like a put-down. Alternatively, if someone has paranoid delusions, harassment or rejection will be perceived through the lens of his psychosis, exaggerating the magnitude of the situation. Finally, a child traumatized by abuse may experience bullying, school failure, or discipline as the final victimization that spurs him or her into violence.

Beyond the typology, there were other influences that shaped the behavior of school shooters. These factors will be discussed throughout the book as the lives of the shooters are presented and compared. All the school shooters presented in this book had a history of trauma, psychopathic personalities, or symptoms of a schizophrenia-spectrum disorder. When life's stresses became overwhelming, the result was rampage.

2

PSYCHOPATHIC SECONDARY SCHOOL SHOOTERS

A WORD ON PSYCHOPATHIC PERSONALITIES

From the days of Shakespeare to contemporary Hollywood, audiences have been fascinated by portrayals of people without a conscience. Psychopaths—or sociopaths, as they are sometimes called—seem like a fundamentally different kind of human being. Unfortunately, despite years of research into psychopathy, it remains an elusive concept. For example, psychopathy is not a formal psychiatric diagnosis. The closest official diagnosis is antisocial personality disorder, but this is not synonymous with psychopathy. Adding to the confusion, there are many types of psychopaths, from violent criminals to white-collar psychopaths.

I draw on the work of several researchers to shed light on psychopathic personalities. Dr. Samuel Yochelson and Dr. Stanton Samenow wrote about what they termed the *criminal personality*, which is akin to psychopathy. Though not all criminals are psychopaths, people with a criminal personality share many features with psychopaths.

Dr. Robert Hare has identified many common traits in psychopaths, including deceitfulness, "impression management," grandiosity, a strong drive for excitement, and a lack of empathy, guilt, and remorse.[1] Using a different approach, Dr. Theodore Millon and Dr. Roger Davis identified subtypes of psychopaths based on different combinations of personality disorders. For example, someone with narcissistic and antisocial traits will differ from someone with sadistic and antisocial traits.[2]

Drawing on the findings of these experts, I emphasize several core features. First, psychopaths are egocentric—they live for themselves and meet their own needs with no regard for the impact their behavior has on others. Psychopaths are also often egotistical, with an inflated sense of their own importance and self-worth. Focused on themselves, they lack a normal capacity for empathy, guilt, and remorse. They not only do not care if they hurt people, but they may experience a rush of euphoria by doing so. This is sadism—the thrill of having power over others.

Psychopaths are often chronic liars who are very good at *impression management*, meaning they make a good impression while hiding their true intentions. This is what makes con artists successful. Charming, witty, and at times remarkably charismatic, they use these abilities to deceive their victims.

Psychopaths march to the beat of their own drum; they have no regard for social norms, morality, ethics, or the law. They are a law unto themselves. As a result, they often have a particular dislike for those who represent authority, whether police officers, schoolteachers, or their own parents. Psychopaths are impervious to fear. Nothing fazes them. They can remain calm in situations that would overwhelm other people.

One of the most striking features of psychopaths is their inability to take responsibility for their own behavior. Even when they admit to their crimes, they tend to blame their victims and paint themselves as "the good guy." They often experience punishment as injustice, feeling that they are being wronged. This, apparently, is a consequence of their narcissism—in their mental world, they ought to be able to do whatever they want. They are ultimately entitled.

Their narcissism is often so fragile, however, that they are hypersensitive to anything that is perceived as a slight. Yochelson and Samenow discuss this extreme reactivity to what they call *put downs*: "Wherever [the psychopath] goes, he is vulnerable, in that anything that is not in line with his inflated image of himself as a powerful person is viewed as a threat. To be told what to do by others is a putdown. To have to ask a question of someone is a [put down], because it reveals ignorance. . . . The criminal is put down by any adverse event over which he does not have control."[3]

Understanding this dynamic is essential because it sheds light on why psychopaths felt justified in killing girls who rejected them, teachers who failed them, or anyone else who frustrated the gratification of their desires.

ATTACKS BY PSYCHOPATHIC SECONDARY SCHOOL SHOOTERS

Robert Poulin

"I don't want to die before I have had the pleasure of fucking some girl."

Date: October 27, 1975   **Killed**: 2
Age: 18   **Wounded**: 6
School: St. Pius X High School   **Outcome**: Suicide
Location: Ottawa, Canada

Robert Poulin's life revolved around sex and violence—at least, he wanted it to. He fantasized about robbing people at gunpoint, as well as committing arson, rape, and murder. On the last day of his life, he committed three of these four crimes.[4]

Poulin grew up with guns in the house and was trained in the use of firearms. His father was a former pilot with the Royal Canadian Air Force who had left the military and become a schoolteacher. Poulin aspired to follow in his father's military footsteps. Unfortunately, he was born with a pigeon chest (pectus carinatum), a deformity that results in a convex chest. He also had poor vision, which interfered with his desire to be a pilot.

Poulin went to church regularly, delivered newspapers, and worked in a pizza shop. Behind the facade of normality, however, Poulin was obsessed with sex and pornography. His collection of pornography included 250 books and magazines, as well as a scrapbook filled with photographs of nude men and women.[5] He maintained an index of pornographic magazines and kept a detailed record of his ratings of photographs and advertisements: "Police found eleven looseleaf [*sic*] binder pages containing nearly one thousand separate entries on pictures and ads."[6]

Poulin also had books on bondage that contained photographs of women handcuffed to bedposts. After his attack, police found four pairs of handcuffs in his room. They also found women's lingerie, an inflatable sex doll, Poulin's writing about his disappointment with the sex doll, a condom-type vibrator, and the names of eighteen girls. Several of these girls had received obscene telephone calls that stopped after Poulin's death.[7]

Poulin apparently engaged in other criminal sexual behavior beyond his alleged harassing phone calls. There were complaints of indecent assaults and attempted rapes along the paths of an apartment building near his home. The descriptions of the assailant fit Poulin. Some women reported that the assailant wore nothing but a balaclava (a type of hat covering the head and lower portion of the face). Poulin had written in his diary about wearing a balaclava if and when he raped someone.[8]

Poulin applied to the military and was devastated by his rejection for officer training when he was found to be "immature."[9] Following this, Poulin joined a government-sponsored militia where he received training in a range of military skills. In the militia, he "sat alone in the camp lunch room staring into space, and the only time he talked to anyone was when they talked to him."[10] He became more engaged with his fellow soldiers over time but remained low-key. If other soldiers joked around, Poulin might smile, but he did not laugh.

Poulin was depressed and intermittently suicidal before his rampage. On April 7, 1975, he wrote in his journal that he was suicidal but added, "I don't want to die before I have had the pleasure of fucking some girl."[11] In the same entry, he recorded his discovery of a sex doll that would allow him to simulate having intercourse. He wrote, "Now I no longer think that I will have to rape a girl, and am unsure as to whether or not I will still commit suicide."[12]

The same diary entry contained his thoughts about two illegal acts. He noted, "I have a half hatched idea about using the gun to rob people at night."[13] It is not known if he attempted this. More disturbingly, he wanted to make his family suffer. He considered murdering his parents but decided instead to burn down their house. "I was going to make sure, though," he wrote, "that I burned the place down soon after payday so that they would lose the largest possible amount of money. I was also planning on having all my earthly possessions with me so that they wouldn't gain one red cent from me."[14] He gave no hint as to why he wanted to make his family suffer.

Nor did he record why he wanted to die. He wrote about death as something positive, commenting, "death is the true bliss."[15] His suicidal feelings, however, may have resulted from his shyness. As early as September 1972 (over three years before his rampage), Poulin wrote, "There are some girls at school that I would love to be good friends with but I know that I am still too shy to go up and talk to any of them. I wish I could overcome this fear of women."[16] Perhaps Poulin overcame his fear of women by objectifying them as sexual objects and trying to force himself on them. He had a crush on a girl named Kim Rabot, but she was dating another boy.[17] On the day of his attack, Poulin lured her into the house, handcuffed her to his bed, raped her, and stabbed her to death.

Poulin maintained his composure under tremendous stress. His bedroom was in the basement, separated only by a curtain from the rest of the cellar. On the morning of the attack, while Kim Rabot was dying or dead, Mrs. Poulin came down to the basement. She asked if she could talk to him, and he said, "yeah, but don't come in."[18] She told him she had scheduled an eye appointment for him. About an hour later, Poulin came upstairs and asked his mother for a peanut butter sandwich. He sat down and watched a quiz show as he ate. His mother noticed nothing unusual about him.

If Poulin had been able to feel any guilt or remorse, he would have been overcome by emotion after the attack. But the casualness of his behavior after having raped and killed a girl he knew indicates a remarkable lack of empathy. After he ate his sandwich and his mother went out, Poulin did what he said he would do: he set the house on fire. Then he went to school, shot random students, and killed himself.

* * *

Poulin was not charming and charismatic, but he managed to hide his dark side, suggesting excellent impression management. Using the personality types identified by Millon, Poulin fits the description of a "nomadic antisocial." Such people exist on the periphery of society, lacking the social skills necessary to meet their needs. They are bitterly unhappy. They lack empathy and are willing to violate the rights of others to gratify themselves. According to Millon, such people may act out "their pent-up frustrations in brutal assaults or sexual attacks upon those weaker than themselves."[19] This is exactly what Poulin did.

But why rape and kill a girl he knew? Perhaps the words of David Berkowitz, the notorious serial killer, can shed some light:

> I was literally singing to myself on my way home, after the killing. The tension, the desire to kill a woman had built up in me to such explosive proportions that when I finally pulled the trigger, all the pressures, all the tensions, hatred, had just vanished, dissipated, but only for a short time. I had no sexual feelings. It was only hostile aggression. . . . I wanted to destroy her because of what she represented . . . a pretty girl, a threat to me, to my masculinity. . . . I couldn't handle her sexually.[20]

Like Berkowitz, Poulin felt powerless in the presence of an attractive girl. He lacked the skills to engage her in a mutual relationship. This was a threat to his identity, to his masculinity. The very existence of an attractive girl beyond his reach was a put down to Poulin—it made him feel powerless. In response, he obliterated the threat by killing Kim Rabot.

Poulin clearly lacked empathy and met his own needs at the expense of others. Also, tricking a girl he knew into his home and then binding her, raping her, and stabbing her fourteen times was deceptive and sadistic. Similarly, his idea to rob people at gunpoint suggests that he wanted power over others—not just sexually, as in rape, but also by making them cower in fear. Poulin's rampage differed from other school shootings in that it included a sexual assault, arson, and murder at his home.

Brenda Spencer

"I just did it for the fun of it."

Date: January 29, 1979   **Killed**: 2
Age: 16   **Wounded**: 9
School: Cleveland Elementary   **Outcome**: Surrendered,
School   prison
Location: San Diego, CA

At 5'1" and eighty-one pounds, Brenda Spencer was not an intimidating presence—unless she was describing her dream of being a sniper and her obsession with killing cops. Unfortunately, she fulfilled her dream. Spencer committed a school shooting from her home, gunning down people at her former elementary school across the street. She killed the principal and a janitor and wounded eight children and a police officer.

Spencer was the youngest of three children. In 1972, when she was nine, her parents separated and subsequently divorced. Her brother and sister chose to live with their father; the judge wanted to keep the children together, so Spencer went with them. By 1976, Spencer's siblings had moved out of the home.

Mr. Spencer was a conscientious father who spent a great deal of time with Brenda.[21] He was a navy veteran who had trained his daughter to become an outstanding marksman. For Christmas 1978, her father gave her a .22 caliber semiautomatic rifle with a telescopic sight. She soon told friends she planned to turn her garage into a fortress. She also talked about an upcoming event that would be "big" and "will be on television and everything."[22] On January 29, 1979, she committed her attack, shooting at the school across the street from the safety of her own home.

The most unusual aspect of Spencer's attack was her remarkable nonchalance. There was no indication of rage, anguish, or distress. Rather, she seemed to regard murder as an entertaining activity. A quick-thinking reporter identified the Spencer home as one that was near the school. He called the house in hopes of finding a witness to the attack, not knowing he was calling the perpetrator's home. Spencer answered the telephone, giggling and bantering with the reporter. She said, "I just started shooting. That's it. I just did it for the fun of it."[23] The reporter described her as calm and matter-of-fact. When told she may have killed three or four people, she said, "Is that all?"[24] Before hanging up, Spencer said, "I have to go now. I shot a pig [police officer], I think, and I want to shoot more."[25] Even the reporter's interruption did not deter her.

It is noteworthy that Spencer specifically wanted to kill police. She reportedly enjoyed seeing cops shot in television shows. She and a friend, Brent Fleming, whose father was a police officer, talked at length about strategies for killing police.[26] When an officer got her on the telephone, Spencer continued to banter and laugh, saying, "I'm having a lot of fun."[27] She seemed excited about being taken out in handcuffs. She asked about being on television, and, when told that there were reporters in the area, she said, "That's great!"[28] This was a sixteen-year-old girl in an armed standoff, surrounded by police and SWAT teams, with helicopters circling above her house. Most people would have been shaken to their core, but she was completely cool, unruffled, and pleased with herself. The cool calm of a psychopath.

Prior to the attack, she had used a BB gun to shoot out windows at her elementary school. She also had broken into the school with Brent Fleming, with one or both of them committing vandalism inside the school.[29] Fleming said Spencer had talked to him about doing "major things, such as sniping or burning or blowing things up."[30] Though Fleming had eventually moved away, he'd visited Spencer only two days before the attack. She had told him, "Wait until Monday, and see what I'm going to do. It might even be big enough to make the news."[31] Spencer's desire to become well known was not new. Long before the attack, she had "stated on occasion that she would be famous."[32]

Spencer once had a "major fight" with her father, "concerning whether she would have to go to school. She said it was boring."[33] Though her sister thought their father was too easy on Brenda, she also commented, "My dad, however, required her to conform somewhat to house rules. I think she was a headache to him in that she often talked back."[34] When Spencer was talking with the police officer during the standoff, he asked if she had a message for her father. She said, "Yes, I do. Tell my dad to go get screwed." She had no message for her mother, but added, "I don't like her either."[35] She might have been angry about their divorce seven years earlier, or she may have resented them simply because they were authority figures. Her best friend said Spencer "hated all authority."[36] Brent Fleming's mother commented that Spencer and her son "Used to sit around and talk about what a rotten place the world is . . . about how everybody hassles you—But nobody hassled them."[37] For psychopaths, even the normal expectations of parents and teachers can be intolerable.

Spencer's psychopathic behavior continued after the attack. Her mother reported that while in prison, Spencer "mentioned she was being kept in room confinement, because the authorities had found a knife in her cell. She said it took her two weeks to make it. She did not plan on using it. She just wanted to break the rules."[38]

Maybe she did plan on using the knife, or maybe not. Either way, she demonstrated a flagrant disregard for prison regulations.

Spencer's deceitful and manipulative style was apparent during two parole hearings where she denied responsibility for her actions, fabricated stories, and tried to make herself the victim. At her first hearing, fourteen years after the attack, Spencer claimed she had been high during the shooting, with hallucinations of commandos attacking her house. She said she'd shot people in self-defense.[39] This is contradicted by two sources. First, her conversations with the reporter and police officer during the attack were completely at odds with this. Second, after her arrest she tested negative for drugs and alcohol.

Spencer also claimed that the children she shot were actually shot by police. In reality, all victims were hit before the police arrived; the police never fired a shot. Spencer's statements were not only false but also contradictory: she claimed that she hadn't shot anyone and also that she'd shot people because she'd been hallucinating.

At her second parole hearing, twenty-two years after the attack, Spencer claimed that her father beat her and committed incest.[40] Whether this occurred is unknown, but there is no evidence that Mr. Spencer mistreated any of his children. When the parole board commented that Spencer never mentioned incest in her counseling sessions, she said she tried but her therapists ignored her. The board was not convinced.[41]

In addition, Spencer said she thought her father gave her a gun because he wanted her to kill herself. She also said, "I had failed in every other suicide attempt. I thought if I shot at the cops, they would shoot me."[42] First, according to her sister, Spencer begged her father for a long time to buy her a rifle. Her mother confirmed this, stating, "Brenda told me that is what she wanted."[43] Second, I have found no reference to any suicide attempts by Spencer, and there is no indication that she was suicidal at the time of the shooting. In fact, she was having fun and made no effort to kill herself. Finally, if she had wanted the police to kill her, she could have committed the attack outdoors instead of from inside her home.

Spencer's claims during her parole hearings demonstrate her dishonesty, refusal to take responsibility, and desire to be seen as a victim. Psychopaths often pose as misunderstood victims. Dr. Martha Stout, in her book about sociopaths, observed, "The most universal behavior of unscrupulous people is not directed, as one might imagine, at our fearfulness. It is, perversely, an appeal to our sympathy."[44]

※ ※ ※

Brenda Spencer seems to be the most cold-blooded school shooter. Other school shooters experienced various degrees of emotional distress. Many were depressed; virtually all were angry. She alone acted without any hint of anguish or rage. She seemingly enjoyed shooting people, got a kick out of seeing wounded children writhing on the ground, and was particularly excited about shooting at police. There was no element of revenge in her attack—just a sadistic thrill and narcissistic delight at her instant fame.

Spencer appears to be an example of a *risk-taking psychopath*. These psychopaths are thrill seekers, people for whom ordinary life is dull beyond endurance and who need extreme excitement to make them feel alive. Millon and Davis described them as "substantially fearless, unblanched by events that most people experience as dangerous or frightening . . . dauntless, intrepid, bold, and audacious."[45] This aptly describes Spencer's excitement about being surrounded by police, helicopters, and SWAT teams.

It is interesting that Spencer had previously vandalized her elementary school. Perhaps her attacks expressed her disdain for any institution that put expectations and limits on her behavior. Her hostility toward police, as well as toward her parents, indicates her rejection of those who represented authority.

Barry Loukaitis

*"It's like I pictured myself doing it or something. I never really
pictured myself doing anything else."*

Date: February 2, 1996   **Killed**: 3
Age: 14   **Wounded**: 1
School: Frontier Junior High   **Outcome**: Held class hostage.
School   Overpowered. In prison
Location: Moses Lake, WA

Mrs. Loukaitis confided too much in her son. Her marriage had fallen
apart, and her husband became involved with another woman. Mrs.
Loukaitis planned to get revenge against her husband and his girlfriend;
she wanted to tie them up, tell them how much they'd hurt her, show
them that she had a gun, frighten them into thinking she was going to
kill them, and then shoot herself.[46] She said, "If he didn't remember my
life, I was going to make him remember my death."[47] She shared this
plan with her son, and on the last weekend in January, told him that she
was going to kill herself on February 14—Valentine's Day—because
she knew she could catch her husband with his girlfriend.[48] On February 2, just a few days after she told Loukaitis her plan, he committed his
school shooting.

What was Loukaitis like prior to his rampage? Through his elementary school years, he was reportedly outgoing and popular. He served
on student council in sixth grade, and numerous friends visited his
house.[49] In seventh grade, he'd become more withdrawn, and fewer
friends came over. His mother said he had a bad temper and would hit
walls in anger. According to his parents, Loukaitis's withdrawal coin-
cided with the onset of their marital problems.[50] It may also have coin-
cided with the onset of puberty.

During middle school, Loukaitis was arrogant and intimidating.
When he crossed paths with his peers, he would "curse them, tell them
to shut up or order them out of his way."[51] He loved the random
violence in the movie *Natural Born Killers* and liked to quote from it:
"Murder is pure. People make it unpure."[52] He talked about his desire
to kill somebody before he died. Loukaitis was drawn to the idea of
murder, saying "It would be cool to kill people . . . to try to get away
with it."[53]

He also felt superior to his peers and viewed murder as a way of
eliminating inferior people. He told a female classmate, "Some people
don't deserve to live; some people should just die or be killed."[54] Later
on, Loukaitis yelled at the girl and asked, "Do you think you deserve to

live?"[55] Murder was also a way of getting back at people. In seventh grade Loukaitis asked a girl out; she turned him down. When they crossed paths in ninth grade, Loukaitis said he was going to kill her.[56]

Loukaitis focused his hostility on two authority figures—a married couple who both worked at the school. Mr. Caires was the vice principal, and Mrs. Caires taught algebra. Two days before the shooting, Mr. Caires gave Loukaitis detention for repeated tardiness. Loukaitis told his friends he hated Mr. Caires. He also talked about hating Mrs. Caires and made threatening comments about her.

On February 2, Loukaitis entered his algebra class and shot Manuel Vela, Mrs. Caires, and two other students. There were reports that Vela had harassed Loukaitis, yet Loukaitis himself denied this, stating, "It's not like he [Vela] was a bully or anything."[57] Loukaitis, however, reportedly had a crush on Vela's girlfriend. She said that Loukaitis would stare at her and Vela would tell him to stop, but the two boys never tangled. It seems likely that Loukaitis shot Vela out of jealousy.

Having shot four people, Loukaitis held the class hostage. During this time, Loukaitis was said to be at ease. When the police arrived and wanted to negotiate with him, he reportedly was not afraid but annoyed.[58] Loukaitis was apprehended after a teacher ripped a gun out of Loukaitis's hands. Once in custody, a detective commented on how unruffled Loukaitis was: "He was acting shockingly calm. . . . I expected to see a look of remorse."[59] An officer commented that when he read Loukaitis his rights, "He looked up at me and cracked a smile and said, 'I know my rights, man.'"[60] His taped confession was so matter-of-fact that a reporter said, "He could have been describing an errand to the grocery store."[61] After giving his confession, he curled up in his cell and had a nap.[62] Later that day, Loukaitis's father described him as "Vicious. No emotion. Not crying."[63] A psychiatrist who evaluated him after the attack commented that his "eerie, weird icy-cold emotion . . . gave me the willies."[64]

❋ ❋ ❋

Loukaitis, like other psychopathic shooters, had a particular dislike for authority figures, including the vice principal and a teacher. Though Loukaitis had talked about going on a killing spree for a long time, the dissolution of his family and his mother's impending suicide may have been the immediate triggers to the attack.

Loukaitis's interest in going on a killing spree for fun suggests the personality of the *risk-taking psychopath*. This subtype pursues antisocial activities "for the sense of feeling alive and involved in life, rather than for such purposes as material gain or defense of reputation."[65]

Rather than do this, however, Loukaitis killed people who apparently made him feel small—his teacher and a boy dating the girl he was interested in. This suggests the *malevolent psychopath*, a subtype that is "particularly vindictive and hostile," with "a cold-blooded ruthlessness, an intense desire to gain revenge."[66]

Andrew Golden

"You're all going to die."

Date: March 24, 1998   **Killed**: 3
Age: 11   **Wounded**: 7
School: Westside Middle   **Outcome**: Apprehended. In
School   prison until turned 21, then
Location: Jonesboro, AR   released

When the children in Andrew Golden's class were asked to draw a picture representing their families, Golden drew guns. When asked to write a skit, he wrote one about guns. Guns were the center of Golden's world—after all, his parents led a local pistol club and his grandfather was a game warden and hunter. Golden handled guns before he could walk, received his first gun as a toddler, and had a rifle at age six.[67]

Golden may have been particularly drawn to guns because of his small size. His grandfather noted that although Golden wanted to play football and basketball, he was "too slight for one, too short for the other. Shooting was what he did best."[68] At the time of his attack, Golden was eleven years old and "barely four feet tall."[69]

Guns were the center of his world, and he was the center of his parents' world. Golden's mother had had a tubal ligation after having two children with a previous husband. When she remarried, she had the procedure reversed so she could have a child with her new husband; when their son, Andrew ("Drew") was born, he was treated as their extra-special child. Multiple people reported that Golden was "overindulged and rarely subject to discipline" and that his parents "seemed to feel that he could do no wrong."[70]

When Golden was very young he cursed in front of his family; his father and grandfather laughed and thought it was cute. A neighbor saw it differently, commenting that when Golden was five years old, "You'd walk by and he'd be cussing, and he'd flip you off."[71] Based on interviews conducted by Dr. Katherine Newman's research team, Golden's parents "were defensive when he got in trouble and actively intervened to prevent Westside Middle School from using what administrators regarded as appropriate punishment. . . . If Andrew did poorly in a particular class, or got in trouble with one teacher, his family just arranged for him to be moved to another."[72]

From an early age, Golden was impervious to authority. In first grade, a teacher confiscated a toy gun Golden brought to school. Golden was warned he'd really be in trouble if he touched the gun. Unfazed, he persuaded a peer to retrieve the toy. At recess, Golden filled the gun with gravel and mud and shot it at a girl, hitting her in the eye.[73]

Years later, Golden persuaded another peer to collude in antisocial behavior, convincing his thirteen-year-old friend Mitchell Johnson to join him in a school rampage. The boys stole Johnson's parents' van and took guns belonging to Golden's father and grandfather. Golden pulled a fire alarm so people would evacuate the school. The two boys then gunned people down from a hill overlooking the school.

Golden's sense of entitlement might shed light on his motive. Mitchell Johnson said, "Andrew was mad at a teacher. . . . He was tired of their crap."[74] Their "crap" apparently meant their expectations that he behave himself in class. For someone who was used to doing whatever he wanted, the rules at school must have been infuriating. During the attack Golden shot and wounded a teacher. Golden also shot Jennifer Jacobs, "who had recently gone out with [him] and who had also rejected him."[75] Both his teachers and Jennifer apparently enraged him by thwarting the gratification of his desires.

If Golden was so entitled, why wasn't he more of a behavior problem in school? Because he was very good at impression management. He knew how to make himself look good. A neighbor said, "Andrew was a sweet child whenever his parents were around . . . but whenever he was away from his parents he was a little demon. . . . I feared that child."[76] Outside of school, Golden was frequently nasty, threatening, and belligerent. Some children were forbidden to play with him. He hit girls, cursed at other children, and threatened to shoot kids with his BB gun. Golden was smart enough to hide his most disturbing behavior from adults. Neither his parents nor his teachers had any idea, for example, what he did to cats: "He killed a cat by starving it in a barrel. He pushed the heads of kittens through a chain-link fence. He shot bottle rockets and BBs at cats, tied one to a clothesline and shot BBs at it, and slit the throats of others."[77]

Such cruel and sadistic behavior indicates a profound lack of empathy and a disregard for living things. Golden may have displaced his anger onto animals, sought excitement to relieve his boredom, or enjoyed the power to torture and kill.

Golden's behavior during his trial also indicated a remarkable lack of feeling, especially considering he was only eleven years old and was on trial for murder. Several reporters commented on his carefree demeanor. One paper noted that "One of the boy killers sat in court yesterday looking relaxed and even smiled at his parents. Drew Golden didn't seem to have a care in the world as he listened to the charges that he committed multiple murders. In contrast his thirteen-year-old friend Mitchell Johnson sobbed."[78]

It could be argued that Golden's composure was a result of his being too young to understand his situation. He was a bright boy, however, and old enough to recognize that he was in serious trouble. In fact, his extreme youth could be expected to have increased his distress, being arrested, placed in detention, and hauled before a judge and jury. In fact, he showed no concern.

❀ ❀ ❀

Andrew Golden stands out among all the school shooters because of his extreme youth. Eleven-year-old mass murderers are extraordinarily rare. He did not, however, act alone. Whereas Spencer had peer support for murder in her friend Brent Fleming, Golden found even more active support by recruiting Mitchell Johnson to join him in his attack.

Golden seems to be an *unprincipled psychopath*. Such people are charming—or, in Golden's case, cute—hiding their hateful and vindictive natures behind a pleasant facade. Exhibiting a combination of narcissistic and antisocial traits, they "expect special recognitions and considerations."[79] Golden seemed to think he deserved special treatment, that rules shouldn't apply to him, and that discipline for misbehavior was an affront.

Eric Harris

"Natural selection needs a boost, like me with a shotgun."

Date: April 20, 1999   **Killed**: 8
Age: 18   **Wounded**: 13
School: Columbine High   **Outcome**: Suicide
School
Location: Jefferson Co., CO

Eric Harris was a self-hating narcissist. This takes some explaining. On the one hand, he liked to write *"Ich bin Gott,"* German for "I am God."[80] Harris did not actually believe he was God, but he felt godlike compared to virtually everyone else. For example, he wrote, "It never ceases to amaze me how stupid and ignorant people can be. . . . I am ashamed to be a part of the same species as some of these people."[81] He also wrote, "I feel like God and I wish I was, having everyone being OFFICIALLY lower than me."[82]

Harris's condescending and contemptuous attitude dominates his journal. And yet, there are glimpses of a very different side of him. He once wrote, "I have always hated how I looked, I make fun of people who look like me, sometimes without even thinking sometimes just because I want to rip on myself. That's where a lot of my hate grows from. The fact that I have practically no self-esteem, especially concerning girls and looks and such."[83]

In fact, Harris's journal ends on a note of surprising vulnerability: "I hate you people for leaving me out of so many fun things. And no don't fucking say 'well that's your fault' because it isn't, you people had my phone #, and I asked and all, but no. no no no don't let the weird looking Eric KID come along, ooh fucking nooo."[84] After pages of arrogant rants and violent fantasies, the journal ends with this woeful note. What is the significance of this?

Harris was not in love with himself but with an image of himself. He concocted a grandiose self-concept, apparently in response to feeling inadequate. Millon described this dynamic in what he called the *compensatory narcissist*—one who compensates for his insecure identity with an image of superiority.

But why was Harris so insecure? Girls reportedly thought he was cute and dated him. He was athletic and played soccer on two teams. He was bright and academically successful. What accounts for his core of inadequacy? Perhaps it was rooted in his two birth defects: a leg problem that apparently was resolved early in life and a chest deformity (pectus excavatum) for which he had surgery at ages twelve and thirteen. A sunken chest can be damaging for any boy's self-concept. As the son of a veteran with military aspirations of his own, Harris may have been particularly vulnerable to feeling damaged and inadequate.

How did he seek to overcome his sense of inadequacy? Power. He wrote, "I would love to be the ultimate judge and say if a person lives or dies—be godlike."[85] On April 20, 1999, his wish came true. Though he did not survive to report what that experience felt like, the words of a serial killer may capture how Harris felt. "I stood there looking at him on the ground, and I was suddenly overcome with feelings of power. I realized I held this man's life in my hands. . . . I thought 'I'm like God . . . I too have the power to give life or take it away.' . . . I never thought it would be so easy to kill a person, or that I would enjoy it. But it was easy and I was enjoying the feeling of supremacy. A supremacy like I had never known before."[86]

Harris himself made the connection between guns and godhood. When he bought his first guns, he wrote, "I am fucking armed. I feel more confident, stronger, more God-like."[87] Guns gave him the power to play god. Without firearms, he was just "the weird looking Eric kid."

Harris didn't just want to kill people; he wanted to experience having power over them. He wrote longingly about his desire to rape and torture people. He referred to himself as a "crazy fuckin . . . rapist" and wrote about wanting to "overpower" girls and get them into a vulnerable situation through impression management: "Who can I trick into my room first? I can sweep someone off their feet, tell them what they want to hear, be all nice and sweet, and then 'fuck 'em like an animal.'"[88]

Following this passage, Harris described his desire to torture and mutilate people. He referred to a video by the music group Nine Inch Nails: "The one where the guy is kidnapped and tortured like hell." He added, "I want to do that too."[89] His comment about torturing someone is followed by a gruesome passage:

> I want to tear a throat out with my own teeth like a pop can. I want to gut someone with my hand, to tear a head off and rip out the heart and lungs from the neck, to stab someone in the gut, shove it up to their heart, and yank the fucking blade out of their rib cage! I want to grab some weak little freshman and just tear them apart like a wolf, show them who is god. Strangle them, squish their head, bite their temples in the skull, rip off their jaw, rip off their collar bones, break their arms in half and twist them around, the lovely sounds of bones cracking and flesh ripping, ahhh . . . so much to do and so little chances.[90]

Elsewhere he wrote about his plan to torture people prior to his school attack. "First we will go to the house of ——— and ——— in the morning before school starts and before anyone is even awake," Eric wrote. "We go in, we silently kill each inhabitant and then pin down ——— and ———. Then take our sweet time pissing on them, spitting on them, and just torturing the hell out of them."[91] On the day of the attack, when Harris and Klebold were shooting students in the school library, Harris was laughing.[92] At one point he looked under a table where a girl cowered in terror. Harris said, "Peekaboo," and shot her.[93] This was sheer sadistic glee, getting a kick out of killing people. This was the culmination of Harris's sadistic strivings.

Why is someone sadistic? According to psychoanalyst Erich Fromm, "He is sadistic because he feels impotent, unalive, and powerless. He tries to compensate for this lack by having power over others, by transforming the worm he feels himself to be into a god."[94] So it was with Eric Harris. Having the power to kill people transformed him from the "weird-looking Eric kid" into a godlike being with control over who lives and who dies.

Harris, like Brenda Spencer, was completely unfazed by the police during his rampage. When he saw police cars through the windows of Columbine High School, he showed no concern. Just the opposite. One student reported that Harris said, "there's a cop—let's get that cop," and another heard him say, "let's go kill some cops now."[95] Harris shot at the police but did not hit anyone. If he had, he presumably would have been particularly excited. Long before the attack, Harris answered an online question about the one person he hated the most by writing, "are cops one person?"[96]

Why hate cops? Perhaps because they had arrested him (and Klebold) for breaking into an electrician's van and stealing equipment. Harris was taken to the police station and later had to appear in court. He said this was the most embarrassing incident in his life. Faced with the power of the legal system, Harris must have felt small and helpless. More generally, he probably hated the police because they represented law and order, goodness, justice—everything that Harris rejected as artificial and meaningless.

In 1941 Dr. Hervey Cleckley published a groundbreaking work on psychopathy. He described a psychopath he worked with by saying, "Beauty and ugliness . . . goodness, evil, love, horror, and humor have no actual meaning, no power to move him."[97] Harris expressed the same sentiment in his own style: "Fuck money, fuck justice, fuck morals, fuck civilized, fuck rules, fuck laws. . . DIE manmade words. . . . There's no such thing as True Good or True evil."[98] He wrote repeatedly about his rejection of morality and values. In their place, Harris celebrated instinct: "Don't follow your dreams or goals or any of that shit, follow your fucking animal instincts. If it moves, kill it, if it doesn't, burn it."[99]

In rejecting morality and celebrating instinct, Harris formulated a psychopathic philosophy. In his mind, he should not be bound by any external constraints. He wanted the freedom to rape and kill without consequences. He created a belief system as a rationalization for his own psychopathic behavior. Here, in a nutshell, is Harris's justification for hating cops and all that they stand for: "Instincts are deleted by laws."[100]

Harris's celebration of instincts was mingled with his celebration of "natural selection," which to him meant the elimination of inferior beings. His writings on natural selection reveal his narcissism and his profound lack of empathy. "NATURAL SELECTION. Kill all retards, people with brain fuck ups, drug addicts, people who can't figure out how to use a fucking lighter. Geeeawd! People spend millions of dollars on saving the lives of retards, and why. I don't buy that shit like 'oh, he's my son, though!' so the fuck what, he ain't normal, kill him. Put him out of his misery. He is only a waste of time and money."[101]

On the day of the attack, Harris wore a shirt that read, "Natural Selection," telling the world the purpose of his rampage.

✢ ✢ ✢

Eric Harris stands alone among the psychopathic secondary shooters in creating an ideology that justified massive violence. Like other psychopathic shooters, he rejected laws, social norms, and authorities, having a particular hostility toward the police. Like the *explosive psychopath*, Harris was prone to tantrums of rage. For these psychopaths, such outbursts "discharge pent-up feelings of humiliation and degradation."[102] Harris's rage may have been sparked by his bodily defects, teasing at school, rejection by girls, or the reality that the world did not grant him the status he craved.

Explosive psychopaths are "hypersensitive to feelings of betrayal,"[103] and Harris was known to erupt in fury at his friends over minor issues. He actually vandalized the homes of former friends.[104] These psychopaths can also direct their rage toward people who symbolize their frustrations and failures: "the resulting violence is a desperate, lashing out against symbols rather than reality."[105] The attack against Columbine High School can be viewed as Harris's attempt to obliterate a symbol of the world that failed to grant him the status he desired.

The sadism in Harris's character is associated with *tyrannical psychopaths*. This subtype "derives a special sense of satisfaction from forcing victims to cower."[106] Harris gleefully mocked cowering students and then shot them at point-blank range, giving him the thrill of ultimate power. He got to play god.

Robert Steinhäuser

"I'm going to be really big one day."

Date: April 26, 2002   **Killed**: 16
Age: 19   **Wounded**: 7
School: Gutenberg   **Outcome**: Suicide
Gymnasium
Location: Erfurt, Germany

Robert Steinhäuser was good at deceiving people—but not good enough. In the end, it was his downfall.

A peer described Steinhäuser as having a rich social life, "meeting friends daily and going to the disco at weekends."[107] Another peer described him as charismatic and rebellious: "He was insubordinate in school, attracting attention. Students loved it. Everybody got on with him, and everybody liked him. I remember that he once told me that one time he wanted everybody to know him and just be famous."[108]

Steinhäuser's insubordination and desire for fame suggest narcissism. He described himself as someone "who is sometimes difficult to bear" and noted that people's opinions of him ranged from "likable" to "cannot stand him."[109] Even his father described him as arrogant and opinionated.[110] He reportedly was rude to teachers, and his report card included comments such as "doesn't respond to discipline well."[111]

For instance, Steinhäuser was caught smoking a cigar and drinking whiskey on a school field trip. Though smoking and drinking are legal in Germany at age sixteen, they were forbidden during the trip. A teacher confronted Steinhäuser, who formed a gun with his hand, pointed it at the teacher, and said, "Rat-a-tat-a-tat-a-tat, you're dead."[112] When Steinhäuser went on his rampage, he killed this teacher.

At school, Steinhäuser had high aspirations but poor performance. He just did not put much effort into anything. Despite this, he made comments like, "I'm going to be really big one day," "Everybody will talk about me," and "I'm going to be a politician."[113] Yochelson and Samenow described grand aspirations without the effort to achieve them as part of the criminal personality. They wrote, "He thinks he can become anything if he will only set his mind to it; to become a doctor, an astronaut, the president of a corporation, or anything else awaits only his decision. With this certainty in mind, he does not consider it incumbent on him to prove anything to anyone—at least, not by working hard."[114]

According to Yochelson and Samenow, someone with this personality doesn't blame his lack of success on his failure to make an effort; rather, he "reacts as though it were someone else's fault. To his way of thinking, it should not be possible for him to fail at anything."[115] This was Steinhäuser's response.

Steinhäuser's failures were significant. He flunked exams and twice failed entire grades. For someone who thought he was going to be "really big," these failures hit him hard. One of his dreams was to study computer science, but he failed his computer class and subsequently abandoned the dream.[116]

Throughout high school Steinhäuser became more and more interested in firearms. His father had an air gun and allowed Steinhäuser to shoot at inanimate objects.[117] Guns are not easy to obtain legally in Germany, but Steinhäuser met the requirements, followed the procedures, and bought himself guns. He also joined a gun club. To speed up the process of getting his firearms license, he forged the number of hours he'd spent practicing at the gun club.

This was not Steinhäuser's only forgery. After a long history of truancy, he forged a physician's note to avoid taking a test he had failed to prepare for. Something about the note was suspicious; the school called the physician, discovered the forgery, and expelled Steinhäuser on October 4, 2001.[118]

Steinhäuser responded to his expulsion from school by covering it up through deception. He never told his parents he had been expelled, and because he was over eighteen, the school did not inform the family. For six months, Steinhäuser left his house each morning as if he were going to school.[119] To further cover his tracks, he forged a report card and presented it to his parents in December 2001. He kept his expulsion secret from his friends and even his brother. He told at least three different stories to friends to explain why he was no longer attending his former school.

Steinhäuser did not take responsibility for his expulsion; instead, he felt like the victim despite confessing his forgery. At a meeting with administrators, he said, "You don't know what you've done to me."[120] What *you've* done to *me*. . . . As if he were innocent. As if he were the victim. Even after this, the school tried to help him continue his education, but he skipped meetings and failed to follow through on opportunities.

Steinhäuser was fascinated by the attack at Columbine and admired Harris and Klebold's methods.[121] Many of his friends knew he had guns and heard him talk about getting revenge by shooting teachers. No one took him seriously.[122] Unlike most school shooters, Steinhäuser specifically targeted the faculty. He killed twelve teachers, an administrator, a police officer, and two students who were hit accidentally.[123]

* * *

Steinhäuser, like other psychopathic shooters, hated authority figures. Unlike the other shooters, however, he made them the primary targets in his attack. He had no ideology like Harris and did not gun people down for fun like Spencer. He felt wronged by the teachers and administrators at his school, and he wanted vengeance.

Steinhäuser had an inflated sense of himself. He did not take responsibility for his own actions, blamed others for his failures, and felt like a victim. He was skilled in deception and used this skill regularly. He demonstrated a blatant disregard for rules and social norms. When caught in a trap of his own making, his response was to commit mass murder against those he blamed for his predicament.

Steinhäuser appears to have been an *unprincipled psychopath*. As noted in the case of Andrew Golden, this type of person is skilled at impression management and deception. Such people expect to receive special treatment without earning it. They are not deterred by punishments or the consequences of their actions. They have a "devious and guileful style, plotting and scheming in their calculations to manipulate others."[124]

Tim Kretschmer

"Shall I get out now, shoot a bit, have a bit of fun?"

Date: March 11, 2009   **Killed**: 15
Age: 17   **Wounded**: 9
School: Albertville-Realschule   **Outcome**: Suicide
Location: Winnenden,
Germany

At eight years of age, Tim Kretschmer told his father what he wanted for Christmas: to play against the European table-tennis champion. His coach thought this was absurd, but his father flew the champion in from Croatia, and Kretschmer's desire was fulfilled.[125] Kretschmer came from a wealthy family and was reportedly given anything he wanted.[126] He was a competitive table-tennis player, and over the years his coach became close with the family. According to him, Kretschmer's father was of the attitude that you can buy anything with money and that nothing is as important as one's own desires.[127]

Besides being spoiled with material possessions,[128] Kretschmer's parents reportedly set no limits on his behavior. Kretschmer had tantrums, cried, and threw his paddle when he lost table-tennis matches. He denigrated his own teammates and "was a poor loser and would always blame his losses on outside circumstances."[129] When his coach talked to Mrs. Kretschmer about these behaviors, she reportedly defended her son. After the attack, however, she said he was not a likable person.[130]

His coach noticed that Kretschmer wanted people to do what he told them to do.[131] He was stubborn and arrogant. On one occasion, Kretschmer refused to join a team because he believed he was far superior to the other players. It struck the coach as inappropriate for a child to challenge his judgment, but the mother's response was, "If my son thinks so, then it's right."[132]

Kretschmer was obsessed with firearms. His father had a firing range in their basement where Kretschmer used air-soft guns to shoot at a human silhouette with targets marking the head and chest. Kretschmer reportedly was good at hitting the head.[133] Mr. Kretschmer was very active in a local gun club and began taking Kretschmer there when he was ten years old.[134]

Kretschmer reportedly wanted people to notice him and talked about being famous, but he did not stand out among his peers.[135] Teachers said he was quiet and shy. Through high school some of his friends drifted away as he became "crazy about weapons."[136] Kretschmer joined an arm-wrestling team but did not make any friends there. He reportedly was a poor loser, and his teammates saw him as grouchy and domineering.[137] He was not popular with girls and had no female friends. Shortly before the attack, Kretschmer expressed interest in a girl at a party, but she rejected him.

Female classmates occasionally teased Kretschmer about his clothes and glasses, but he was not bullied. After all, he was a competitive arm wrestler. As he stated, "Nobody will do anything to me [at school]—I'm the strongest."[138] A girl reported that Kretschmer had recently complained to her that teachers ignored him.[139] This, apparently, was a put-down for Kretschmer and suggests thwarted narcissism, a desire for greater recognition than he deserved.

During his adolescence Kretschmer became depressed and had five psychotherapy sessions. He told his therapist that he hated humanity and had fantasies of killing people, but in the next session he retracted these statements.[140] He withdrew from his family and spent much of his time alone in his room. He became active in an online chat room about school shootings and posted a message stating, "the funny thing is that even when that person announces it, nobody believes him."[141]

Kretschmer was fascinated by pornography and had two hundred photographs on his computer. More than half of them involved bondage, reportedly showing naked women tied up.[142] One source, however, said that the photos depicted women degrading men.[143] Perhaps there were photographs of both types of bondage.

Kretschmer demonstrated impression-management skills in preparing for his attack. In January 2009, he wanted to buy ammunition but was unable to do so because he was underage. To get around this, he told his father he wanted to buy him ammunition for his birthday. Mr. Kretschmer was excited about this because his son typically was very stingy with his money and did not buy gifts for anyone in the family. Kretschmer went with his father, bought him a thousand rounds of ammunition, and secretly kept ninety rounds for himself.[144] On the day of the attack, Kretschmer lied to his parents, telling them his school had a two-hour delay. He acted excited that morning as he had breakfast, giving the impression that he was in a good mood because of the school's late start.[145]

Kretschmer did not attack the business school he was currently attending but the high school he had graduated from the previous year. Though some officials reported he shot people randomly, he appears to have targeted females. He shot twenty-three people at the school; eighteen were female.[146] One of the first victims in the school attack was the girl who had recently rejected his advances.[147] In fact, of the twelve people who died from their wounds, eleven were female. Though some may have been random victims, "several were killed with carefully placed shots to the head."[148]

Kretschmer then fled the school, hijacked a car, and shot other people. He was on the run for three hours, killing himself only after the police shot him twice. Kretschmer exhibited psychopathic nonchalance during his flight from the school. When the kidnapped driver asked why he was killing people, Kretschmer said, "Because it's fun." He acted carefree and at one point asked the driver, "Shall I get out now, shoot a bit, have a bit of fun?"[149] This calmness during a murderous shooting spree showed a profound lack of empathy, and his pleasure in killing revealed his sadistic nature.

✿ ✿ ✿

People described Kretschmer as spoiled and narcissistic but also as shy and insecure. Perhaps he was a *nomadic antisocial* like Poulin. He may also have had elements of the *unprincipled psychopath*, expecting to be treated as special without having earned any distinction. He complained teachers treated him unfairly and shot five of them. His primary targets, however, appear to have been female students. This is interesting in light of his fascination with sexual bondage, an interest shared by Poulin. Kretschmer's attack may have been an assertion of manhood, seeking power over females with whom he otherwise felt powerless.

COMMENTS

The seven shooters presented in this chapter shared a number of features. With the apparent exception of Poulin, the psychopathic shooters demonstrated an inflated sense of themselves. They expressed hostility or resentment toward people who had power over them, and at least four of them sought fame.

Interestingly, Poulin and Harris, the two shooters with chest deformities, both fantasized about raping girls they knew. For them, rape seemed to be a way of asserting their masculinity, proving that they were whole, not damaged. Besides his rape fantasies, Poulin was obsessed with sexual bondage. So was Kretschmer. Poulin apparently tried to rape multiple women prior to his attack, finally finding an outlet for his rage in the girl whom he bound, raped, and murdered. Kretschmer appears to have vented his rage against women by targeting them in his attack. Thus, the two psychopathic shooters obsessed with having power over women through bondage both targeted females in their attacks. Golden also shot a girl who had rejected him. Thus, nearly half of this group targeted females. This is not surprising. Perhaps no failure is as deflating to young males as rejection by a female. For narcissists this is particularly devastating, as they are not used to the helplessness they experience when thwarted in love or lust. The psychopathic shooters targeted two groups of people: girls and authority figures. These were the people with the power to make them feel small, to put them down.

Peer influence played a part in most of these shootings. Except for Robert Poulin, these shooters had either direct or indirect peer support for their rampages. In addition, the only two shooters to successfully recruit partners for their attacks were psychopathic (Golden and Harris), providing them with support for their rampages.

These shooters were motivated by revenge for perceived wrongs, by their pursuit of fame, by the desire for power or domination, and by seeking a sadistic thrill. Their self-righteous entitlement, devastating lack of empathy, and callous disregard of human life mark them as psychopathic shooters.

3

PSYCHOTIC SECONDARY SCHOOL SHOOTERS

A WORD ON PSYCHOTIC SYMPTOMS

Psychosis is often misunderstood. It is not unusual for someone to say of a school shooter, "he's not psychotic—he planned this." Psychosis is not the inability to engage in purposeful action. During Kip Kinkel's trial, an attorney who was questioning a psychologist pointed out that after Kinkel killed his parents he made himself a bowl of cereal. The attorney then asked, "Did that indicate anything to you?" to which the psychologist replied, "Probably that he was hungry." The attorney apparently was questioning if psychotic people can engage in meaningful behavior. Psychotic symptoms vary considerably and may be chronic or episodic, broadly debilitating or narrowly problematic.

Though psychotic symptoms can occur with several diagnoses, including major depression and bipolar disorder, the psychotic shooters presented in this chapter appeared to have had either schizophrenia or schizotypal personality disorder. Of the two conditions, schizophrenia is more severe. Schizophrenics experience hallucinations and/or delusions, the former being false perceptions and the latter being false beliefs. They also struggle socially, are often desperately lonely, and are prone to depression.

Those who are schizotypal may have strange ideas, beliefs, and perceptual experiences, but these tend not to be as severe as hallucinations and delusions. Schizotypals are usually seen as odd in appearance, speech, or behavior. They also have significant impairment in their social functioning.

What is it like to be schizophrenic? It can be terrifying: "My greatest fear is this brain of mine. . . . The worst thing imaginable is to be terrified of one's own mind, the very matter that controls all that we are and all that we do and feel."[1] This and the following quotations are from people living with schizophrenia. Though none of them are school shooters, their comments shed light on psychotic experiences.

To not trust one's own brain has devastating consequences. "What then does schizophrenia mean to me? It means fatigue and confusion, it means trying to separate every experience into the real and the unreal and not sometimes being aware of where the edges overlap."[2]

Delusional beliefs can seem so obviously true that they are held with great conviction: "In college, I 'knew' that everyone was thinking and talking about me and that a local pharmacist was tormenting me by inserting his thoughts into my head and inducing me to buy things I had no use for."[3]

In addition, psychosis either causes, or is a result of, profound disturbances in identity. In *Psychoanalytic Diagnosis* Nancy McWilliams writes that "People whose personalities are organized at an essentially psychotic level have grave difficulties with identity—so much so that they may not be fully sure *that* they exist, much less whether their existence is satisfying. They are deeply confused about who they are."[4] Several psychotic shooters struggled with the fundamental question of whether or not they were human, and, if they were human, who were they?

Schizophrenia causes altered perceptions of the world, impaired social interactions, and a shattered sense of self. It is no surprise that people with schizophrenia are often depressed and suicidal. In fact, the suicide rate for schizophrenics is approximately one out of ten.[5] The overall rate for the nation is approximately one out of ten thousand.[6] In other words, schizophrenics are a thousand times more likely to kill themselves than the general population.

Though I have not personally evaluated any of the shooters in this chapter, they appear to have been either schizophrenic or schizotypal. Though none of them was diagnosed with these disorders prior to their attacks, several who survived their attacks were so diagnosed afterward. In each case, I explain the rationale for their categorization as psychotic shooters.

ATTACKS BY PSYCHOTIC SECONDARY SCHOOL SHOOTERS

Luke Woodham

"If they could give the death penalty in this, I deserve it."

Date: October 1, 1997   **Killed**: 3
Age: 16   **Wounded**: 7
School: Pearl High School   **Outcome**: Tried to escape.
Location: Pearl, MS   Apprehended. Prison

When Luke Woodham stated, "I am not insane! I am angry. This world has shit on me for the final time. . . . I killed because people like me are mistreated every day,"[7] many people believed that his attack was retaliation for bullying. The truth about Luke Woodham, however, is not that simple.

On October 1, 1997, Luke Woodham killed his mother in their home. He then drove her car to school and shot his former girlfriend and her best friend and then opened fire on others. He then got back in his mother's car and tried to drive away but was blocked and apprehended.

Woodham's father had left the family when Luke was young; Luke reportedly was devastated by this abandonment. His older brother, John, reportedly harassed Luke, but there is no evidence of anything out of the ordinary. When Woodham flunked ninth grade, his mother reportedly exhorted him to be more like his brother, whom Woodham referred to as "Mr. Popular."[8] Woodham complained that his mother was intrusively involved in his life but also that she was so absent that he felt neglected. Friends of his testified that Mrs. Woodham was "just a normal mom."[9]

Woodham was said to endure chronic taunting at school, reportedly being teased about being overweight. A peer commented, "Everybody picked on him. I felt real sorry for him."[10] One of Woodham's friends, however, stated that other kids had it far worse.[11] This doesn't mean that Woodham was not badly mistreated, but, as is often the case, it is difficult to know what really occurred.

All his life Woodham loved his pets. He spent hours playing with and taking care of them. On April 14, 1997, however, under the direction of his friend Grant Boyette, Woodham engaged in a series of horrific acts against his dog, Sparkle, and eventually killed him.[12]

Despite claiming his attack was revenge for mistreatment, Woodham did not target anyone who picked on him. The only targeted victims were his mother and Christina Menefee, his former girlfriend.[13] A few weeks before the attack Woodham had asked Christina to get back together—she said no. The date of Woodham's rampage was the one-year anniversary of their breakup. During his taped confession, Woodham said his rampage was due to the breakup with Christina.[14] This is a crucial point. In the immediate aftermath of the attack, he did not blame bullying; he blamed Christina's rejection.

Despite Woodham's conflicting reports about his mother's behavior toward him, he confessed to the police, "I didn't want to kill my mother; I do love my mother. I just wanted revenge on Christina and my mother—like, she wouldn't just say 'Go ahead, take the gun, take the car.'"[15] Thus, the only reason he gave for killing his mother is that she would not have let him take a gun to school and drive her car.

Though before the attack Woodham wrote, "I am not insane!" afterward he claimed that demons influenced him to commit murder: "I remember I woke up that morning and I'd seen demons that I always saw. . . . They said I was nothing and I would never be anything if I didn't get to that school and kill those people."[16]

Of all the factors that influenced Woodham, however, perhaps Grant Boyette was the most important. Boyette was the leader of the Kroth, a peer group that Woodham affiliated with, whose interests included Hitler, the occult, black magic, and Satanism.[17] Under Boyette's influence, Woodham became interested in the occult. His interest intensified after he cast a spell on a boy and two days later the boy's friend was killed by a car. At this point, Woodham became a believer in magic: "One second I was some kind of heartbroken idiot, and the next second I had complete control or complete power over a lot of things."[18] Why was the idea of power so alluring? Woodham saw himself as "a short little fat boy with a crew cut and thick brown glasses. I was nothing, and I knew it."[19]

Woodham testified about Boyette's directives in court: "He told me I had to kill my mom. He told me I had to get the gun and the car and get my revenge on Christy and cause a reign of terror."[20] Boyette reportedly hammered these ideas into Woodham, repeating them for hours. Woodham stated, "Everything I did was influenced by Grant. . . . I tried so hard to get his acceptance."[21] Woodham's claims about Boyette's influence were supported by peers. One testified that Boyette was fascinated by Hitler's ability to manipulate people and that he was able to influence Woodham.[22] Based on peers' testimony, Boyette was charged with accessory to murder.

Was Woodham really psychotic? If, as he sometimes claimed, he both saw demons and heard them talking to him, then he experienced visual and auditory hallucinations that suggest schizophrenia. In the initial aftermath of the shooting, however, Woodham said nothing about demons. Perhaps he did not want to appear "crazy," or perhaps he invented the symptoms later to excuse the attack. Even if he did not have hallucinations, however, there is evidence that Woodham was delusional.

A friend said that Woodham believed Boyette had power over demons, and Woodham reportedly believed that one of these demons was outside his room one night.[23] Woodham also believed he caused a boy's death with a spell. These beliefs could constitute delusions or "magical thinking," a less-severe disturbance in cognitive functioning. Such beliefs are in keeping with schizotypal personality disorder. For example, schizotypals "may be superstitious or preoccupied with paranormal phenomena" or "may believe that they have magical control over others."[24]

Woodham, as is common among schizotypals, had significant social difficulties. He struggled to fit in with a peer group and did not do well with girls. He dated Christina Menefee but quickly alienated her. Schizotypals often strike people as odd, and this was true of Woodham: "During Luke's infrequent appearances at school, he was so odd, disagreeable, and generally frightening that his teachers kept their distance."[25] Even his friends found him "quite difficult to understand. Sometimes he seemed like he was from another planet."[26]

When reality becomes too harsh, schizotypals often withdraw into themselves and create a fantasy world in which they are superior beings. Woodham, who had repeated ninth grade, believed he was intellectually superior to his peers. He was also interested in ideologies of power, including Nazism, magic, Satanism, and the works of Nietzsche. In fact, he cited Nietzsche's *Gay Science* in his manifesto, and also used the term *superman*, referring to Nietzsche's ideal of the man who stands above the masses.[27] Floundering in adolescence, Woodham was drawn to ideologies of power the same way he was drawn to the dominant personality of Grant Boyette. These sources of strength supported Woodham's inadequate identity.

* * *

Woodham appears to have multiple features of schizotypal personality disorder: significant social difficulties, oddness that alienated both peers and adults, unusual perceptual experiences, and beliefs in demons and his own magical ability to control the lives of others. He also exhibited features that we will examine in other psychotic shooters: an inadequate sense of self, the search for strength through powerful friends or ideologies of power, and the attempt to transform himself from a helpless nobody into a superior being. He was so insecure that he tortured and killed his own pet and murdered his mother and the girl he claimed to love just so Boyette would accept him.

Michael Carneal

"I think I'm an alien but I'm not sure."

Date: December 1, 1997   **Killed**: 3
Age: 14   **Wounded**: 5
School: Heath High School   **Outcome**: Surrendered.
Location: West Paducah, KY   Prison

Michael Carneal's psychosis began at a young age. The average age of onset for schizophrenia in males is in their twenties, but some people exhibit symptoms in their teens. Carneal's symptoms, consisting primarily of paranoia, appear to have begun when he reached puberty. According to the research conducted by Dr. Katherine Newman and her colleagues, Carneal was afraid to sleep in his bedroom and was terrified that monsters were under the bed and that strangers would climb through the windows. He covered the bathroom's heat vents so snakes could not get him. In an effort to avoid being grabbed by monsters, he jumped from one piece of furniture to another.[28] When metal tools were found under his mattress after his rampage, Carneal explained they kept his legs from being cut off by a man with a chainsaw who lived under the house.[29] Carneal not only was delusional, he also had auditory hallucinations. The voices criticized and threatened him and eventually began commanding him to do things. On the day of the attack, the voices reportedly told him, "Do this for yourself."[30]

Prior to the attack, Michael wrote a short piece titled "The Secret," in which he wrote, "I have been led to believe that there is a secret in my family that my parents and my sister know. . . . I overheard my parents debating 'whether they should tell me or not.' I still don't know what they were talking about. I think I'm an alien, but I'm not sure."[31] It is not clear if the writing was fictional or autobiographical. If the latter, then Carneal doubted he was human.

Though Carneal's family was by all accounts loving and supportive, there was a history of mental-health problems on the father's side: "in previous generations, several relatives had been institutionalized for severe mental-health problems—including one who had been violent toward others and eventually committed suicide."[32] By itself, however, schizophrenia does not account for Carneal's rampage. What other factors were involved?

The family history of mental-health problems hit only Michael, not his older sister, Kelly. Kelly Carneal was an outstanding young woman who graduated as the class valedictorian. In addition, "she was musically talented, served as a section leader in the marching band, and made the all-state choir. She was also articulate, attractive, and popular with her peers."[33] Michael Carneal, on the other hand, was a socially awkward kid whose odd behavior alienated many of his classmates. He was painfully aware of the disparity: "I have an overachieving sister, Kelly, who is a senior. I hate being even compared to her. . . . I am seriously mad at the world."[34] Carneal apparently raged against the injustice of his situation. He and Kelly had the same parents and grew up in the same household, but she was a star and he, through no fault of his own, had significant problems. It wasn't fair, and it made him mad.

Sibling rivalry was not the only factor that caused him distress. Though Carneal was not gay, a gossip column in the student newspaper implied that he was. This was devastating and sent him into a deep depression. Also, his peer relationships were problematic, but sorting out the truth is difficult. Carneal reported significant bullying. At 5'2" he was short, and other students allegedly pushed him around and harassed him.

Classmates and teachers, however, maintained that Carneal's behavior was just as bad as what he endured. A peer said that "He also picked on other people. . . . [He was] always the one who teased everyone else."[35] A teacher commented, the "media want to make it look like kids that become shooters are picked on until they just can't take it anymore. But he was a picker, not a kid who was picked on."[36] Dr. Katherine Newman concluded, "From his classmates' perspective, Carneal was not picked on any more or less than other students, and he quite consistently picked on other students himself."[37]

Dr. Dewey Cornell, who evaluated Carneal after his attack, said, "Other students experienced similar treatment . . . but Michael seemed more troubled by it."[38] Dr. Newman and her team reached a similar conclusion: "We believe that his [Carneal's] paranoia, fears, and misreading of social cues contributed to the shooting. They magnified the extent and meaning of the teasing and bullying that occurred."[39]

Perhaps a bigger problem than bullying was envy. During his attack, Carneal did not target anyone who had picked on him; he targeted a group of popular, high-achieving students who met each morning for prayer before school: "He said he was envious of their popularity and

their friendships and felt rejected by them."[40] Besides the victims' popularity, he had a crush on one of the girls, and another had rejected his
request for a date. Perhaps he targeted them both because he envied
their status and because they did not return his feelings.

Carneal's group of friends may have influenced him by talking about
getting guns and taking over the school or a mall. Carneal initially told
police that it was a well-formed conspiracy and named his friends and
who would use what kind of gun. He then stated that this wasn't true,
saying he told the police what it seemed they wanted to hear. Dr.
Newman wrote, "We know that Michael's capacity to read the subtleties
of other people's intentions was limited. He might well have imagined
that they were planning to join in when they were merely contributing
to hypothetical scenarios."[41]

Carneal did, however, talk to his friends about his ideas for attacks.
One friend said, "Michael has told me before that he thought it would
be cool to walk down the hall shooting people."[42] Another said Carneal
talked about shooting school administrators: "We should go into their
office . . . and shoot 'em while they're in their offices."[43] Because his
friends listened to these ideas without objecting and without reporting
Carneal to any adults, he may have taken this as approval. He may also
have found encouragement in their conversations about taking over the
school, even if they were just joking. Additionally, Ted Kaczynski, the
Unabomber, might have been an influence—Carneal had his work on
his hard drive.

As external stresses took their toll and Carneal's internal world deteriorated, he began his downward spiral. "He found an old handgun in
his father's closet and considered using it to end his life. He took a
sewing needle and gouged a large mark on his arm. In his depressed
and paranoid state, he came to feel that all of his former friends had
turned against him and that students whispering and laughing in the
hall were whispering and laughing about him. In the weeks before the
shooting, he began to hear voices telling him to stand up for himself."[44]
Tragically, Carneal listened to the voices.

❈ ❈ ❈

Two mental health professionals who evaluated Carneal after his attack
concluded that he suffered from schizophrenia.[45] In addition, Carneal's
life contained multiple factors that appear in the lives of other psychotic
shooters: the early onset of psychotic symptoms; an outstanding older
sibling and the resulting comparisons and failure to measure up; peer
issues including harassment, rejection, and envy; romantic failures; peer
support for violence; and a role model for violence.

Andrew Wurst

"I died four years ago. I've already been dead and I've come back."

Date: April 24, 1998   **Killed**: 1
Age: 14   **Wounded**: 3
School: Parker Middle School   **Outcome**: Surrendered.
Location: Edinboro, PA   Prison

Andrew Wurst did not live in the world we know—he dwelled in a delusional realm that resembled a bizarre science-fiction story. He believed that only he was real; everyone else was "unreal." Other people were "programmed to act and say what the government, mad scientists, or a psycho want them to say."[46] Only he could actually think his own thoughts. He had returned from the future to carry out a mission, but an archenemy was trying to thwart him. His parents were not really his parents; he was brought to Earth when he was four years old and placed with them. Finally, "We are all in reality in hospital beds being monitored and programmed by these mad scientists."[47]

We know that Wurst did not invent these symptoms after his attack in order to plead insanity because he had shared his delusions with his girlfriend a couple of months before his rampage. The conversation reportedly was so disturbing that she asked him to stop telling her such things. In addition to his multiple delusions, Wurst had auditory hallucinations. A letter written before the attack said, "the voices are coming again."[48] What the voices said to him is not known.

Wurst was so delusional that in the immediate aftermath of the shooting he was babbling, "I died four years ago. I've already been dead, and I've come back. It doesn't matter anymore. None of this is real."[49] Later, he stated that he was in jail for killing an unreal person. There was nothing wrong with this, he said, because the victim was already dead or unreal.

The victim was John Gillette, a teacher whom Wurst had never had. The shooting occurred at a school-sponsored dinner dance at a local venue named Nick's Place. Wurst killed Gillette and wounded another teacher and two students. He had planned to kill himself and even left a suicide note at his home. When James Strand, the owner of Nick's Place, pointed a shotgun at Wurst and told him to drop his gun, Wurst hesitated but then complied.

Wurst reportedly told peers he planned to shoot at least one girl who had rejected him and possibly two others. This did not happen. Gillette was not a premeditated target, but he may have been singled out. Why?

Perhaps because he had announced that Wurst won a door prize. After the attack, Wurst disclosed that this made him uncomfortable.[50]

There were no reports that Wurst had been bullied. He hated the "popular students" and athletes because he viewed them as stuck up.[51] As with Michael Carneal, Wurst apparently envied more popular peers. Though he was not popular, he had friends. He reportedly was known for being weird and saying strange things, so no one took him seriously when he talked about going on a rampage. He even tried to recruit a friend to join him. As with other shooters, the lack of objection to his plans from his peers may have served as encouragement.

Wurst also had active encouragement to kill. A teacher overheard a student talking to Wurst about killing his—Wurst's—mother: "We'll wait until she gets back, and as she's coming in the door, that's when you'll shoot her, and we'll just say we didn't know who she was, that we thought she was an intruder."[52] Whether or not this boy also encouraged Wurst to commit a school shooting is unknown.

Wurst had also talked to a girl about shooting his parents. He had conflict with his father, but there is no evidence that he was abused. Perhaps he wanted to kill his parents because he believed they were not really his parents and had thus deceived him his whole life. Or maybe his anger was an exaggerated response to normal parent/teenager conflict. Writing to a friend, Wurst said of his parents, "Fuck them thanks to them I'm in my shit life on the edge of insanedity [sic], murder and suicide."[53]

How bad was Wurst's family? There is no indication of violence or abuse in the home. There was depression on both sides of the family, however, and a paternal aunt had been in a psychiatric hospital for years. His parents disagreed about how to raise Wurst; his mother was more lenient and his father more strict. Wurst had two older brothers who showed none of the symptoms their younger brother struggled with. They helped out in their father's landscaping business, and, though Wurst tried to help, he was not as good a worker. His father saw him as lazy, which Wurst resented. He made disparaging comments to his friends about his parents, saying his father was an alcoholic and his mother was a prostitute. There is no evidence to support these statements; perhaps he lied out of anger, or perhaps he believed what he said.

Like Woodham and Carneal, Wurst had role models for violence and ideological influences, including Napoleon, Hitler, and the Antichrist.[54] In addition, Andrew Golden and Mitchell Johnson's rampage in Jonesboro, Arkansas, seems to have influenced Wurst. The Jonesboro attack occurred on March 24, 1998. Shortly after this, Wurst "said he was going to do something like that someday." He also remarked, "That

Jonesboro thing, that would be like me bringing a gun to the dinner dance."[55] Wurst committed his attack on April 24, 1998, exactly one month after the Jonesboro shooting.

Why did the attack occur when it did? There may have been several factors. Wurst's girlfriend broke up with him, and two other girls turned down his invitation to the dinner dance. He began using marijuana and drinking alcohol. For someone who was already out of touch with reality, substance abuse may have exacerbated his psychosis. At least one peer encouraged him to commit murder. His interest in Hitler and the Antichrist may have helped him to justify murder. Finally, the shooting in Jonesboro may have provided the impetus to actually carry out the attack.

❀ ❀ ❀

The psychiatrist who evaluated Wurst after the attack concluded that he was psychotic but was too young to be labeled schizophrenic; he described Wurst as "preschizophrenic."[56] Wurst had many features in common with Luke Woodham and Michael Carneal, including the early onset of psychosis. Like the others, he had higher-functioning older siblings and resented being compared to them. Three girls rejected him shortly before the attack. Peers encouraged him to commit violence. He was hostile toward high-status classmates. He had role models for violence and was influenced by ideologies of power. Also, where Carneal may have thought he was an alien, Wurst firmly believed that he was. This indicated a profound disturbance in his identity.

Kipland Kinkel

"I wish I had been aborted."

Date: May 20–21, 1998   **Killed**: 4
Age: 15   **Wounded**: 25
School: Thurston High School   **Outcome**: Intended suicide;
Location: Springfield, OR   tackled, apprehended. Prison

Like Andrew Wurst, Kip Kinkel was impressed by the Jonesboro shooting. He, too, said the attack was "cool" and that "somebody should do that around here."[57] Also like Wurst, Kinkel tried to recruit a peer for his rampage, saying he had a better plan than Golden and Johnson, but the boy did not take him seriously. Two months after Jonesboro, and one month after Wurst's attack, Kinkel killed his parents. The following day he went to school and shot twenty-seven people.

Even before the attack in Jonesboro, Kinkel had talked about bringing a gun to school and shooting people.[58] He also admired the Unabomber and had even given an oral report on making bombs. After his attack, his neighborhood had to be evacuated because of the numerous explosives he left in his house. Thus, external influences on Kinkel included the Jonesboro attack, his admiration for the Unabomber, and his friends' passive encouragement. Why was he vulnerable to these influences? Based on Kinkel's testimony, by the time he committed his attack at age fifteen, he had been psychotic for three years.

The Kinkel family had a history of severe mental-health problems. At least nine relatives had been institutionalized.[59] A great-uncle believed a police officer was a Nazi soldier; the officer shot him in self-defense when the uncle tried to stab him. Two paternal uncles were institutionalized with schizophrenia. His mother's nephew believed he was the Second Coming of Christ and threatened his workplace with a homemade bomb. Other relatives were depressed to the point of being suicidal or had auditory hallucinations.[60] Clearly, Kinkel was born with significant genetic loading for major psychological problems.

Kinkel first had hallucinations when he was twelve. "I was on my driveway, looking at some bushes," he told his psychologist, "and a voice said, 'You need to kill everyone, everyone in the world.' . . . It scared the shit out of me. I was confused. It seemed like something was seriously wrong. I ran into the house and cried in my room."[61] Kinkel said one voice was authoritarian and commanding, a second was very critical of him, and the third repeated what the others said. Sometimes he heard them talking to each other about him.

Kinkel also had multiple delusions. He believed the United States was facing an imminent invasion by China; he sought to arm himself in preparation for the attack. He believed a plague was imminent; he wanted to stockpile supplies for when society broke down. He believed he had a computer chip in his brain and wondered if the chip broadcast the voices he heard: "when they did an MRI, I thought they would find a chip or something in my head put there by the government. . . . Maybe that's the way they are controlling me."[62] Though Kinkel saw a psychiatrist and a psychologist for depression prior to his attack, he deliberately kept his psychotic symptoms secret to avoid the stigma of being seen as "crazy." As a result, his schizophrenia was not diagnosed until after his attack.[63]

Kinkel's sister, Kristin, was untouched by schizophrenia. She was five and a half years older than Kip and was pretty, athletic, and popular. She received a cheerleading scholarship to the University of Hawaii.

In comparison, Kip repeated first grade due to physical and emotional immaturity. Though he was bright, he struggled in school and was eventually diagnosed with dyslexia. He did not have an easy time growing up. He reportedly was "hyperactive, insecure, extremely sensitive and likely to have temper tantrums from his earliest years. He cried easily and was smaller than others his age."[64]

Kinkel's academic struggles were particularly problematic in his family; his parents were teachers who valued academic success. His father also valued athletic prowess; unfortunately, Kinkel was not a good athlete. As a result, he and his father had a very conflicted relationship. His sister's successes made things even harder for him. As Kristin said, "I know he felt compared. I'm sure it was hard."[65]

Was Kinkel bullied? No. In fact, he had an explosive temper, and some students feared him. Once a peer reportedly pushed him, and Kinkel, who was trained in martial arts, kicked the boy in the head, resulting in a two-day suspension. Shortly after that, he threw a pencil at a boy and was suspended for three days. Kinkel made fun of other kids but reacted with fury when someone dared to disparage him: "Kip's experience of being the victim of such taunts was minimal, probably less than what passes for 'normal' in many schools. Instead, he was more often the one who intimidated others."[66]

He had multiple friends but despite this felt very alone. He wrote in his journal, "I feel like everyone is against me, but no one ever makes fun of me, mainly because they think I'm a psycho."[67] He also got drunk on occasion, and this probably did not help his state of mind. Kinkel had homicidal thoughts toward a star football player who was dating the girl Kinkel was interested in. He apparently hated him out of envy.

Kinkel knew there was something very wrong with him. He wrote in his journal, "Why aren't I normal?"[68] He was devastated by his sense of being damaged. He even seemed to question his identity. One of the first things he wrote in his journal was, "I don't know who I am."[69]

❀ ❀ ❀

Kinkel shared several features with the other psychotic shooters: a family history of mental-health problems, early onset psychosis, a much higher-functioning older sibling, peer encouragement, substance abuse, and role models for violence, including the Unabomber, Andrew Golden, and Mitchell Johnson. He also exhibited homicidal envy toward at least one peer. Finally, he was painfully aware that he was psychologically impaired and struggled to understand who he was.

Dylan Klebold

"I just want something I can never have—The story of my existence."

Date: April 20, 1999   **Killed**: 5
Age: 17   **Wounded**: 10
School: Columbine High   **Outcome**: Suicide
School
Location: Jefferson Co., CO

Dylan Klebold was a complicated person. As a child, he was unusually shy and insecure. He lacked confidence to initiate activities, so he followed his peers. According to a childhood friend, "I always had to say, 'We're going to go here to play. We're going down to the creek now,' or whatever."[70] In adolescence, Klebold experienced profound social anxiety. He frequently wrote in his journal about his loneliness, emotional suffering, and insecurities. Based on his journal and the reports of people who knew him, he appears to have had avoidant personality disorder, which is characterized by "a pervasive pattern of social inhibition, feelings of inadequacy, and hypersensitivity to negative evaluation."[71]

Klebold was so ill equipped to deal with the social realities of his life that his mental functioning deteriorated. According to Dr. Theodore Millon, schizotypal personality disorder can emerge through the deterioration of an avoidant personality. This appears to be what happened with Klebold. Unfortunately, Klebold kept his psychological difficulties to himself and thus was never diagnosed or treated.

People with schizotypal personalities have difficulty functioning in reality. They withdraw into their own mental worlds and create alternative realities to compensate for their inadequate identities. In Millon's words, this is a process of "constructing new worlds of self-made reality."[72] For example, though Klebold was painfully shy and insecure, he developed an internal world in which he looked down on the masses of humanity as inferior "zombies."

Klebold had other schizotypal traits, too. He struck many people as odd, goofy, or weird,[73] which is common for schizotypals. His journal reveals a fragmented sense of self and profound identity issues. Like Carneal, Wurst, and Kinkel, Klebold struggled to understand who he was, apparently feeling—if not believing—that he was not human. For example, Klebold wrote, "I lack the true human nature that Dylan owned."[74] This is characteristic of Klebold's writings—writing about himself as if he were somehow apart from himself, as if *I* and *Dylan* were separate entities. We see this again in his comment, "I wonder how/when I got so fucked up w[ith] my mind, existence, problem—when Dylan Benet [*sic*] Klebold got covered up by this entity containing Dylan's body."[75] Klebold once began a journal entry by writing his name: "Dylan Klebold." He then crossed out his name and wrote, "Fuck that," with an arrow pointing to the crossed out name. Underneath this, he wrote, "Me."[76] Again, he seemed to think that *me* and *Dylan Klebold* were separate beings.

Klebold also wrote about being nonhuman: "Being made a human/ Without the possibility of BEING human."[77] In another passage, he wrote, "Does that make me a non-human? YES."[78] Thus, like Michael Carneal who may have believed he was an alien, and Andrew Wurst who was convinced he was an alien, Klebold also seemed to believe he was not human. In fact, Klebold often referred to himself as a god. He wrote, "I am a true god," referred to "the one thing that made me a god," and declared, "I am the god of everything."[79] This exemplifies how schizotypals create alternative realities to give themselves the status that is so sorely lacking in their real lives.

Klebold's extreme dependence is also significant. In *Why Kids Kill* I wrote about the extent to which he presented himself differently in Eric Harris's presence than he did with other people or in the privacy of his journal. Klebold felt so desperately alone and inadequate that he couldn't risk losing Harris as a friend. As a result, he was willing to do anything—even kill people—to win Harris's approval. This parallels Luke Woodham's willingness to do anything to gain the acceptance of Grant Boyette.

Klebold also appears to have absorbed ideas from Charles Manson. He wrote a paper about Manson for school, his writings echoed Manson's romanticized ideas about death, and he even imitated Manson's followers by spray-painting "Death to Pigs" on a local pawnshop.[80]

Apparently to compensate for his inner emptiness, Klebold created an internal identity as a superior being, and an external relationship with Eric Harris that required him to become a cold-blooded killer. If this conceptualization is accurate, it explains how shy, anxious Dylan Klebold transformed himself into a figure of power to compensate for his woeful, inferior self.

The change in Klebold was evident well before the attack. In his last two years of high school he became markedly angry and belligerent. For a life-long introvert, this was a drastic change in behavior. There are numerous reports of Klebold's being aggressive, intimidating, and threatening. He openly made derogatory comments about teachers, swore in class, walked out of class and slammed the door, bullied other students, vandalized the homes of classmates, and generally alienated many peers and teachers.[81]

Despite the widespread belief that he and Harris were bullied mercilessly by jocks, Klebold's journal makes clear that he admired and envied jocks for living the kind of life he dreamed of for himself. He wrote, "I see jocks having fun, friends, women, <u>ALIVE</u>,"[82] and that he "hated the happiness that they have."[83] Though he did not complain about jocks, he did complain about being picked on by various relatives (but not his parents). Klebold apparently resented his brother, Byron, for being popular and athletic, and because Byron "ripped" on him.[84]

Klebold sank into a deep depression in which he exaggerated and obsessed about his misery. At times he recognized how good his life was: "let's see what I have that's good: A nice family, a good house, food, a couple of good friends, & possessions."[85] Despite this, he later lost all perspective: "Let's sum up my life . . . the most miserable existence in the history of time."[86] He also wrote, "I am in eternal suffering, in infinite directions in infinite realities."[87] It is no surprise that he wanted to die.

※ ※ ※

Klebold resembles other psychotic shooters in many ways. He was the youngest child with an older sibling he resented, he had peer influence for murder (Eric Harris) as well as a role model for violence (Charles Manson), and he developed grandiose ideas about himself. He smoked marijuana and drank frequently. He wanted desperately to have a girlfriend and had crushes but never established a romantic relationship; this was a devastating failure for him. He felt profoundly alienated from, and envious of, his peers. His alienation was so severe that he did not even feel like a human being. Finally, he was deeply depressed, obsessed with his own suffering, and suicidal.

Alvaro Castillo

"I believe that I was stopped from suicide by God because
I have to do another massacre."

Date: August 30, 2006   **Killed**: 1
Age: 18   **Wounded**: 2
School: Orange High School   **Outcome**: Suicidal.
Location: Hillsborough, NC   Surrendered. Prison

Alvaro Castillo wanted to kill people in order to save them. He was profoundly delusional with a moralistic ideology that drove him to protect people from the evils of the world by murdering them.[88]

Castillo's family structure differed from that of the previous psychotic shooters, who were the youngest and most troubled children in their families. Castillo was the oldest surviving child in his family (his father had a son from a previous relationship who died young in El Salvador). After the father left El Salvador, he moved to California where he met his future wife, Vicky, who had emigrated from Spain. Together they had Alvaro and two daughters. One daughter reportedly suffered from bulimia; the other was diagnosed with autism.[89]

His mother's family had significant psychological disturbances: "Vicky and seven of her nine siblings suffer[ed] from severe mental illness."[90] This reportedly included depression, schizophrenia, and other psychotic disorders.[91] Vicky experienced panic attacks, and after her marriage she became depressed.[92] Though there is no information about the mental health of the father's side of the family, he was a disturbed man who physically abused his wife.[93] Castillo was too afraid to intervene, but his younger sister, Victoria, would sometimes step in to stop the violence. Because of Castillo's fear of his father, his mother called him a coward.[94] Castillo may have resented his sister for being more courageous than he was.

When the children were sick, instead of seeking medical services the father reportedly made them take cold showers, believing that cold water was a cure-all. When Castillo turned five years old, his father told him that childhood was over and he could no longer have friends. This man was so controlling and violent that Vicky wanted to leave with the children and return to Spain. The father threatened that if she left, he would kill her.[95] Despite the stress at home, Castillo was reportedly an excellent student who was well behaved and eager to please at school. He did not fit in well with his peers, seeming shy and odd.

At age eight, Castillo was disgusted when a friend showed him pornography. At fifteen, he babysat a toddler and reportedly felt sexually aroused; this caused overwhelming guilt, and he worried that he might be a pedophile. He was so disturbed that he "resorted to self-flagellation with a stick, prayer, rigid eating, and exercise to cope with his agitation."[96]

In adolescence, Castillo became obsessed with guns, mass murderers, and school shooters, particularly Eric Harris. Despite his extreme discomfort with sexuality, Castillo wrote in his journal, "Eric is just so good-looking. I can't believe he couldn't get a date for the prom. If I was a girl, I would have gone to the prom with him. Does that sound

gay, straight or bi[sexual]?"[97] Castillo also became obsessed with a girl
he knew, but apparently there was no romantic relationship. After graduating from high school, Castillo joined the National Guard so he could
learn to use weapons. This was a miserable experience for him, so his
psychiatrist got him discharged.

Castillo planned to kill himself on April 20, 2006, the seventh anniversary of the Columbine attack. His father, however, intervened, and
Castillo was hospitalized. He was diagnosed with depression, anxiety,
and possible psychosis.[98] Castillo interpreted his father's intervention in
his suicide to mean that God wanted him to live so that he could carry
out his own rampage attack. Perhaps to inspire himself, he convinced
his mother to take him from their home in North Carolina to Littleton,
Colorado. They visited Columbine High School, the house where Eric
Harris had lived, and the pizza shop where he had worked. While there,
Castillo bought a trench coat in imitation of Harris.

Castillo had multiple psychotic symptoms. A court report detailed
some of his paranoid delusions, saying that "He believed he was being
watched through cameras in air vents. He believed that he was being
watched by a picture of a woman in the bathroom; he turned the picture over whenever he used the bathroom. His belief that he was being
watched led him to keep the blinds in his room closed. He was afraid
that the FBI or the CIA was watching him, and he wore a jacket and a
hat to conceal himself from them."[99]

Castillo was obsessed with sin and sacrifice. He viewed the world as
a sinful place and believed that murdering students would protect them
from the world's evil. He wrote, "Sacrifice will occur and those children
will be freed from evil. . . . We have to die and leave this sick, drinking,
sex-crazed, drug using, sadistic, masochistic world."[100] He also wrote, "I
think I must do a massacre. . . . And I'm not doing it for revenge. I love
that school. I'm doing it to save them."[101]

He carried out his attack on August 30, 2006, because it was Kip
Kinkel's birthday. He shot his father seven times and wrote about feeling both happy and remorseful. He then went to his former high school,
set off smoke bombs, and opened fire outside the school. He wounded
two students before being stopped by an armed officer who told him to
drop his weapon and lie down. Castillo did as directed, but told the
officer, "Shoot me. Shoot me. You'll love it."[102]

On the day of his attack, Castillo recognized that it was morally
wrong: "I am sorry! Sorry for everything. I am sick. Mentally ill."[103]
After the attack, however, when his mother asked if he wanted to go to
confession, Castillo said, "what do I have to confess about? I didn't do
anything bad. I did the right thing."[104]

While he was in prison, Castillo reported more psychotic symptoms. "He told a doctor at the hospital that he had an imaginary twin named Red who had told him to commit the shootings at Orange High School. He said that Red told him to do terrible things all the time—to hurt and rape people and to make people rape Alvaro. He said it was the first time he had ever acted on any of Red's orders."[105] Though prosecution and defense typically argue about psychosis, in this case, "Every mental health expert who examined Alvaro Castillo after the shootings agreed that he was psychotic."[106]

✿ ✿ ✿

Castillo resembles other psychotic shooters in his paranoid delusions, his poor social functioning, and his obsession with other killers. He differs, however, in a number of ways. Unlike the other psychotic shooters reviewed so far, Castillo was neither the youngest nor the most impaired child in his family. Also, according to multiple reports, Castillo was an emotionally abused child. Nevertheless, he is categorized as a psychotic shooter rather than a traumatized shooter for three reasons. First, though his father abused his mother, it is not clear how abusive he was to Castillo. Second, the family did not have many features associated with those of traumatized shooters. Third, Castillo's school rampage was driven by his psychotic thoughts.

Castillo also differs in having had no peer influence to commit the attack. Also, there is no evidence of substance abuse. Finally, his delusions were such that he believed he was doing God's will and saving innocent people. His motivation was fundamentally different from that of other shooters.

Pekka-Eric Auvinen

"I can't say I belong to same race as the lousy, miserable, arrogant, selfish human race! No! I have evolved one step above!"

Date: November 7, 2007   **Killed**: 8
Age: 18   **Wounded**: 12
School: Jokela High School   **Outcome**: Suicide
Location: Jokela, Finland

Pekka-Eric Auvinen did not view his attack as a school shooting but as political terrorism. In his mind, he was instigating an international revolution to topple totalitarian regimes.[107] In reality, he shot people at his high school.

Auvinen reportedly came from a stable family that included his parents and a younger brother. Auvinen progressed normally in school and had friends, but during adolescence his friends became fewer and his school performance declined. The official report by the Finnish Ministry of Justice states that in the upper grades he had no friends,[108] though the same report noted that Auvinen talked to friends about shooting and buying a gun.[109]

Auvinen was taunted at school. This may have been because of his size: "He suffered from the fact that he was quite short."[110] In addition, "he dressed more neatly than others, he expressed his extreme opinions vociferously, and his interests were generally different from those of other youngsters. He was also bullied for his insecurity and involuntary blushing."[111]

It is noteworthy that his interests and opinions triggered some of his harassment. Auvinen was fascinated by school shootings and discussed Columbine and other rampages at home, at school, and online. He admired the Unabomber and believed that violence was an acceptable way to solve problems. Auvinen even hinted that he would carry out a rampage attack. He also became interested in the Communist Party and, later, the Nazis.[112] These interests did not endear him to his peers: "Statements by teachers and students confirm that politically radical views did not help Auvinen to socialize with other young people."[113]

Auvinen apparently was also influenced by Finnish ecologist Pentti Linkola, who is well-known in Finland for his extreme views. Auvinen went so far as to make a video tribute to him that included the following Linkola quotes: "A minority can never have any other effective means to influence the course of matters but through the use of violence," and "I wish that death to mankind comes soon."[114]

In 2007 Auvinen had his military call-up examination: "His fitness classification was E for mental-health reasons, which would have meant deferment for three years."[115] He reportedly did not mention his depression or suicidal thoughts. Given that he hid his depression from the examiner, it is not known why he was deferred.

According to his diary, Auvinen had been planning his attack since March 2007.[116] He wrote that "he was going to initiate an operation against humanity with the purpose of killing as many people as possible."[117] His parents reported that in the months preceding the attack, Auvinen's grades declined, he increasingly isolated himself in his room, and he spent much of his time on the computer.[118] His mother noted that Auvinen became even more fearful of social situations in the summer of 2007.[119] A peer noticed that he was acting strangely and that "he withdrew into his shell."[120]

In August 2007 "other youngsters noticed that his behaviour had become unusual and told a youth worker about their concern. This youth worker received similar reports from several young people up to the end of October 2007. The perpetrator behaved threateningly toward other youngsters, saying that they would die as a result of a white revolution."[121] What Auvinen meant by a *white revolution* is not clear; perhaps he wanted to rid Europe of nonwhite people.

In the summer of 2007, Auvinen found an online girlfriend. When she found a new boyfriend in the fall, Auvinen became verbally aggressive, and he, the young woman, and her new boyfriend exchanged insults online. Interestingly, the night before his attack, Auvinen apologized for his behavior.[122]

Auvinen was very active online and posted many videos, often celebrating Hitler and the attack at Columbine. In addition, some of them included "sadomasochistic sexual fantasies."[123] This material included "violent pornographic video clips and fantasies of near-rape. . . . The videos portray innocent-looking nude or semi-nude women helplessly bound, gagged, and struggling to get away. These pictures are coupled with his fantasies of abducting women and forcing them to submit to his will."[124] Auvinen commented in one of his videos that women "are cheating whores, lying sluts and manipulative bitches. They are best when they are dominated, bound & gagged."[125] Despite his misogyny, he did not appear to target women in his attack.

Though Auvinen committed his rampage at his school, he had considered other sites for his attack. He reportedly posted online "that he might commit a spree killing in the Finnish parliament because of the corrupt nature of politicians."[126] It was also reported that he "even considered going on a shooting rampage in a shopping centre but thought that school would be better because shooting in a school would give him more public attention."[127] These comments, along with his reference to a "white revolution," indicate that he had no particular rage toward people in his school.

Auvinen left several pieces of writing, including his YouTube profile, a manifesto, his likes and dislikes, and information about his upcoming attack.[128] Much of what he wrote echoes the writings of Eric Harris. In fact, one of his screen names was NaturalSelector89, borrowing from Harris's rants about natural selection.

Auvinen's social anxiety and frequent blushing suggest that, like Dylan Klebold, he had avoidant personality disorder. He became increasingly withdrawn through adolescence, the same time that he developed an interest in extreme ideologies.[129] This may have been the withdrawal into the self that schizotypals often experience.

Though he was never diagnosed as schizotypal, Auvinen had multiple features of this disorder. For example, he exhibited an odd combination of traits that resemble those of other schizotypal school shooters: he was socially anxious and yet was so vocal about his extreme political views and his interest in violence that he generated hostile responses. This was noted with Dylan Klebold, as well, and suggests poor interpersonal skills.

Auvinen was also teased about his clothing. His peers reported that he "often wore the same clothes to school—brown leather jacket, black trousers and checkered shirt—and usually he carried a briefcase."[130] Schizotypals often have an odd appearance, including unusual clothing: "Many dress in strange and unusual ways, often appearing to prefer a 'personal uniform' from day to day. . . . The tendency to keep to peculiar clothing styles sets them distinctively apart from their peers."[131] There were also multiple reports that his behavior became unusual, and though this could mean many things, it may have been the eccentric behavior that is seen in schizotypals.

Finally, Auvinen's ideology revealed the distorted thinking that is in line with schizotypal functioning. He was insecure and prone to blushing in public, yet he created an internal reality in which he was a godlike being who looked down on the masses of humanity, whom he called "retards," "robots," and "vegetables." He wrote, "I can't say I belong to same race as the lousy, miserable, arrogant, selfish human race! No! I have evolved one step above! . . . Compared to you retarded masses, I am actually godlike."[132]

He not only had a grandiose conception of himself but of his attack as well. "My enemies will run and hide in fear when mentioning my name," he wrote. "Long live the revolution. . . . We must rise against the enslaving, corrupted, and totalitarian regimes and overthrow the tyrants."[133] This bears no connection to what he actually did. He shot people at his high school, but he believed he was initiating the overthrow of national governments. There was no congruence between his view of himself and reality. He was not a hero or martyr or revolutionary; he was a psychotic young man gunning down innocent people.

❊ ❊ ❊

Auvinen, like Woodham and Klebold, fits the model of schizotypal young men who felt like social failures and created alternative identities for themselves as superior beings. Whereas Woodham and Klebold had actual friends who led them to murder (Grant Boyette and Eric Harris, respectively), Auvinen modeled himself on Eric Harris. Though he did not have any direct peer encouragement, he did talk extensively about school shootings with his peers. Where Woodham was attracted to the ideas of Nietzsche, and Klebold studied Charles Manson, Auvinen was influenced by the writings of Pentti Linkola, the Nazis, and Eric Harris.

COMMENTS

As noted earlier, my analyses are based on the available information. In addition, what is known about each shooter varies in consistency and quality. Keeping these limitations in mind, I conceptualize Michael Carneal, Andrew Wurst, Kip Kinkel, and Alvaro Castillo as schizophrenic and Luke Woodham, Dylan Klebold, and Pekka-Eric Auvinen as schizotypal.

Though all seven shooters had serious psychological disturbances, only three—Kinkel, Castillo, and Auvinen—received mental-health treatment prior to their attacks. They were treated for depression or anxiety. Castillo was diagnosed with possible psychosis; none of the others was identified as psychotic prior to his attack.

All the psychotic shooters had frustrating love lives, with breakups and rejections that contributed to their anguish and rage. Though these are common experiences for adolescents, the shooters' mental-health problems presumably exacerbated the impact of these events. The psychotic shooters all drew inspiration from notorious figures or ideologies of power. Several used these external influences to transform themselves from weak, anxious adolescents into formidable figures. In addition to attaching themselves to, or imitating, figures of power, these shooters also created alternative identities for themselves.

Dr. Theodore Millon notes that schizotypals tend to create unreal identities out of their fear of losing their sense of self. This fear "may overwhelm these patients, driving them into a bizarre psychotic state in which they create tangible illusions to which they can relate, self-referential ideas that give them a significance they otherwise lack."[134]

Millon also describes what happens when schizotypals are stressed beyond their ability to endure. "Many schizotypals," he writes, "have stored up intense repressed anxieties and hostilities throughout their lives. Once released, these feelings burst out in a rampaging flood. The backlog of suspicions, fears, and animosities has been ignited and now explodes in a frenzied cathartic discharge."[135] This explains how shy, anxious people can ultimately commit murder.

Three of the shooters killed family members prior to their school attacks. Luke Woodham killed his mother, Kip Kinkel shot both his parents, and Alvaro Castillo murdered his father. It is unclear why Woodham killed his mother; it may have been simply because Grant Boyette told him to. Kinkel may have killed his father out of hatred and his mother out of love (in his mind). Having killed his father he didn't want his mother to have to live with the agony of knowing that her son killed her husband. Castillo apparently killed his father in revenge for years of domestic violence. Though Andrew Wurst did not kill his parents, he had talked about doing so. His motivation for wanting to murder his parents remains unclear. He may have sought revenge for his perceived mistreatment by his father or been motivated by his delusion that his parents were not really his parents.

In fact, several of these perpetrators had problematic relationships with their fathers—Wurst, Kinkel, and Castillo. Luke Woodham also had a troubled relationship with his father—not because of mistreatment but because Mr. Woodham left the family, leaving a gaping wound in Luke's life. There is no evidence that Carneal, Klebold, and Auvinen had troubled relationships with their parents.

Several of these shooters were unusually sensitive to being hurt. They had an exaggerated sense of the wrongs they suffered. Dr. Cornell commented about Michael Carneal that, "because of his personality and mental condition, Michael was sensitive to feeling mistreated and may have reacted strongly to incidents that other students were able to tolerate." [136] A forensic psychiatrist who evaluated Carneal stated, "He hoarded these perceived injustices and dwelled on them rather than letting them go as many kids would." [137]

Similarly, a psychiatrist who evaluated Andrew Wurst noted personality features that "caused him to be hypersensitive to the rejection of others, as well as the demands placed upon him by his family." [138] Luke Woodham was also unusually sensitive to being hurt—he took things harder than other kids and obsessed about his misfortunes. Dylan Klebold magnified his adolescent angst into "the most miserable existence in the history of time." [139]

These shooters had masochistic personalities, meaning they dwelled on their misfortunes, exaggerated their suffering, and obsessed about being victims. As described by Dr. David Shapiro, such people "are chronically aggrieved, constantly preoccupied with their suffering. They complain a great deal about having been victimized or unfairly treated." [140] They engage in "the chronic, usually bitter exaggeration and 'nursing' of humiliations, defeats, and injustices." [141] The FBI identified school shooters as often being "injustice collectors," people who go through life keeping a mental account of all the wrongs they've suffered. This is another name for a masochistic personality.

Speaking generally, the psychotic secondary school shooters grew up in the shadow of higher-functioning siblings. They struggled socially and failed in their attempts at romance. They were alienated from their peers and misfits in their families. They did not recover from being hurt, holding onto and magnifying their pain. They questioned their identities, as many teenagers are wont to do, but often took it further and even questioned their status as humans. To compensate for their fragile, inadequate identities, they attached themselves to sources of strength in the form of dominant peers, infamous role models, or ideologies of power. Several shooters were encouraged by their peers to kill. As they progressed through adolescence, they heard voices, developed paranoid delusions, and created internal realities where they were superior beings. The combination of anguish and alienation, rage at the injustice of their existence, envy of their peers, and active or passive encouragement put them on the path toward rampage.

4

TRAUMATIZED SECONDARY SCHOOL SHOOTERS

A WORD ON TRAUMA

Most school shooters, contrary to what people often think, did not have terrible family lives. This chapter, however, presents some who did. Traumatized school shooters were not simply abused children but experienced multiple difficulties that caused unstable, overwhelmingly stressful lives.

Though physical and sexual abuse occur at all levels of society, the shooters presented here were at the lower end of the socioeconomic spectrum. Some grew up in poverty and filth. Others had better living conditions with at least one working parent. One shooter, Mitchell Johnson, had two working parents but lived in a filthy, unkempt environment.

These shooters experienced significant disruption and loss within their families. They often lost parents through separation, divorce, prison, brain damage, or death. Even when parents were physically present, they were often emotionally absent due to alcoholism and drug addiction. Addicts can wreak havoc in families due to financial problems, arrests, and unsavory characters passing through the home. Children in these families often endured frequent relocations and changing caregivers, adding further instability and uncertainty to their lives.

These shooters were traumatized by physical, and sometimes sexual, abuse. But what is *trauma*? In psychology, a traumatic event is a dangerous or disturbing situation that may be life threatening or that causes intense fear for one's safety. The trauma may be something done directly to us or something that we witness happening to others. Trauma can result in posttraumatic stress disorder (PTSD). No attempt is made here to formally diagnose the shooters with PTSD because many of the diagnostic criteria are internal experiences that we do not have access to. Nonetheless, an understanding of PTSD is important because it can account for many behaviors these shooters displayed.

People with PTSD feel extreme anxiety, especially in the presence of anything that reminds them of the trauma. A teacher's yelling may trigger memories of a parent's drunken rages, causing severe distress in the student. People with PTSD often can see no future for themselves, feeling as if their lives have come to an end. In fact, the affliction often results in depression and suicidal thoughts. PTSD may also involve shame, feeling permanently damaged, problems managing one's emotions, withdrawal from relationships, impaired social skills, hostility, suspicion, impulsive behavior, and substance abuse.

Physical abuse can cause both physical and emotional pain, with the emotional pain often lasting far longer. Children may feel unloved and unwanted. A drunken adult raging through the house, damaging property and assaulting family members, can leave children feeling terror, helplessness, and hopelessness. Sexual abuse may have all of these effects and more. Issues of shame, secrecy, and confusion can make sexual abuse far more damaging than physical abuse. Male children who are molested by males often have concerns about being gay, causing additional anxiety and depression.

It is crucial to keep in mind the impact that experiencing and witnessing violence can have on children. These shooters were not just kids with strict parents who used harsh punishments. They were children whose lives were full of disruption, chaos, violence, shame, hopelessness, terror, and, ultimately, rage.

ATTACKS BY TRAUMATIZED SECONDARY SCHOOL SHOOTERS

Eric Houston

"If I die today please bury me somewhere beautiful."

Date: May 1, 1992
Age: 20
School: Lindhurst High School
Location: Oliverhurst, CA

Killed: 4
Wounded: 10
Outcome: Held 70 students hostage for 8 hours, gradually let them go, and then surrendered. In prison

Eric Houston was born into a family plagued by incest, alcoholism, physical abuse, suicide, and murder. His mother was physically abused by multiple relatives. His aunt was molested by Houston's grandfather. His uncle murdered three people in a fight. A grandmother died by suicide. Houston's father was a violent alcoholic who abandoned the family. On top of this, Houston himself suffered encephalitis, meningitis, and severe pneumonia in infancy; perhaps as a result, his development was delayed.[1]

Houston's mother described her home in dark detail. "My husband was drinking and running around with other women; fighting," she said. "There was a lot of fighting going on. A lot of really bad scene[s]. I went through some suicidal things myself and tried to hold my marriage together. It wasn't working."[2] Later in his life, Houston lived briefly with his father and stepmother; both had drinking problems, and the father used "a lot of heavy drugs."[3]

According to Dr. Jonathan Fast, Houston suffered "violent physical abuse."[4] Was Houston also sexually abused? His grandfather was a sex offender; it would not be unusual for there to be unreported victims. Even if the grandfather did not molest Houston, another victimized family member might have. One molested family member often molests others.

During Houston's trial there was discussion about a photograph of him at approximately age three. He was wearing a girl's dress and hat. The back of the photograph said, "To Daddy. Love Christopher." Christopher was Houston's middle name. It was also written, "See, daddy, Chris was a good girl. You never believe he's a boy."[5] If Houston was only three, who wrote these messages? Did Houston dress himself up as a girl, or did somebody do this to him? Sexual abuse and being dressed as a girl could have had a profound impact on his identity development.

Another identity issue for Houston was his belief that he had been adopted. His parents said this wasn't true.[6] Regardless, what matters is that he believed he was adopted, which also meant he believed his parents lied to him and hid the truth.

Between second and third grade Houston was identified as "learning handicapped" and started attending special classes. At the end of third grade he was still performing as a beginning first grader; after three years of school he was three years behind. His academic difficulties were likely compounded by his family's frequent relocations around California. Moving disrupted not only his education but also his friendships; he was repeatedly the new kid on the block and in the classroom.

When Houston was twelve or thirteen years old, he became fascinated with the military, weapons, and SWAT teams. In light of the photograph of him dressed as a girl, his fascination with ultramasculine activities beginning around the onset of puberty is interesting. Perhaps his masculinity was threatened, driving him to overcompensate by seeking to establish a powerful male identity.

In 1988, around age sixteen, Houston had a girlfriend. When the relationship ended, he attempted suicide. In 1989, Houston reportedly was molested by his teacher, Robert Brens. Though Houston's allegations were challenged in court, he provided detailed accounts of the events. Also, a friend reported that Houston had disclosed his molestation prior to the rampage, providing corroboration for Houston's testimony.

There were two significant outcomes of the relationship with Mr. Brens. First, Houston was traumatized and questioned his sexual orientation. He became "obsessed with what this meant, what did it mean about him."[7] Following the molestations, Houston had a single homosexual encounter with a friend and also went to a gay bar at least once. A friend reported that Houston "blamed the teacher for his feelings of homosexuality."[8]

The second significant outcome was that Brens failed Houston in his course. This meant that Houston did not graduate with his class in 1989. In fact, he never did graduate. This would loom larger over time, preventing him from joining the military as he desired and limiting his job opportunities. Though the abuse occurred in 1989, Houston did not commit his attack until 1992.

What triggered his attack? Houston had been doing temporary work at Hewlett-Packard with his half-brother, Ron Caddell. Houston, however, was not employed by Hewlett-Packard but placed there through an agency. When his contract expired, Hewlett-Packard was not able to hire him because he lacked a high school diploma. He ended up on unemployment and became increasingly depressed. Caddell commented that Houston would "every now and then . . . get into these quiet spells where he didn't want to talk to me or my mom and kind of go like by himself."[9] These depressive episodes became worse once he was out of work.

Other stresses were piling up. The friend he had a homosexual experience with wanted Houston to be his sexual partner, but Houston wanted to date women. This caused conflict between them. Houston found a girlfriend, but she left him shortly before his attack. He had poor relationships with family members. His mother pressured him to move out and support himself. Faced with the prospect of being self-sufficient, the lack of a diploma became more significant. This fed his rage toward Brens. Houston also reportedly drank, tried marijuana, and, according to his mother, had probably tried other drugs.

Houston began talking to a friend about going back to his high school and shooting people. This reportedly began as joking around. Houston, however, was fascinated by military tactics and had accumulated weapons and ammunition, and his fantasy of committing a rampage attack became more and more real. On May 1, 1992, Houston turned the fantasy into reality. He shot and killed Brens, shot random people, and held seventy students hostage for up to eight hours. Houston claimed the attack was revenge against Brens for ruining his life. He also wanted to make the public aware that he had been molested at the school so no other students would go through what he did.

Houston was surprisingly concerned about his hostages. He had Advil brought in for students who had headaches. He asked if anyone was hungry, and when students said yes, he exchanged hostages for pizza and soda. He sent a student to help carry wounded victims out of the building. He sent another student to search the school and tell people they could leave. He let students leave who were not feeling well, were extremely upset, or were pregnant. When the last hostages left, he shook their hands and apologized.

※ ※ ※

What caused Houston's rampage? Perhaps it was the accumulation of stresses: being raised in a chaotic and violent family, frequent relocations, being molested by his teacher, confusion about his sexual orientation, failing twelfth grade, breakups with girlfriends, unemployment, pressure to move out on his own, and his struggles with PTSD and depression. Also, a friend talked with Houston about shooting people, providing peer support for Houston's violent thoughts.

Houston's behavior was notable for its contradictions. He shot random people but was kind to his hostages. He committed murder, but part of his motivation was to bring attention to his molestation to prevent it from happening to other students. He blended murderous rage with compassion and virtuous aspiration. Unfortunately, he had poor judgment and was not thinking clearly, and his desire to do good was lost amid the tragedy of his violence.

Gary Scott Pennington

"The worst day of my life was the day I was born."

Date: January 18, 1993   **Killed**: 2
Age: 17   **Wounded**: 0
School: East Carter High   **Outcome**: Held class hostage
School   for 20 minutes, then
Location: Grayson, KY   surrendered. In prison

Gary Pennington was an honors student who reportedly was smarter than just about any other kid in the county. In seventh grade he won a science competition for the eastern region of Kentucky. In high school, he taught himself calculus over the summer.[10] Why, then, did he gun down his English teacher and a custodian and hold his class hostage?

Though Pennington was the opposite of Eric Houston in terms of academic achievement, the two had many things in common. Pennington's father was an alcoholic and drug abuser[11] whose substance abuse caused mental impairment.[12] Mr. Pennington was on disability and his family survived on public assistance and whatever odd jobs he could find. The family was so poor that "Pennington was embarrassed by the family's dilapidated wooden house with no telephone, toilet, or running water."[13]

The father physically abused both his wife and Pennington.[14] An aunt commented about Pennington and his father, saying that "there was no relationship. . . . There was just nothing there."[15] Once when he was addressed as Gary, Pennington declared, "I want to be called Scott. . . . My father's name is Gary, and I hate my father."[16] Making matters even worse, Pennington's mother was reportedly psychotic.[17]

In addition to the difficulties at home, Pennington was bullied at school. After the attack, a student testified that he had once beaten up Pennington while fifteen students had watched.[18] Another student recalled Pennington's sitting silently on the school bus as kids called him "nerd, geek, and dork."[19] One student admitted that he punched Pennington in the nose and mouth and kneed him in a fight.[20] A week before the attack, a bully teased him and then beat him up.[21]

Why was Pennington picked on? Perhaps because he was a shy kid who stuttered. Perhaps because of his intelligence. Maybe because he was new to the school that year, having relocated after his family had been evicted.[22] Being the new kid may have been part of the problem, but a friend said Pennington had been tormented at school since sixth grade.[23] Pennington's aunt testified that even other children in his family made fun of him for stuttering.[24]

In a writing assignment for his teacher, Deanna McDavid, Pennington wrote, "The worst day of my life was the day I was born . . . the day I realized that no matter what I did, Dad would never love me . . . the day when I discovered I had no friends, my stuttering became more pronounced . . . I realized what hell life was . . . I have been serving 11 years of hell."[25] Just before Christmas, McDavid gave Pennington a C on his English midterm. He was upset by the low grade and asked her to change it, but she held firm. Pennington told friends he hated McDavid and contemplated either putting a bomb in her mailbox or shooting her.[26] He suffered another blow when his first girlfriend broke up with him shortly before Christmas.[27]

Not long after winter break, Pennington walked into McDavid's class several minutes late. He shot at her and missed, then shot her again, killing her. A custodian heard the noise, entered the room, and confronted Pennington; Pennington shot and killed him. Then he taunted the class, saying, "Do you like me now? . . . Do you think I'm crazy? . . . What's the matter, cat got your tongues?"[28] Though he initially threatened the students by saying he had enough bullets for each of them, he then said, "You don't have to worry. The next person I shoot will probably be myself."[29] He did not, however, shoot himself or anyone else. He gradually let the students leave and after about twenty minutes surrendered to police.

Pennington hated his violent, alcoholic, drug-addicted father, but he didn't target him. He may have hated the bullies who beat him up, but he didn't target them. He targeted the teacher who gave him a C. What sense does this make? Perhaps he tolerated his dysfunctional family; after all, this was all he had ever known. Perhaps he never expected to be liked by his peers and was used to being picked on. The one area in which he excelled, however, was academics. His intelligence was the foundation of his identity. When this was threatened by a poor grade, it apparently was more than he could tolerate. But the C was not the only factor. He might have endured the low grade if his girlfriend hadn't left him. Similarly, if he hadn't been raised in a chaotic family, if he hadn't felt abandoned and unloved by his father, if he hadn't been harassed for years by his peers, maybe a C wouldn't have mattered so much.

❈ ❈ ❈

Pennington's family, like Houston's, was rife with parental violence and substance abuse. Though Pennington may not have had frequent relocations, he was a new kid at his school. Whereas Houston was molested by a teacher, Pennington was harassed and assaulted by his peers. Thus, both were victimized at home and at school. Pennington, like Houston, had several stressors shortly before his attack: a breakup with his girlfriend, conflict with a teacher, and being beaten up the week before his rampage. Finally, both Houston and Pennington targeted teachers due to real or perceived victimization.

James Rouse

"Mama, people are dead because of me."

Date: November 15, 1995   **Killed**: 2
Age: 17   **Wounded**: 1
School: Richland High School   **Outcome**: Apprehended.
Location: Lynville, TN   In prison

Jamie Rouse's father was an alcoholic and a drug addict. On four occasions he spent the night in jail, twice for reckless driving and twice for driving under the influence. His drinking got him fired from multiple jobs. Cocaine was a daily habit for years; he also used marijuana, quaaludes, amphetamines, and crystal meth. His substance abuse nearly bankrupted the family. At one point, he came home to find his wife and kids gone, and a long letter from his wife waiting for him. After that, he decided to turn his life around.[30] By the time his son, Jamie, committed a rampage attack, Mr. Rouse had been clean and sober for a year and a half.

By then, however, the damage had been done. The father had been a violent man who beat his kids with belts and paddles.[31] He punched holes in the walls of their home during drunken rages. He once blasted six pet cats with a shotgun and flung the carcasses into trees. Rouse lived in terror of his father's violence. Recalling one incident of abuse, Rouse said "My Daddy came in there, and he raised me by the arm, and [he started whipping] the back of my legs, and my butt too, and he just kept doing it. I had bruises and welts, even a few days afterward. I just lay there and cried on the floor."[32] Rouse's father was a truck driver; he was on the road the day of the shooting. He later commented, "To this day, I still believe if I'd been home that day, I'd been the one that died."[33] He knew that his son had reasons for hating him to the point of wanting him dead. And yet, if Rouse had wanted to kill his father, he could have done so.

Instead, he shot two teachers and aimed at a coach but missed him, killing his best friend's sister. Why shoot teachers? Rouse had talked to friends about killing a girl at school, the principal, and a state trooper who had twice caught him speeding. Yet, when asked immediately afterward what was on his mind as he entered the school, he replied, "Kill all the teachers."[34] This was a mystery to Rouse himself. "Those people, the victims, hadn't ever done nothing to me," he said. "It would have been different if they had picked on me, but they never picked on me or nothing."[35] It is interesting that his father had four teachers in the family: his parents, his sister, and his brother-in-law. Perhaps Rouse associated teachers with his father's family and instead of killing his father, killed innocent people who represented his father.

But what drove Rouse to want to kill in the first place? After all, his father had been clean and sober for eighteen months. This was the most stability the family had ever known. Why go on a rampage when he did? As with Houston and Pennington, there were multiple stressors. In eleventh grade Rouse began going out with a girl. This relationship lasted several months. It isn't clear when it ended, but she broke up with him. Rouse felt devastated and admitted that he had thoughts of killing her.[36]

In twelfth grade, Rouse wanted to drop out of school and get his GED. His parents, however, objected and pressured him to stay in school. In addition, Rouse worked eight hours after school, from 2 p.m. until 10 p.m. To manage this grueling schedule, he used MaxAlert to stay awake and then Tylenol PM to get to sleep. He also drank alcohol and used marijuana.[37]

Not surprisingly, given his substance use, Rouse got four traffic tickets within nine months and lost his license. When he got his license back, he had further trouble. On November 12, three days before his attack, he backed his father's pickup into a car at a service station. When the girlfriend of the man who owned the car heard him talking about it, she confronted him angrily and said, "I hope you've got insurance." Rouse, panicked about further legal trouble and losing his license again, responded with, "You'd better have life insurance." Later, he recalled, "I almost felt like I could kill her."[38]

On top of this, Rouse was incorrectly marked absent at school, and a truancy officer called his mother. This was not a major issue, but it was one more upsetting event. Rouse was overworked, abusing substances, and worried about losing his license again. In addition, he had a lifetime of fear, trauma, and rage built up from his home life. He later recalled his mental state, "I was so stressed out, I guess. I don't know. I had a lot of conflict, and mostly, at that time, I guess I just had kind of a panicked feeling. I was angry, depressed, worried, all at one time. I'd get extremely angry, and in a split second I'd feel like crying, and then I would go back to being extremely angry."[39] The movie *Natural Born Killers* was another possible factor in Rouse's psychological state. After his attack, he commented of the film, "It made killing look easy and fun . . . it fascinated me."[40] He talked about why violence was appealing: "I guess for so long I'd felt helpless and weak, and with violence, you know, you have control."[41] Control had been noticeably absent from his life. In taking control for a few brief moments, however, he committed acts that destroyed him emotionally.

While in prison, Rouse tried to kill himself. When his mother asked him why, he said, "Mama, people are dead because of me."[42] This was the first of many suicide attempts. Rouse literally could not live with what he had done.

✳ ✳ ✳

Houston, Pennington, and Rouse all targeted teachers. Rouse's attack was different, however. Whereas Houston killed the teacher who molested him and failed him, and Pennington killed the teacher who had given him an unacceptable grade, Rouse shot random teachers for no known reason. This makes his attack harder to comprehend. His attack seemed to be the most impulsive, the least planned, the most driven by immediate emotion.

All three of these shooters discussed their ideas for attacks with friends. It seems the friends did not actively encourage the shooters to kill, but neither did they object to the talk of murder. The shooters may have taken this as tacit approval for the attacks.

Evan Ramsey

"I don't know who my parents are; that was another thing that hurts. It seemed like all my friends knew their fathers."

Date: February 19, 1997
Age: 16
School: Bethel High School
Location: Bethel, AK

Killed: 2
Wounded: 2
Outcome: Intended suicide, but decided against it. Surrendered. In prison

Evan Ramsey's father was known as "the Rambo of Alaska." Donald Ramsey went on an armed rampage when Evan was five years old because the publisher of the *Anchorage Times* did not print an advertisement he had paid for. Mr. Ramsey also believed the publisher had his apartment set on fire in an attempt to kill him. Heavily armed, Mr. Ramsey stormed the newspaper building, looking for the publisher. He chained the doors shut and set off a smoke grenade, starting a fire. He found the publisher and his daughter, who struggled with Mr. Ramsey, eventually subduing him. [43] "The Rambo of Alaska" served ten years in prison. Evan Ramsey called his father's legacy "the family curse." [44]

The family curse also hit Ramsey's older brother, John. Five days before Ramsey's attack, an armed John Ramsey robbed a porn shop. [45] John had been racking up criminal charges since he was twelve years old, including theft, assault, and the illegal use of firearms. [46] In addition, a man named Willie Billy, one of Ramsey's mother's boyfriends, had a long list of criminal charges including misconduct with a weapon. [47] At least three men in Ramsey's family constellation used guns illegally; his friends, however, convinced him to kill.

Ramsey told two buddies he wanted to take a gun to school, scare people, and then kill himself. His friends, James Randall and Matthew Charles, talked him into murder. They showed him how to use a shotgun and said he would become famous. Randall reportedly told him, "Don't kill yourself. . . . You got to live the fame and the fortune." [48] Charles urged Ramsey over and over again to kill the principal, Ron Edwards. Randall pressured Ramsey, saying, "You can't go back, everybody would think you're nothing. Everybody would just have one more reason to mess with you." [49]

Ramsey, depressed, confused, and pressured by his peers, did as he was told. He shot Ron Edwards, killing him. He also shot and killed Josh Palacios, a boy who had reportedly harassed him. Besides picking on Ramsey, Palacios was a star basketball player who was handsome and attractive to girls.[50] Ramsey may have shot him out of revenge, out of envy, or because his friends told him to.

What events drove Ramsey to suicidal thoughts and homicidal actions? Whereas the previous three shooters had fathers who were violent substance abusers, violence and substance abuse were split among Ramsey's father, mother, and mother's boyfriends. Mr. Ramsey's rampage at the newspaper building showed his violent nature. Ramsey's mother, Carol, had a serious alcohol problem that became devastating after Donald was imprisoned. She often drank from morning to night, passing out and neglecting her three children—John, Evan, and William.[51] Carol was arrested once for drunk driving and another time for public drunkenness. Once a social worker found the boys huddled in the apartment with their mother drunk and unconscious. There was no heat in the apartment; outside, the temperature was twenty-two degrees below zero.[52]

After her husband's incarceration, Carol moved in with a man in another town, bringing her three boys with her. This boyfriend was violent. Carol then moved in with another man in a different town. This boyfriend was also violent.[53] One of these boyfriends may have been Willie Billy, or perhaps he was a third violent boyfriend. Carol went to court over Mr. Billy's domestic violence. In fact, Willie Billy crossed paths with the legal system in two dozen different incidents from 1983 to 2000, for reasons including intoxication, assault, criminal trespass, misconduct with a weapon, attempted sexual assault, and failure to register as a sex offender.[54] It would not be surprising if he physically or sexually abused the Ramsey boys.

When Ramsey's mother sunk into chronic drunkenness, her three sons were removed from her care and placed in foster homes. Ramsey moved through eleven homes in two years. In one home, an older boy assaulted Ramsey, leaving bruises on his face and neck. The boy also molested Ramsey and urinated in his mouth.[55]

Eventually, Ramsey ended up in foster care with the school superintendent. She had an adult adopted son who had pleaded "no contest to sexual abuse of a minor."[56] Though it was against state law to have a sex offender living with foster children, this situation slipped through the cracks. Ramsey never reported being molested in this home; perhaps there was no molestation, or perhaps he kept silent to protect his foster mother. He described her as "the nicest person I've ever met."[57] She took him in and was like a mother to him.

At age ten, Ramsey reportedly attempted suicide.[58] He was suicidal again at fourteen.[59] Not everything in his life was bleak, however. He had a group of friends with whom he hung out, talked, and smoked marijuana. Despite his tumultuous childhood, Ramsey was generally seen as a polite and likable young man. He had angry outbursts at school and at home, but by age sixteen his behavior had improved.[60]

What triggered Ramsey's violence? As with other shooters, several events occurred shortly before the attack that exacerbated his distress. There was girlfriend trouble: "all of a sudden, she said no more, [expletive] you, and left town. It was a pretty depressing situation."[61] He also had a CD player confiscated at school the week before the attack. It was a minor incident, but it bothered him.

Perhaps more important were the family events. His father finished his ten-year sentence on January 13, 1997.[62] On February 9, he called Ramsey and announced he was out of prison.[63] We can only speculate about how this affected Ramsey. Was he excited or perhaps terrified? Would his father expect him to move in with him? The prospect of living with "the Rambo of Alaska" might have been overwhelming. A few days after his father's call, Ramsey's brother was arrested for armed robbery. Did this suggest that all the men in his family were destined to be violent?

Though Ramsey intended to kill himself during the attack, he did not do so. He put a gun under his chin but didn't shoot.[64] He surrendered to the police and is in prison for the rest of his life.

❁ ❁ ❁

Ramsey shares many features with the previous shooters in terms of family history and trauma. In addition, like the other shooters presented so far, Ramsey targeted an adult at the school. Unlike the other shooters, Ramsey also sought out and killed a boy who had harassed him. How much this was his idea versus his friends' remains unknown.

What stands out in Ramsey's case was the significant criminal activity in his family, the number of violent men in his life, and the multiple role models for the misuse of firearms. Another prominent feature was the extent of his friends' influence on his attack. In fact, without peer influence, there apparently would have been no attack. He planned to only kill himself at school; his friends convinced him to kill others. This is the first case where the idea of committing a school shooting did not originate with the shooter. The following case presents a different twist on this dynamic.

Mitchell Johnson

"I felt cornered. I felt like I didn't have anywhere to go, nothing to do. I thought my life was at an end."

Date: March 24, 1998
Age: 13
School: Westside Middle School
Location: Jonesboro, AR

Killed: 1
Wounded: 3
Outcome: Planned escape. Apprehended. In prison until he turned 21, then released. Back in prison on other charges (not violent crimes)

According to Mitchell Johnson, the school shooting was not his idea. His friend, Andrew Golden, recruited him.[65] This appears to be the case, even though Golden was only eleven years old to Johnson's thirteen. Johnson fired his rifle five times while Golden fired twenty-five shots, which implies that Golden was indeed the aggressor.[66] Johnson used a high-powered rifle with a telescopic sight, so he could clearly see his targets.

Who were his targets? One was Candace Porter, a girl he went out with briefly who broke up with him shortly before the attack. After the attack several students reported that Johnson had talked about killing all the girls who rejected him.[67] Another girl who had rejected his advances was also shot, but ballistics could not determine whether Golden or Johnson had shot her. This is where facts give way to speculation.

As noted, Johnson fired five shots, hitting either four or five people. According to an article in the *New York Times*, ballistics experts reported that Shannon Wright, a teacher, was hit twice by bullets from Johnson's gun.[68] Elsewhere it was reported that Wright was hit inadvertently. However, if Johnson hit Wright twice, this suggests that he was aiming for her. This would mean that Johnson was not the one who killed the second girl who rejected him. Thus, Johnson may have targeted one girl and a teacher, or else he may have targeted two girls and hit the teacher by mistake.

But why target anyone? As with other traumatized shooters, there were both long-term factors and recent stresses. Johnson's parents had a stormy marriage that had ended in divorce after eleven years. Mr. Johnson smoked marijuana and had been fired from one job because of theft. He also had an explosive temper, punching holes in walls and abusing his son. Of his father's treatment, Johnson said, "He cussed me all the time. Used to hit me, fight with me. . . . Punch me in the face, slap me around, throw me against the walls."[69] His father sometimes terrified Johnson to the point of vomiting.[70]

Not only was he physically abused at home, but an older boy reportedly sexually abused him from ages eight to twelve.[71] This boy violently raped Johnson and threatened to kill his grandmother if he told. Johnson suffered both from the abuse itself as well as fearing for his grandmother's safety. The perpetrator also molested Johnson's younger brother, which presumably exacerbated Johnson's helplessness and rage. During his deposition, Johnson referred to the molestations: "That had a lot to do with my anger, had a lot to do with why I was so mad all the time."[72]

After his parents' divorce, Johnson's mother moved from Minnesota to Arkansas. She married her third husband, an ex-convict who had served time for a variety of charges, including a firearms violation.[73] Johnson reportedly admired his stepfather, thinking it was cool that he had been in prison. Johnson lived with his mother in Arkansas during the school year and spent summers with his father in Minnesota. According to Johnson, "Me and my dad never got along, me and my real dad, Scott. I would go up there [to Minnesota], and I hated it."[74]

In the year leading up to the shooting, Johnson had one problem after another. In sixth grade, he lost his temper at school and slammed a thermostat with his fist, breaking the glass. Shannon Wright, the teacher he later killed, gave him in-school suspension.[75] Then, over the summer, a girl in Minnesota broke up with him, and he became suicidal. That same summer, he was caught molesting a two-year-old girl while changing her diaper; he admitted he stuck his finger in her vagina and was charged in juvenile court.[76] Perhaps it was this summer, if not earlier, that he began smoking marijuana.

A month before the shooting he was caught using his father's credit card to call telephone sex lines; he had run up several hundred dollars worth of calls. His father was furious. He reported his son to the police, accused his ex-wife of unfit parenting, and threatened to have Johnson live with him. This prospect left Johnson feeling hopeless.[77]

Other stresses piled up. A few weeks before the attack he wore a baseball cap to school. This violated school policy, but when teachers confronted him, he refused to remove it. They tussled and ripped the hat from his hands. He was suspended again. "Mitchell was humiliated, furious, and unrepentant."[78]

Not long after this, he was either kicked off the basketball team for self-mutilation or else tried out and didn't make the team—stories differ.[79] Johnson had peer conflicts, but he was not bullied. Some people said he *was* a bully. He bragged about being a gang member, claiming he was in the Bloods; when kids didn't believe him, he flew off the handle. Perhaps the final straw was that shortly before the attack he went out with Candace Porter but she broke up with him.[80]

Years after the shooting, Johnson recalled how he felt in the period leading up to his rampage: "I remember feeling like I was trapped, like no one understood me. . . . I felt cornered. I felt like I didn't have anywhere to go, nothing to do. I thought my life was at an end."[81]

❅ ❅ ❅

What factors led Johnson to participate in the attack? Physical abuse by his father, four years of brutal sexual abuse, legal troubles, disciplinary issues, rejection by girls, the threat of having to live with his father again, and Andrew Golden's persuasion to join the attack. Like Evan Ramsey, Mitchell Johnson would probably not have committed an attack without peer influence. Both boys faced possible reunification with violent fathers, a potentially terrifying prospect. Johnson, like other traumatized shooters, had a family role model for the misuse of firearms. Finally, if Johnson did target Shannon Wright, the teacher he killed, then like the previous traumatized shooters, he targeted school personnel.

Jason Hoffman

"I got to thinking, 'What the hell is the point of life?'
It was like I dove off a cliff."

Date: March 22, 2001   **Killed**: 0
Age: 18   **Wounded**: 5
School: Granite Hills High   **Outcome**: Intended
School   "suicide by cop."
Location: El Cajon, CA   Was shot and wounded.
                                     Died by suicide in prison

Contrary to popular opinion, most school shooters were not loners; Jason Hoffman, however, came close. He apparently had one friend, and when the boy moved away, Hoffman was essentially alone.[82] Apart from his lack of friends, Hoffman's case resembles those reviewed so far. His childhood was unstable and violent. His parents, Ralph Hoffman and Denise Marquez, never married. His father was an alcoholic with criminal charges of public drunkenness and malicious mischief. As noted by a social worker's report, "The situation has been unsafe for Jason since virtually his birth."[83]

Mr. Hoffman reportedly threw his three-month-old son at Ms. Marquez during a fight;[84] fourteen months later he was arrested. "Jason Hoffman came to the attention of authorities when he was just seventeen months of age after an incident in which his father was drunk, took the minor into a swimming pool, threw him toward the deep end . . . and continuously submerged the minor for a period of approximately fifteen minutes even though the minor was obviously terrified."[85]

Mr. Hoffman's comment at the time was, "The kid loved the water . . . and besides, I didn't let him stay under that long."[86] Mr. Hoffman also reportedly assaulted Ms. Marquez and banged her head against the wall. When Jason Hoffman was seven years old, his father reportedly urinated on him in the shower.[87]

There is minimal information about the years between Hoffman's childhood and his attack. During high school he reportedly kept to himself. He was generally silent, had a quick temper, and was not bullied. One student said, "He had this hate-the-world walk. . . . Most of the kids were afraid of him."[88] Another student said, "He was always trying to start fights with people."[89] He was a large, intimidating young man. He was arrested in tenth grade for hitting a peer in the head with a racquet during an argument.[90]

What drove Hoffman to commit a rampage attack? First, he was chronically unhappy and angry. Second, academics were not his strength. At some point he had been in special-education classes.[91] He was supposed to graduate in 2000 but did not have enough credits and had to repeat his senior year. It was also reported that he did not have enough credits to graduate in 2001.[92] He took a math class at a community college and did not do well. He also lost his job at McDonald's for failing to learn to use the cash register.[93]

Perhaps in response to these failures, he tried to enlist in the navy. Unfortunately, he was rejected. The following day he committed his attack.[94] When he arrived outside the school, he saw the vice principal, Dan Barnes. Hoffman cried, "I've got you."[95] He shot at Barnes but missed. He went on shooting, however, wounding two teachers and three students. He was wounded twice by a school resource officer and apprehended. Hoffman said he had intended to commit "suicide by cop." Failing in this, Hoffman killed himself in jail.[96]

After the attack, Hoffman told investigators he wanted to kill Barnes because he blamed him for his rejection by the navy. For some reason, Hoffman believed Barnes was out to get him. Barnes had met with him four times regarding counseling and disciplinary issues but said their last meeting on February 23 had been positive.[97]

One other fact may be of importance. On March 5, 2001, just over two weeks before Hoffman's attack, Charles "Andy" Williams committed a school shooting at Santana High School in Santee, California. Not only were the attacks less than three weeks apart, they were also less than five miles apart. Was Hoffman influenced by the attack by Williams? He left no statements to this effect, but the proximity in time and place is striking.

* * *

Hoffman differed from other traumatized shooters because he did not discuss his plans with friends. Indeed, he doesn't seem to have had any friends at the time of his attack, and this sets him apart from other traumatized shooters. His attack was also not preceded by a breakup with a girlfriend because he apparently never had a girlfriend. He did, however, experience other rejections: his impending failure to graduate at the end of his second senior year, failure at the community college, failure at McDonald's, and rejection by the navy.

Though the details of his life are few, they match the family history of other traumatized shooters. His father was an abusive alcoholic, and Hoffman grew up amid domestic violence and threats to his safety. Also, like other traumatized shooters, he targeted an adult at the school. One feature of Hoffman's case is new and will be seen in many other cases—military failure. Rejection by the military apparently was a devastating blow to Hoffman; he committed his attack less than twenty-four hours later.

Jeffrey Weise

"Sixteen years of accumulated rage."

Date: March 21, 2005   **Killed**: 9
Age: 16   **Wounded**: 7
School: Red Lake High   **Outcome**: Shot by police
School   during attack.
Location: Red Lake, MN   Died by suicide

Jeffrey Weise was a writer; he had a way with words. He posted his zombie fiction online and also posted personal material about himself. Though many details of his life are missing, we have a glimpse into his internal world through his writings. [98]

Weise's parents, Joanne Weise and Daryl Lussier Jr., were Native American. They were not married when Jeffrey was born and may never have lived together with Jeffrey. When Weise was three months old, his mother, who lived in Minneapolis, gave him to his father, who lived on the reservation at Red Lake, Minnesota. For three years, Weise was raised by his father and his father's parents. Then, he went back to live with his mother in Minneapolis. Weise's life was characterized by relocations and changing caregivers.

Very little is known about Weise's father. He reportedly was "a real nice guy when he was sober,"[99] which implies that he was often not sober and that he was not a nice guy when drunk. One crucial fact is that Lussier killed himself during an armed standoff with tribal police. This incident was particularly heartrending because Lussier's father was one of the officers trying to resolve the standoff. Daryl Lussier Sr. was not able to talk his son into surrendering; Lussier Jr. shot himself and died. Jeffrey Weise was eight years old.

At this time, Weise lived with his mother and her boyfriend, Timothy Desjarlait. Joanne and Timothy had two children together and eventually married. Life for Weise, however, was not good. He wrote, "My mom used to abuse me a lot when I was little. She . . . used to drink excessively, too. She would tell me I was a mistake, and she should say so many . . . things that it's hard to deal with them or think of them without crying."[100] In addition, "Weise was disciplined by being locked out of the house, locked in the closet, or made to kneel for hours in the corner."[101]

Joanne Weise was jailed once for driving while intoxicated and again for misdemeanor assault.[102] Less than a year after marrying Tim Desjarlait, Joanne and her cousin were out drinking and had a car accident; the cousin was killed, and Joanne suffered brain damage. Desjarlait separated from Joanne and took their two children. He did not take Jeffrey. "Within two years, Jeffrey lost his father to suicide, his mother to brain damage, and his stepfather and half-siblings to separation."[103]

There is no information regarding the impact of these events on Weise, but these were clearly overwhelming losses. A few years later, Weise flunked eighth grade. One source said he was "held back a couple of grades."[104] During his adolescence, he drank and used marijuana. He became depressed and engaged in self-mutilation, using the metal end of a pencil to scratch himself. When he was fifteen, he attempted suicide by cutting his wrists. Of the incident he wrote, "I had went through a lot of things in my life that had driven me to a darker path than most choose to take. I split the flesh on my wrist with a box opener, painting the floor of my bedroom with blood I shouldn't have spilt. After sitting there for what seemed like hours (which apparently was only minutes), I had the revelation that this was not the path."[105] When Weise was fifteen years old, he joined an online discussion forum about the Nazis. The idea of a Native American Nazi may be odd, but

Weise wrote, "I've always carried a natural admiration for Hitler and his ideals, and his courage to take on larger nations."[106] For someone who had been physically abused and spiritually beaten down, perhaps Hitler represented strength.

Though some people said Weise was a loner, this is wrong. He belonged to a group of kids who called themselves "The Darkers." He played in a band. He hung out with friends. In fact, he apparently was well liked by his peers. One girl said, "He was the one I talked to about my problems. . . . He was trustworthy, and he always understood what I was going through."[107] Another peer said, "Jeff often said his friends were the only thing he had in life."[108] A girl named Michelle said, "He was funny. He was cool. . . . Any time I felt sad, he made me feel happy. . . . He always made me laugh."[109]

Was Weise harassed? Reports vary significantly. His maternal grandmother said that three years before the attack, Jeffrey told her that kids punched and tripped him.[110] His aunt said he was picked on because of his appearance, but not badly.[111] A classmate said he was "terrorized" by people who thought he was weird.[112] His paternal grandmother reported, "Kids would say stuff about his mom. . . . They'd say things to him about not having a mother, about not having a dad."[113] In contrast, another peer "denied the contention of other students who said Weise . . . was a target of teasing."[114]

It appears that he was harassed when young, but perhaps not after he became physically imposing. Some sources say he was six feet tall and weighed 250 pounds; others said he was 6'3" and weighed close to three hundred pounds. He liked to style his hair into two "devil horns" on the top of his head. Between his Nazi interest and his deliberately odd appearance, he may have either invited comments or discouraged them. Weise said, "You encounter a lot of hostility when you claim to be a National Socialist, but because of my size and appearance people don't give me as much trouble as they would if I looked weak. . . . I try not to be aggressive in most situations. I'll use force if I have to, but I'm not about to go out and pick a fight. I'm mostly defensive; I'll defend myself if someone tries something."[115] We do not know what role—if any—peer harassment played in his attack. When it came time for his attack, he did not target any particular students.

After slicing his wrist with the box cutter, Weise tried to turn his life around, but there was no stability. With his father dead and his mother incapacitated, Weise bounced back and forth between relatives and foster homes. At some point he was put on homebound instruction, but why this was done is not clear.[116] Whatever the cause, Weise was not attending his school at the time of his attack.

Despite his efforts at getting out of "the grave I'm continually digging for myself,"[117] his depression returned. On January 4, 2005, Weise posted a comment: "I'm starting to regret sticking around, I should've taken the razor blade express last time around. . . . Well, whatever, man. Maybe they've got another shuttle comin' around sometime soon?"[118] Just a few weeks later, his mood sank even further. "So fucking naive man," he wrote despairingly, "so fucking naive. Always expecting change when I know nothing ever changes. I've seen mothers choose their man over their own flesh and blood, I've seen others choose alcohol over friendship. I sacrifice no more for others, part of me has fucking died and I hate this shit. I'm living every man's nightmare and that single fact alone is kicking my ass, I really must be fucking worthless. This place never changes, it never will. Fuck it all."[119] A couple of friends heard him say, "That would be cool if I shot up the school."[120] In addition, Weise had been communicating with his cousin and best friend, Louis Jourdain, for months about carrying out some kind of attack.[121] It is not clear if Jourdain planned on joining Weise's attack or if he were just a sounding board. Whatever their plan might have been, Weise carried out the attack on his own on March 21, 2005.

Alone among traumatized shooters, Weise killed members of his family, shooting his paternal grandfather, Daryl Lussier Sr., and Lussier's girlfriend, Michelle Sigana. After killing his grandfather, he drove Lussier's police cruiser to the school, got out, and began shooting. Weise ended up in an armed standoff with police—just like his father. And just like his father, he chose death.[122]

Weise had written reflections on suicide. He once wrote, "Most people have never dealt with people who have faced the kind of pain that makes you physically sick at times, makes you so depressed you can't function, makes you so sad and overwhelmed with grief that eating a bullet or sticking your head in a noose seems welcoming."[123] In another passage on suicide, he may have been thinking of his father, or perhaps he was anticipating his own death: "It takes courage to turn the gun on yourself, takes courage to face death. Knowing you're going to die and actually following through takes heart."[124]

* * *

Jeffrey Weise resembles other traumatized shooters in his history of abuse, frequent relocations, use of alcohol and marijuana, and peer influence to go on a rampage. Also, like some other traumatized shooters, there was peer harassment. There is no clear evidence that he targeted school personnel, but one account suggested that he pursued Neva Rogers, a teacher who was killed.[125]

Unlike other shooters, Weise's mother was physically abusive. Also, he was the only traumatized shooter to target family members. He was the only one to be attracted to Nazi ideology or any ideology of power. Like Jason Hoffman, there is no record that Weise ever had a romantic relationship; thus, he did not experience the distress of a breakup.

The other traumatized shooters typically had multiple stresses that accumulated shortly before their attacks. If Weise had such stresses, they have not been identified. Perhaps he was angered about being put on homebound instruction, but he left no record of this. It seems that his rampage was driven by all the pain he had endured throughout his life: "16 years of accumulated rage suppressed by nothing more than brief glimpses of hope, which have all but faded to black. I can feel the urges within slipping through the cracks, the leash I can no longer hold."[126]

Eric Hainstock

"I face less abuse in prison than I did at school or at home."

Date: September 29, 2006   **Killed**: 1
Age: 15   **Wounded**: 0
School: Weston High School   **Outcome**: Apprehended.
Location: Cazenovia, WI   Prison

Eric Hainstock shot and killed the principal of his school.[127] Though he only shot one person, he appears to have intended to kill more. He carried two loaded firearms plus additional ammunition. He also had made references to Columbine, which suggests he was planning a large-scale attack.[128] When he showed up at the school, a janitor saw him aiming a shotgun at a teacher and wrestled it from him.[129] Hainstock got away from the custodian, shot the principal, and was immediately apprehended. If things had gone differently, there might have been many more victims.

The Hainstock household was filthy and cluttered.[130] There were indications that his mother had problems with alcohol.[131] His father was unemployed and on disability.[132] In addition, home was a violent place. His father abused Hainstock by hitting him with a piece of wood and whipping him with a belt. The father was charged with felony child abuse, though the charge was later reduced and eventually dismissed.[133] A woman who dated the father got one restraining order against him to protect herself and another to protect her children.[134] According to a reporter, "Hainstock says both parents beat him, kicked him, slapped him, and threw things at him. His dad made him hold hot sauce and peppers in his mouth, which burned so bad 'I couldn't breathe or swallow,' and run laps in the yard, sometimes for hours. He couldn't stop to urinate; 'I would have to pee in my pants or pull it out while I ran.'"[135] Hainstock reportedly was also physically abused by his adoptive mother and his stepfather and sexually abused by his stepbrother, including fondling and anal penetration. Hainstock exhibited inappropriate sexual behavior when he was four years old.[136] Besides the abuse, Hainstock said his father treated him like a slave, making him do housework until midnight. He also reported strange punishments, such as having to stand with his nose touching a wall and one leg lifted in the air.[137]

When Hainstock came to school with a split lip, Mr. Hainstock was investigated for abusive behavior, but the allegation was dismissed. Once Hainstock showed up at school without a shirt and another time was "filthy and smelling."[138] Both times the school filed reports of neglect; both times the allegations were dismissed. Hainstock also had to deal with moving to a new home eight times in nine years.

Hainstock's mother apparently wanted nothing to do with him. She gave up her parental rights when he was eight years old.[139] She apparently dropped out of his life and wasn't even on his list of visitors when he was in prison after his attack. Regarding his home life, Hainstock said, "I would accept all the beatings if I could have just heard one 'I love you' or 'Good job, Eric.'"[140]

In addition to the abuse at home, Hainstock reported severe bullying at school: "I would be slapped, hit all over the body, pushed in bushes or thrown to the ground, my head was stuck in dirty toilets."[141] Hainstock was gay,[142] and he reported chronic harassment about his sexual orientation: "Every day the same thing. They would call me names in the hall, in class, at lunch, before school and after."[143]

Other students, however, challenged his reports and said that Hainstock was a bully himself. He admitted to harassing a couple of students but claimed the mistreatment he received was far worse than what he did to others. A peer, however, said that Hainstock "would push people more than he got pushed."[144] In addition, a guidance counselor who knew Hainstock said he enjoyed playing the role of victim and that his accounts of abuse at school were not accurate.[145] Finally, Hainstock's credibility is damaged by his postattack statements that he never meant to kill the principal.

Hainstock struggled with academics. In seventh grade he functioned at a fourth- to fifth-grade level.[146] His academic performance presumably was not helped by his drug use, which by his report included marijuana, cocaine, LSD, psychedelic mushrooms, and heroin.[147]

Two weeks before his attack, Hainstock quarreled with a student and threw a stapler at his special-education teacher. The principal, John Klang, suspended Hainstock for three days.[148] Hainstock was also charged with disorderly conduct, criminal damage, and recklessly endangering safety. A few days later he had a fight with his adoptive mother in which she reportedly bit him. The day before the shooting, Klang gave him an in-school suspension for bringing tobacco to school.

After the attack, Hainstock said he had brought a gun to school to force Klang to listen to his complaints about being bullied. He denied homicidal intent, claiming that his gun went off accidentally when Klang grabbed him from behind. The court did not accept this. Weeks before the shooting, Hainstock made comments to at least two peers that the principal would not live much longer. The morning of the attack, he reportedly said he was there "to fucking kill somebody."[149] He also had confessed to the police that he deliberately shot Klang three times.[150] Klang was not the only target, however, because Hainstock initially tried to shoot a teacher. Despite his claims of harassment, he made no attempt to kill students.

❈ ❈ ❈

Hainstock resembles other traumatized shooters in multiple ways: his abusive father, the fragmented and dysfunctional family, frequent relocations, sexual abuse, and substance abuse. Also, in addition to the long history of trauma, there were several incidents shortly before the attack that presumably contributed to his rage: a fight with a student, suspension and charges for throwing a stapler at a teacher, a fight with his adoptive mother, and an in-school suspension the day before the attack.

Hainstock differs from the other shooters in the extent of his substance abuse. Also, though Eric Houston experimented with homosexuality, Hainstock is the only shooter discussed so far who identified as gay. He reported severe bullying, but the accuracy of his reports has been challenged. It is not clear if he discussed his attack plans with friends or if peers just happened to hear him remark that the principal would not live much longer. Finally, Hainstock, like most other traumatized shooters, targeted school personnel.

Asa Coon

"Now what have you got to say to me?"

Date: October 10, 2007   **Killed**: 0
Age: 14   **Wounded**: 4
School: SuccessTech Academy   **Outcome**: Suicide
Location: Cleveland, OH

Asa Coon was a bright, well-behaved boy living in horrendous circumstances—at home, at school, and in his neighborhood. Despite growing up amid violence, there are reports that Asa was often polite[151] and ignored his peers' harassment.[152] His father claimed that Asa had been a state chess champion when he was ten years old.[153] His uncle said Asa had won a citywide chess tournament the previous December.[154] Unfortunately, according to the uncle, Coon's intelligence made him a target of his peers.

Coon came from a broken home with a long history of significant dysfunction. His father lived in Florida;[155] it is not known when he left the family. At age four, Coon was the subject of a juvenile court neglect case.[156] The home was described as having a yard littered with dog feces and debris, and Coon often went to school with his face dirty, his clothes shabby, and his hair unkempt. In 2000, the Department of Children and Family Services investigated the home because Coon had scratches on his forehead and burns on his arms.[157] It was difficult to assess the severity of the burns. Why? Because they were covered with flea bites.[158] It was alleged that Coon's brother, Stephen, had burned him, but Coon would not tell what happened.

When Coon was twelve, he was charged with domestic violence for aggression toward his mother. His older brother, Stephen, had a long history of illegal behavior. He had been charged with domestic violence and assault by age thirteen.[159] Later charges included intimidation, burglary, assault, sale of counterfeit drugs, and weapons charges. He spent two years in prison.[160] Stephen and another brother "threatened neighbors with weapons, including rocks, knives, and a fake bomb."[161] Between 2006 and the attack in October 2007, police made five visits to the home in response to calls about domestic violence, assault, property crime, and a hit-and-run accident.[162] There are consistent reports that Coon was harassed at school and in the neighborhood, including fights and beatings.[163]

Coon had several placements out of the home as his behavior deteriorated. He was sent to a shelter pending a placement in a detention center. While in the shelter, he attempted suicide. After being placed in the detention facility, he was sent to a psychiatric hospital.[164]

A woman who volunteered at the school commented on Coon's unkempt appearance: "shabby shoes and raggedy coat—didn't brush his hair, take a washcloth across his face, hair sticking up all over the place."[165] She also said, "That child was tormented from his classmates every single day."[166] A friend of Coon's said, "I ain't justifying nothing . . . I ain't saying he did the right thing, but I am saying he got pushed for a long time and asked them people for help, help, help, help, but nobody helped."[167]

There are remarkable parallels between Asa Coon and Evan Ramsey. Ramsey's father was in prison for a variety of charges, including the illegal use of firearms. Coon's older brother was in prison for a variety of charges, including the illegal use of firearms. About six weeks before Ramsey's attack, his father was released from prison. About six weeks before Coon's attack, his brother was released from prison.[168] Five days before his attack, Ramsey's brother was arrested for armed robbery. Two days before his attack, Coon's brother was arrested for armed robbery.[169]

In addition to these similarities, both boys had disciplinary problems at school shortly before their attacks. Ramsey had a CD player confiscated, and Coon was suspended for fighting.[170] Furthermore, both were harassed at school, had histories of fighting, and had been suicidal. Finally, both boys gave plenty of warning to their peers of what they were about to do.[171] A friend reported that Coon "said if he did shoot up the school he'd let me and some other dude he knew go."[172] He also made threats at school: "He threatened to blow up our school. He threatened to stab everybody."[173] Students also reported that Coon threatened to come to school with a gun and shoot everyone.

Coon targeted at least one teacher in his attack. He was in danger of failing his history class taught by Michael Grassie. Grassie said Coon had tried to pick a fight with him shortly before the attack. On the day of the rampage, Coon walked into his classroom and said to him, "Now what have you got to say to me?" and then shot him.[174] Fortunately, Grassie survived.

✼ ✼ ✼

Unlike most shooters in this category, there is no evidence that Asa's father was violent or that he abused substances, but this lack of evidence may be due to the virtual absence of any information about his father. Coon grew up amid poverty, neglect, and domestic violence. He was bullied, but there is no indication that he targeted anyone who bullied him. Instead, he targeted a teacher. Nor is there any report of a girlfriend. Like most of the other traumatized shooters, Coon talked about his plan with at least one friend.

Thomas "T. J." Lane

"In a quaint lonely town, sits a man with a frown.
No job. No family. No crown."

Date: February 27, 2012   **Killed**: 3
Age: 17   **Wounded**: 3
School: Chardon High School   **Outcome**: Surrendered.
Location: Chardon, OH   Prison

T. J. Lane's parents, Thomas Lane and Sara Nolan, never married. They had a tumultuous relationship in which both were charged with domestic violence.[175] According to Mr. Lane, Ms. Nolan bit and punched him, was "unable to control herself with respect to the use of alcohol," and engaged "in violent, dangerous conduct."[176] Ms. Nolan's behavior was bad enough that she was jailed. She, however, was not as violent as T. J. Lane's father.

Mr. Lane had multiple violent episodes that are difficult to sort out.[177] He was charged with resisting arrest for fighting with an officer who intervened in a domestic altercation and was later imprisoned for beating and kidnapping a woman. This may have been the attack in which he "held his wife's head under running water, then bashed it into the wall, hard enough to leave a dent in the drywall."[178] In 1997, Mr. Lane was charged with pushing a woman around and threatening to kill her. Five years later, Mr. Lane was imprisoned after he "verbally abused and physically attacked another woman over a period of nine hours in the presence of three young children."[179] He was charged with attempted murder and felonious assault. If T. J. Lane were one of the three children present during this episode, he would have been seven years old. It is no surprise that "more than once, police or courts warned [Mr. Lane] to stay away from the boy and his mother."[180] Because of the family chaos, Lane was largely brought up by grandparents, apparently living with his mother's parents and visiting his father's parents on weekends.

Though at first Lane was said to have been an outcast who was bullied, multiple people who knew him said that this was not true.[181] He reportedly had friends and was not picked on[182] and was said by many to be a nice young man who was easy to talk to.[183]

If the attack was not revenge for bullying, why did he shoot people? Though initial reports said he did not know the victims, it was later reported that he had known some since middle school and was even Facebook friends with them.[184] The best guess as to a motive was that one of the victims was dating Lane's former girlfriend.[185] Lane walked over to the table where this boy was sitting and opened fire on him and his buddies. This may have been a crime of envy and resentment. These themes appear in a poem Lane wrote two months before his attack:

> He was better than the rest, all those ones he detests, within their castles, so vain. Selfish and conceited. They couldn't care less about the peasants they mistreated. They were in their own world, it was a joyous one too.[186]

Lane clearly felt left out of the joyous world that others seemed to live in, and he was bitterly angry about it. His poem ends on a threatening note:

> Now! Feel death, not just mocking you. Not just stalking you but inside of you. Wriggle and writhe. Feel smaller beneath my might. . . . Die, all of you.[187]

※ ※ ※

Lane had two unusually violent parents, both of whom served time. It's not clear how much violence he witnessed versus how much he experienced. Regardless, the instability of the household, his mother's reported alcoholism, violent episodes with both parents, police intervention, and moving among multiple caregivers makes his life resemble those of other traumatized shooters. Unlike most traumatized shooters, however, Lane did not target any school personnel. Nor is there evidence that he discussed his attack plans with any peers.

COMMENTS

All ten traumatized secondary school shooters had overwhelmingly stressful lives, with physical abuse being common and sexual abuse occurring in four cases. At least eight grew up with parental substance abuse. Seven experienced frequent relocations. All of the shooters had fathers who were either absent or had severely impaired functioning. Seven of them had mothers who were absent or impaired to varying degrees. They all had family role models for violence, and at least five of them (six, if Eric Houston's uncle used a gun when he murdered three men in a fight) had older male family members who were role models for the misuse of firearms.

According to Dr. James Garbarino, author of *Lost Boys: Why Our Sons Turn Violent and How We Can Save Them*, "Disruption in the basic relationships of the family figure[s] prominently in the lives of violent boys."[188] This was certainly the case with the traumatized shooters. Garbarino noted two patterns of influence involving fathers and violent boys: "(1) the *presence* of an abusive father and (2) the *absence* of a caring and resourceful father."[189] The traumatized shooters suffered both of these influences.

According to Garbarino, "Many of the boys involved in lethal violence lose their mothers for significant periods in their early years; some lose them permanently."[190] Evan Ramsey lost his mother to alcoholism. Jeffrey Weise lost his mother to alcoholism and brain damage. Eric Hainstock's mother walked out of his life. T. J. Lane's mother was unable to care for him, and he ended up with his grandparents.

One remarkable feature of the traumatized shooters is that at least seven out of ten targeted school personnel (nine, if Mitchell Johnson and Jeffrey Weise targeted the teachers they shot). In comparison, only one shooter targeted a bully, and one targeted family members. Despite the fact that at least five of the shooters were devastated by breakups, only Mitchell Johnson targeted a girl. T. J. Lane, however, apparently targeted a boy who was dating his ex-girlfriend.

Why shoot school personnel? Was this a displacement for the shooters' rage against the abusive adults in their lives? It is noteworthy that all of them had violent adults in their families, but none of them shot a family member who abused them. Perhaps shooting a parent was simply taboo; maybe they displaced their rage from abuse at home onto adults at school.

In addition, at least seven talked to friends about their plans for rampages. In some cases, the friends' apparent tacit approval may have been encouraging. In others, there was direct encouragement, such as with Evan Ramsey, or recruitment by a peer, as with Mitchell Johnson.

The attacks by the traumatized shooters were triggered by an accumulation of stressors, including breakups, legal troubles, disciplinary issues at school, academic failures, bullying, job loss, military rejection, impending relocations, and impending reunions with violent fathers. These recent stresses, on top of the shooters' chaotic and violence-filled life histories, formed a deadly combination.

5

COLLEGE SHOOTERS

Targeted Attacks

Research sometimes yields unexpected results. I had planned to present the college shooters as I did the secondary school shooters, grouping them as psychopathic, psychotic, and traumatized. However, this became problematic when I realized that several of the college shooters were both psychopathic and psychotic. Also, though trauma-tized shooters were the most common type of secondary school perpe-trators, there was not a single traumatized shooter in the college sam-ple.

As I studied the college incidents, I was struck by an alternative organizing principle: whether the attacks were targeted against specific people or were random assaults on strangers. Attacks by secondary school shooters were generally random or mixed, meaning the shooters targeted one or two specific victims while also shooting random people. College attacks, however, were more distinctly targeted or random.

In addition, the pattern of events leading up to targeted attacks was consistently different from that of the random rampages. Furthermore, analyzing the two types of attacks on multiple dimensions, including suicide rates and numbers of people shot, revealed striking differences. Thus, the college shooters are categorized as targeted or random attack-ers. Two shooters whose rampages did not clearly fit either category are discussed as ambiguous attackers. Finally, though the college shooters are organized by attack type, they are also discussed in terms of their psychopathic and psychotic features.

TARGETED ATTACKS BY PSYCHOPATHIC SHOOTERS

Gang Lu

> *"It is believed that there exists no justice for little people in this world, extraordinary action has to be taken to preserve this world as a better place to live."*

Date: November 1, 1991   **Killed**: 5
Age: 28   **Wounded**: 1
School: University of Iowa   **Outcome**: Suicide
Location: Iowa City, IA

In 1985, one of the top physics students in China came to the United States to study for his PhD in physics. His name was Gang Lu. When he arrived at Iowa University, however, he changed his mind and decided to pursue his MBA instead.[1] Why the change in plans? That's where the money was.

Lu was arrogant and abrasive and alienated people. A student said that Lu "argued about everything, and he had this I-must-be-right attitude."[2] A former roommate of Lu's said of him, "He looked down on people and made fun of them behind their back. He believed he was the smartest person in the physics department and felt everyone else should worship him and kowtow to him. . . . [He] was not a nice person."[3]

Lu's manner did not endear him to women. He wanted a girlfriend but had no success in his romantic endeavors. He was very persistent in his pursuit of women, sometimes showing up at their rooms unexpectedly. One woman commented, "He never threatened me, but he did scare me a few times."[4] Once, after a rejection, he came home drunk and kicked a hole in the wall of his apartment. Following a trip to Las Vegas, Lu reportedly showed off photographs of prostitutes and disclosed their fees.

Though Lu wanted to change his major to business, the conditions of his visa prohibited this. He argued with people at the university, but without success. Despite Lu's frustration, he might have accepted his role as the physics department's rising star and perhaps had an illustrious career if it were not for the arrival of Linhua Shan. Shan, another physics student from China, arrived after Lu's first year. Though Lu was brilliant, Shan was even more so. To make matters worse, he was friendly, attractive, and very popular. He also was engaged to a beautiful woman. Socially, Shan was everything that Lu wasn't.

As they progressed in the program, Shan repeatedly outperformed Lu. He outscored Lu on their qualifying exam; when they had a class together, Lu got an A minus, but Shan got an A. Furthermore, even though Shan entered the department a year after Lu, he received his degree sooner.

Besides his rivalry with Shan, Lu became increasingly bitter toward the faculty. He was particularly angry with his adviser, Professor Chris Goertz, by whom he felt unsupported and mistreated. In addition, when Goertz missed deadlines in sending letters of recommendation, Lu blamed him for not being hired.

Lu reached his breaking point, however, when he did not win the Spriesterbach Award—a $2,500 cash award given by the university to the student with the best dissertation. To make matters even worse for Lu, the prize was awarded to Linhua Shan. Lu was both stunned and outraged. He believed he was the most brilliant student in the department and that his dissertation was the best. He believed this with absolute certainty and interpreted his failure to win the prize as an indication that the system was rigged against him. He felt he was the victim of an unfair process.

Lu's failure to get the Spriesterbach Award became the major focus of his life. He waged a campaign in protest, first in the department, then higher up in the university, and eventually tried to take his complaint to the press. Considering that the award had a relatively small cash value and was unheard of outside the university, Lu's rage was striking. He wrote to an administrator that he would take "further action, *whatever necessary*, to protect my rights."[5]

When he did not get satisfaction from the university, he sent letters to the *New York Times*, the *Los Angeles Times*, the *Des Moines Register*, and KGAN-TV in Iowa City. He believed he was the victim of a conspiracy by university administrators and was determined to bring their misconduct into the open. Lu wrote of himself, "Outraged by the downright attempt to cover up, Mr. Lu is more determined to pursue a fair resolution of this matter *at any cost*. And he is considering to take possible legal action if he is left without other choice."[6] None of these letters drew any response.

When all of his efforts proved futile, Lu resorted to violence. He gunned down Linhua Shan, Professor Goertz, other physics professors, and an administrator and her secretary. Then he killed himself. He defended his actions in a statement he left to be read after his death.

Lu's statement justified his violence, explaining that using firearms were a traditional way to protect one's rights in the United States. Lu wrote, "Privately-owned [*sic*] guns are the only practical way for individuals/minority to protect them against the oppression from the evil organizations/majority who actually control the government and legal system."[7] In his mind, he was the victim of injustice, and, therefore, "extraordinary action has to be taken to preserve this world as a better place to live."[8]

Lu was narcissistic, abrasive, insensitive, and envious of Linhua Shan. He believed that his professors interfered with his success and that the university engaged in gross misconduct in denying him the Spriesterbach. After his narcissistic strivings were repeatedly thwarted, he justified the necessity of murder, believing he was making the world a better place.

✿ ✿ ✿

Like other psychopathic shooters, Lu could not tolerate a threat to his narcissism, so he killed the authorities who thwarted him and the rival who "stole" his award. In this way, he resembled Robert Steinhäuser, who also killed teachers and administrators he believed had wronged him.

Lu appears to be an example of an *abrasive psychopath*. Such people "have incessant discords with others, magnifying every minor friction into repeated and bitter struggles."[9] They are quarrelsome, attacking and belittling people who disagree with them. A key feature is their claim of acting on behalf of lofty principles. Lu believed he was righting the wrongs of the university, bringing to light the evil that existed there. For such psychopaths, "Anything personal they have done to others does not really reflect their character but is merely a justified reaction to the uncaring treatment to which they have been exposed."[10]

Valery Fabrikant

"I know how people get what they want, they shoot a lot of people."

Date: August 24, 1992   **Killed**: 4
Age: 52   **Wounded**: 1
School: Concordia University   **Outcome**: Took hostages.
Location: Montreal, Canada   Overpowered and
                                   apprehended. Prison

According to multiple sources, Valery Fabrikant's behavior was chronically outrageous. Much of the information presented here comes from the official report commissioned by Concordia University and written by John Cowan (one of two reports on the incident).[11] Cowan reviewed over nine hundred documents and interviewed more than two dozen people.

An immigrant from Belarus to Montreal, Fabrikant was hired by the mechanical engineering department at Concordia University. His French, however, needed improvement. He took a French class but complained incessantly to, and about, the instructor. He was so verbally abusive to her that many students, as well as the instructor herself, wanted to quit the class. Fabrikant was barred from attending, first by a supervisor, and then by "a legal and proper order."[12] Despite these measures, Fabrikant came to class and tore up the legal order in front of the teacher and classmates. As noted by Cowan, "This is a marvelously clear example of classical insubordination, from a labour law perspective."[13] Afterward, an order came from higher up in the university, and Fabrikant finally complied.

This was not the end of the matter, however. Feeling that he had been victimized, Fabrikant "complained that his career was being damaged by the refusal of the University to let him become bilingual for free."[14] He argued that the university must pay the tuition for another French class. He pushed this issue repeatedly, and it went up the chain of command until legal counsel to the university advised that no concessions should be made.

As demonstrated in this sequence of events, Fabrikant was narcissistic, relentlessly entitled, abrasive, demanding, abusive, and insubordinate yet somehow believed he was the victim and used his status as victim to make further demands.

During his years at Concordia, Fabrikant became embroiled in significant conflicts with his department. Having named colleagues as co-authors on his articles, he later said they did not contribute to the papers. He accused them of acting unethically in allowing their names to be included. He demanded they write letters to all the journals where the articles had been published and retract their authorship. When they refused to do so, he sued two members of his department.[15]

The history of Fabrikant's conflicts with the university is too long and complex to be told here. Besides the issue with authorship, however, there were contract disputes regarding his position and pursuit of tenure. Most relevant are Fabrikant's behavior in creating conflicts and his methods of attempting to get his demands met. As early as 1989—three years before his attack—Fabrikant talked about solving his problems "the North American way": "I know how people get what they want, they shoot a lot of people."[16] He even named people in his department he'd like to shoot. This was taken seriously, and the university had him followed and posted security guards at the homes of two of the intended victims.[17] Despite this, Fabrikant continued to teach at the university.

His outrageous behavior continued. An administrator came home one evening to a voice-mail message from Fabrikant: "You know who I am, and you know what is going to happen."[18] He sent e-mail complaints to people inside and outside the university, sent transcripts of secretly recorded conversations, and made allegations of financial fraud against the department. He even contacted two government agencies about his complaints. More disturbing was the tone of one of his e-mails: "I am no longer afraid of anything or anybody. . . . We all have to die one day."[19]

Fabrikant eventually received media coverage of his complaints against the university. Following this, a woman who had reported to the university in 1982 that she had been raped by Fabrikant[20] contacted the administration to warn them that he could be physically violent.[21] The situation in the department was so tense that surveillance cameras were mounted and secretaries had panic buttons installed in their desks.[22]

During the legal proceedings against his colleagues, Fabrikant was cited for contempt of court.[23] The contempt hearing was scheduled for August 25, 1992. This hearing never occurred, because on August 24 Fabrikant went on a rampage, shooting five people in his department, killing four. Still not satisfied, Fabrikant took two hostages, called 911, announced he had "made several murders," and asked to speak to a television reporter.[24]

An official report about the attack summed up his story, finding that "Dr. Fabrikant was thwarted in his search for a tenured professorship. First, he gathered evidence with which to blackmail his way into an appointment; then he attempted to force the university to appoint him; then he tried to destroy the reputation of those he thought responsible for his rejection; and finally, in despair and anger, he killed four innocent bystanders in cold blood and gravely wounded a fifth."[25] To this day, Fabrikant apparently has no remorse. On the website he maintains from prison he boasts, "I killed not one, but four scoundrels."[26] It seems that as far as he is concerned, he was the victim. Like Gang Lu, Fabrikant appears to think he made the world a better place by killing innocent people.

❋ ❋ ❋

Valery Fabrikant, like Gang Lu, sought revenge when his goals were thwarted. Fabrikant seems most like the *abrasive psychopath*, turning minor issues into major conflicts and pursuing them with a vengeance. Like Gang Lu, he apparently believed he was acting to uphold ethical standards. Even after killing four people, Fabrikant defended the murders on principle as an appropriate response to an inappropriate situation.

Robert Flores

"You better watch your back if you're going to flunk me."

Date: October 29, 2002   **Killed**: 3
Age: 41   **Wounded**: 0
School: University of Arizona   **Outcome**: Suicide
Location: Tucson, AZ

Robert Flores had an anger problem. At times, he was aware of this. Once, when a professor had told him his classroom behavior was unacceptable, Flores replied, "I'm doing better than I used to. In the past I would have bashed someone's head against a curb."[27] Typically, however, Flores apparently viewed his anger as a reasonable response to unreasonable treatment.

According to Flores, he had "marginal parents at best."[28] His father was a police officer who was emotionally distant. Flores joined the army at nineteen and served for eleven years; during his service he qualified as an expert marksman.[29] Flores married, had two children, and became a licensed practical nurse. He moved his family from Texas to Tucson to obtain additional nursing education at the University of Arizona. Once in Tucson, his life began to unravel.

Flores's wife left him, taking their two children with her. He said his wife falsely accused him of being "cruel and abusive,"[30] claiming she manipulated the legal system by stating "all the politically correct buzzwords."[31] He lost a year in his program dealing with the divorce. This led to financial hardships: "Eventually laid off and scraping together temporary work, he struggled to pay credit card debts and student loans."[32]

His interactions with his professors angered him. As a narcissist, Flores liked to be the center of attention; he dominated classroom discussion to the point of being disruptive. He "was belligerent, angry, and rude. . . . He would blow up and call [the instructors] names in class."[33] When one professor didn't call on him, he erupted in fury and challenged her in class. Flores felt so ignored by his professors that he complained to the dean and insisted on making a written statement. His behavior was so belligerent that twice the dean warned him he could be expelled.[34] Unfazed by authority, he continued to threaten and intimidate his professors.

In April 2001 Flores was heard to make a suicidal remark, as well as a comment that he might "put something [like a bomb] under the college."[35] The professor who heard these comments reported them to campus security, but there was no apparent follow-up. Flores's professors encouraged him to seek counseling, but he refused.

One of his instructors, Robin Rogers, failed Flores in his pediatric rotation. She had received four complaints about his behavior from staff and patients. Flores was heard telling Rogers, "You better watch your back if you're going to flunk me."[36] Rogers was so worried about Flores that she talked to family and friends about him and asked her congregation to pray for her safety. Another professor, Barbara Monroe, also failed Flores. A third professor, Cheryl McGaffic, talked to her husband about Flores's anger and intimidating behavior and her fear of what he might do.[37]

These three women—Rogers, Monroe, and McGaffic—were the three women Flores murdered. Shortly before his rampage, however, he announced that he had received a concealed-weapons permit.[38] Perhaps this was his way of making them squirm in fear before he killed them. After killing the three professors, Flores killed himself.

On the morning of the attack Flores mailed a twenty-two-page letter to the publisher of the *Arizona Daily Star*. He referred to his upcoming attack as "a reckoning," making his concern with status clear: "The University is filled with too many people who are filled with hubris."[39] As a narcissist, Flores could not tolerate anyone with status and wanted to bring down the authorities who had power over him.

❉ ❉ ❉

Robert Flores, like Lu and Fabrikant, felt wronged by university authorities and believed he was making the world a better place by murdering those who wronged him. The fact that all three of his victims were female professors may have been a coincidence, but perhaps not. Maybe he could not tolerate women having power over him. He allegedly abused his wife and may have been hostile toward women in general.

Flores's quarrelsome, contentious behavior suggests he was an *abrasive psychopath*. He believed he was upholding high principles in killing people who had wronged him, and he justified his behavior as a reasonable reaction against them. In addition, however, Flores also had features of the *malevolent psychopath*: "These psychopaths often relish menacing others, making them cower and withdraw."[40] Flores threatened and intimidated his professors and apparently enjoyed doing so. Millon and Davis capture key aspects of Flores's character in their description of this kind of psychopath. "Spurred by repeated rejection and driven by an increasing need for retribution," they write, "aggressive impulses will surge into the open. At these times, the psychopaths' behaviors may become outrageously and flagrantly antisocial. Not only do they show minimal guilt or remorse for their violent acts, but they may instead display an arrogant contempt for the rights of others."[41]

COMMENTS

Lu, Fabrikant, and Flores were highly narcissistic, with demanding, obnoxious behavior. They were also paranoid—not in the delusional sense, but in terms of seeing malice or slights where they did not exist. This was a result of their narcissism. They could not accept failure, rejection, or disappointment as having anything to do with their own shortcomings. This simply was not conceivable within their mental worlds. Thus, they viewed their problems as being caused by other people's hostility toward them. They also had the masochistic trait of obsessing about and magnifying their complaints and setbacks, acting as "injustice collectors" who accumulated grievances that in their minds justified revenge.

A noteworthy feature of these three shooters is the lack of charm or impression management that is often seen in psychopaths. They were all openly arrogant and abrasive. Whereas Eric Harris was able to hide his dark side from his teachers under a mask of pleasantness, these psychopathic shooters demonstrated no such ability in impression management. Also, unlike the secondary school psychopathic shooters who often had peer support for their attacks, these shooters had no external support for their rampages.

TARGETED ATTACKS BY SHOOTERS WITH PSYCHOTIC AND PSYCHOPATHIC TRAITS

Peter Odighizuwa

"I was sick, I was sick. I need help."

Date: January 16, 2002   **Killed**: 3
Age: 43   **Wounded**: 3
School: Appalachian School of   **Outcome**: Prison
Law
Location: Grundy, VA

Peter Odighizuwa was afraid of others, and they were afraid of him. His fears for his safety were unwarranted. Others' terror of him was justified.

Odighizuwa was born in Nigeria and came to the United States in 1980 at age twenty-one. He worked in Portland, Oregon, as a bus driver for seven years. His job came to a bizarre end when Odighizuwa was ordered off his bus by a company officer. Odighizuwa refused to comply, drove away in the bus with the officer in pursuit, and crashed the bus. Odighizuwa was fired for "reporting to work under the influence of drugs or alcohol, deliberate destruction of the district's property, and for posing an immediate or potential threat to public safety."[42] Odighizuwa initiated a lawsuit claiming unlawful termination but dropped it after ten days.

In the 1990s, Odighizuwa briefly attended The Ohio State University[43] before going to Central State University in Ohio where he earned a mathematics degree. He then decided to be a lawyer and was accepted at the Appalachian Law School in Grundy, Virginia. He was forty-two, married to a woman from Nigeria, and had four sons. He had no income or money saved. Lack of funds was a chronic stress, and Odighizuwa was frequently desperate, such that "Early in his first semester he brought his four children to a meeting of the Student Bar Association to plead for money to pay his electric bill. Later that semester, he took over the podium in his Civil Procedures class and again appealed for money."[44] Besides his financial stress, Odighizuwa struggled in his classes, failing some and barely passing others. He also had conflicts with faculty and administration. He filed a grievance against a professor and, in an unusual move, sent it to most of the faculty. He also filed a grievance against two people in the Student Services department.[45] At this point, he was paranoid, "complaining of a conspiracy to deny him access to sources of financial aid."[46]

His paranoia manifested in other situations as well. When Odighizuwa found a spent shell casing in his yard, he became convinced his life was in danger. The police found no evidence of a threat, but Odighizuwa was so relentless in pestering them that they threatened to charge him with obstruction of justice.[47]

He became increasingly suspicious. When a tree fell across a road, Odighizuwa thought people had deliberately obstructed his movements. At home, he covered his bedroom windows with cardboard and had multiple locks on his door—a precaution that was not necessary in Grundy, Virginia. Odighizuwa "really started to think that people were out to get him, [that they] just didn't want to see him make it through law school."[48]

Odighizuwa's behavior was abrasive, particularly toward women. The director of Student Services "considered him so abusive and threatening that she barred him from the office unless he was accompanied by one of the Deans or the president of the Student Bar Association."[49] He reportedly refused to sit next to women and "verbally assaulted and threatened female students and staff . . . several students had reported they were afraid of him."[50]

Odighizuwa talked back to professors in class and was prickly and belligerent. One student said, "Peter would snap at you for no reason—even when you tried to reach out to him."[51] Another said, "He always thought he was getting picked on. . . . I had been told to stay away from him."[52] Odighizuwa was nicknamed "Shooter," and a student recalled, "We used to sit around and talk about how Peter's gonna shoot somebody."[53]

Odighizuwa's situation deteriorated in September 2001, when he hit his wife in the face. He was charged with assault; she took their children and moved out.[54] Shortly after this, a physician gave him an undisclosed medication. Odighizuwa's grades for the fall semester were a D+, a D, and an F. He decided to withdraw from school and met with Student Services on January 15, 2002. When he learned that his withdrawal meant his financial aid would end and he would have to begin repaying his student loans, Odighizuwa had a "bitter altercation" with a staff member.[55]

The next day Odighizuwa shot and killed the two professors who had worked with him most closely.[56] He passed through a student lounge and chatted briefly with a classmate and then shot a group of four women, killing one. One source said he only knew one of the women.[57] Another source said Odighizuwa commented that all four had been unusually mean to him, but he was unable to give particulars. This source also quoted Odighizuwa as saying, "I wasn't just shooting all over the place. . . . I saw the people who were menacing me."[58]

Though people had observed Odighizuwa's paranoia before the attack, his comments afterward revealed severe delusional thinking. He reported, "I feel like I'm God sometimes, and I was running demons out of the school. It was like an exorcism."[59] When he was in prison, he stated, "I was taking care of FBI and CIA agents. And the KGB, too."[60] He said, "I was sick, I was sick. I need help."[61] He also said that he didn't have his medication and that he needed it. After the attack, Odighizuwa was diagnosed with schizophrenia.[62]

* * *

Peter Odighizuwa had a history of litigation and problematic behavior at work. He faced severe financial stress. He appears to have had particular hostility toward women, including his wife and women at the university. (In this way he resembled Robert Flores, who also reportedly hit his wife and who focused his anger on women at the university.) Odighizuwa was schizophrenic, with prominent paranoid delusions. Unlike some psychotic shooters, his attack had nothing to do with ideology and he had no role models for murder. His rampage was a response to overwhelming stress, hopelessness, and paranoia.

Besides being psychotic, he also seems like an *abrasive psychopath*, being chronically quarrelsome and belligerent. He could also be seen as an *explosive psychopath*. These are people who are "deeply frustrated by the futility and hopelessness of their lives" and for whom "impotence and personal failure become the source of . . . aggressive acts."[63]

Biswanath Halder

"By doing what I did I saved the mankind."

Date: May 9, 2003
Age: 62
School: Case Western Reserve University
Location: Cleveland, OH

Killed: 1
Wounded: 2
Outcome: Standoff with police for hours. Shot by police. Surrendered. Prison

At age sixty-two, Biswanath Halder was a lonely, isolated man. He had come to the United States from India in 1969 when he was eighteen, eventually becoming a citizen in 1980. He apparently had no friends or family in this country and maintained virtually no contact with his relatives in India.[64] Despite his dreams of success, Halder had "an erratic work history characterized by short-term jobs where he was either terminated or quit because of personality or monetary problems. In addition, Halder had sued many of his former employers, alleging racial discrimination or unfair employment practices."[65]

Halder also had an erratic education history. He completed a bachelor's degree in electrical engineering in India but struggled with graduate education in the United States. He started a business program at New York University, studied mathematics, computer science, and economics at the University of Massachusetts, and later took courses at Boston University. He did not complete a degree at any of these institutions.[66]

Halder eventually received his MBA from Case Western Reserve University in 1999 and continued taking classes there for another year. He wanted to launch an online business and spent twelve to fourteen hours a day in a campus computer lab. His behavior, however, became increasingly problematic. He monopolized multiple computers and was rude to students, and one woman reported that he harassed her in an effort to make her proofread documents for him. He also reportedly wore the same clothes daily and had poor grooming. His behavior was so odd, arrogant, and abrasive that someone created a website called HalderSucks.org, where people posted insulting comments about him.[67]

The situation became serious when someone hacked into Halder's business website and deleted his files and a reported fifty thousand contacts.[68] This constituted cyber crime, and Halder was relentless in pursuing justice. Unfortunately, he believed that Shawn Miller, who worked in the computer lab, was the guilty party. Investigations subsequently showed this was not true,[69] but Halder was fixated on Miller.

Halder was also paranoid. He complained that he was mistreated in the computer lab by "master race" employees because of his "inferior race."[70] As a student in the Weatherhead School of Management, he sent an e-mail to the entire program in which he wrote, "The evil man [Shawn Miller] wiped out everything that it took my lifetime to create. . . . Now, the evil man is on his evil path to destroy Weatherhead."[71] Halder was not only paranoid, he was also grandiose. He claimed that if his site hadn't been hacked, he could have had a business dealing with "billions and trillions" of dollars in less than two years.[72]

Halder fought a legal battle for nearly three years, even after his own attorney tried to convince him that Miller was innocent.[73] Halder also waged a campaign through other channels, posting messages about his situation on his website, sending e-mails to people in the university, and even contacting the FBI and the Judiciary Committees for the United States Senate and House of Representatives.[74]

He said that if he lost his appeal in the case against Miller, he would "fuck those fuckers up."[75] When Miller heard about this, he told his supervisor, "apparently Halder is interested in killing us."[76] Halder lost the appeal on April 29, 2003. This legal failure convinced him that the FBI and legal system were corrupt and deliberately working against him.[77] He also believed that Case Western paid journalists to write negative articles about him. When his attorney withdrew from the case due to Halder's behavior, Halder wrote "a letter to the judge alleging that his opponent [Shawn Miller] had bribed his attorney."[78] After the attack, Halder claimed that his "attorneys were conspiring against him with the prosecutor and with Case Western."[79]

Ten days after he lost his appeal, and nearly three years after his website had been destroyed, Halder went on his rampage. He broke into the building that housed the business school, using a sledgehammer to shatter a glass door. He shot and killed the first person he encountered.[80] He fired at other people, missing some but wounding two. His primary targets were "Shawn Miller and three of his friends,"[81] but they managed to avoid Halder. The police arrived, along with seventy SWAT troops. Halder held them off for seven hours with a reported ninety-three people stuck in the building. Halder shot at the officers and eventually surrendered after he had been wounded by gunfire.

After his rampage, Halder seemed to believe he had put an end to cyber crime and was the salvation of humanity. He said, it "will never be allowed to happen again. . . . By doing what I did I saved the mankind."[82] Even in prison he was unrepentant, claiming "Violence is essential!"[83] He continued to seek publicity, wanting to contact journalists to "tell the entire world the whole truth" and bring to light the "evil objectives" of Case Western Reserve University.[84]

✧ ✧ ✧

Biswanath Halder may be schizotypal or schizophrenic. After his attack, multiple mental health professionals diagnosed him as psychotic.[85] He had poor grooming, had no friends, and maintained virtually no contact with his family. Despite years of education he could barely eke out a living. Halder had paranoid delusions about Shawn Miller, Case Western, the justice system, and even his own attorneys. He also had delusions of grandeur, believing that despite his failure at the age of sixty to achieve financial stability his website would produce trillions of dollars.

His grandiosity was also evident in his claims that he had ended cyber-crime and "saved the mankind."

Like previously discussed shooters, Halder had features of the *abrasive psychopath*, being chronically belligerent and entitled. He had the incessant discords, the quarrelsomeness, and the conviction that what he did was justified because of the treatment he had received. Like other targeted shooters, he waged a campaign both inside and outside the university. He also claimed the moral high ground even as he was suing and threatening to kill someone who was innocent.

Amy Bishop

"Dr. Amy Bishop, Harvard trained."

Date: February 12, 2010
Age: 44
School: University of Alabama
Location: Huntsville, AL

Killed: 3
Wounded: 3
Outcome: Apprehended. Prison

On February 12, 2010, Professor Amy Bishop was in a biology department staff meeting at the University of Alabama in Huntsville. Forty-five minutes into the meeting, she pulled out a Ruger nine-millimeter semiautomatic pistol and shot six of her colleagues, killing three.[86] It was a bizarre act for a professor. Even more bizarre is that it was not the first time Amy Bishop had killed somebody. When she was twenty-one, she had shot her brother with a shotgun, fled the scene, and tried to hijack a car from a car dealership. She claimed the shooting was an accident, and it was accepted as such at the time.[87]

The details of the shooting, however, suggest that she knew what she was doing. Bishop reportedly had fired the gun accidentally previously that same morning, leaving a hole in her bedroom wall. She then took the gun downstairs. Right after her mother told her not to point it at anyone, Bishop turned toward her brother, pointed the gun, and pulled the trigger. She then, allegedly, accidentally fired the gun a third time. The former police chief who handled the case in 1986 commented, "To say someone accidentally fired a shotgun three times is crazy."[88] Furthermore, an article was found in her bedroom about a man who had committed murder with a shotgun, fled the scene, and hijacked a car from a car dealership—the very sequence of actions that Bishop enacted, except that she failed in her attempt to steal a car.[89]

Between killing her brother and murdering her colleagues, she may have also tried to kill someone else. In the 1990s Bishop had worked for

Dr. Paul Rosenberg, a researcher at Children's Hospital in Boston. Rosenberg had wanted her to leave because of her inability "to meet the standards required for the work."[90] She was not stable and had reportedly been violent.[91] While working with Rosenberg, a team of nine researchers had completed a paper for publication, with Bishop listed as second author. She erupted with fury over not having been named the first author. One of the other authors said, "She exploded into something emotional that we never saw before."[92]

Less than a month after Bishop left Rosenberg's laboratory, he received a letter bomb. Bishop and her husband were investigated, but there was too little evidence to convict them. When Bishop talked to a colleague about being interrogated, she "was quite cavalier about it," grinning as she described the interview.[93] Interestingly, Bishop wrote three highly autobiographical novels (unpublished); in all three, the protagonists "fantasize about the deaths of those who have wronged them."[94]

Bishop was unusually status-conscious and often introduced herself as "Dr. Amy Bishop, Harvard trained." She acted as if she were superior and was once arrested when her arrogance got out of control. While dining at the International House of Pancakes she wanted a booster seat for one of her children. Another woman took the last booster seat, and Bishop flew into a rage, shouting, "I am Dr. Amy Bishop."[95] She then punched the woman in the head. Bishop was arrested for assault and battery and disorderly conduct and was given probation.[96]

Besides being arrogant, Bishop's behavior revealed social cluelessness. Whether in a writers' group in her neighborhood or with students and colleagues, she was odd, inappropriate, and abrasive. One neighbor said, he "could just tell she wasn't right. I said to my wife right away, stay away from her. She's bad news."[97] He went on to describe Bishop as "belligerent, confrontational, a bully." When Bishop and her family moved away, the neighbors got pizza and beer and had a celebration; one person said, "Ding, dong, the witch is dead."[98]

Bishop's students at the University of Alabama complained repeatedly to the administration about her. They wrote a letter to the head of the department, met with him in person, and submitted a petition signed by dozens of students.[99] The petition cited her "odd, unsettling ways,"[100] including her failure to make eye contact when speaking with them. Also, "Students and colleagues observed that Bishop was angry, stressed, distracted, disruptive, and displayed inappropriate behavior."[101] Her graduate students frequently switched out of her lab due to her odd behavior and "flip-outs."[102] Bishop reportedly "could be rude and dismissive to students and colleagues alike, and her teaching was often seen as disjointed."[103] A university administrator said that in faculty meetings Bishop rambled about "bizarre" things—"left-field kind of stuff."[104]

One administrator avoided Bishop due to her "harassing" and "hounding" behavior.[105] A professor said he had seen her go "ballistic" and stated that she was "out of touch with reality." He even called her "crazy." When challenged on this, he held his ground: "I said she was crazy multiple times, and I stand by that. . . . The woman had a pattern of erratic behavior. She did things that were not normal."[106]

In April 2009 Bishop was denied tenure. She appealed the denial but lost the appeal in November of that year. She then sued the university for discrimination.[107] During her tenure battle, Bishop threatened people in the department, but the details of these threats have not been released.[108]

Bishop was in crisis. She "threatened suicide to faculty members and coworkers at UAH [University of Alabama, Huntsville], both verbally and in writing."[109] At one point, when Bishop's suicidal comments were brought to the provost, he "immediately summoned the UAH armed police to protect himself and other administration officials by barring Bishop's entrance to the administration building."[110] Perhaps because of Bishop's threats to people in the department, the provost feared that she was both suicidal and homicidal.

Bishop said she was "fighting for my life, and my life has been put squarely in the hands of the department."[111] Facing life as a nontenured professor was devastating to her. Bishop had written a sentence in one of her novels that sheds light on her psychology: "The thought of being some unemployed loser, a non-Harvard, a nonscientist, made her shiver at her loss of identity."[112] Her battle for tenure wasn't just about a job; it was about who she was.

Bishop reportedly knew who had voted in favor of her tenure and who had not. If true, she did not discriminate during the shooting, firing at people who supported her as well as those who voted against her. During the police interrogation, she insisted, "I wasn't there. . . . It wasn't me."[113]

❈ ❈ ❈

Though there was talk of Bishop being schizophrenic,[114] and though she "pleaded not guilty by reason of insanity,"[115] I have not found the results of any formal diagnostic evaluations. Nonetheless, her long history of poor social skills, odd and inappropriate behavior, lack of eye contact, and bizarre and rambling conversation all suggest the possibility of schizotypal personality disorder.

Bishop resembles Peter Odighizuwa and Biswanath Halder in that she had no role models or ideology driving her attack. She was desperate, facing the loss of her position, and believed she had been wronged. Like Odighizuwa and Halder, however, her behavior was so belligerent and abrasive that she, too, seemed to have psychopathic traits. Her quarrelsome attitude and contentious behavior fits that of the *abrasive psychopath*. She could also be seen as having features of the *malevolent psychopath*, particularly the vindictiveness and chip-on-the-shoulder attitude that alienated so many people. Or, like the *explosive psychopath*, her violence could be seen as a result of "repeated failures, humiliations, and frustrations,"[116] with her ultimately exploding against people who symbolized her failures—the members of the department that rejected her.

COMMENTS

Not only were Odighizuwa, Halder, and Bishop either schizophrenic or schizotypal, they were also belligerent and abrasive. They alienated people with their demanding, arrogant ways. Thus, they resembled the three shooters who were solely psychopathic (with no psychotic symptoms) who engaged in targeted attacks. This is significant. Most people who are schizophrenic or schizotypal are not belligerent and abrasive. They may be shy and self-effacing, pleasant and eager to please, or have any other personality traits. Instead, Odighizuwa, Bishop, and Halder resemble Lu, Fabrikant, and Flores with their caustic personalities.

All six shooters in this chapter felt they were victims of injustice and obsessed about having been wronged. They were injustice collectors, nursing their grudges until they felt justified in committing murder. Author Stanton Samenow provides insight into the dynamics behind such attacks in his book *Inside the Criminal Mind*. "Criticism or interference with the criminal's plans," he finds, "constitutes a monumental threat, because it signifies to him that he is not the omnipotent person he thinks he is. Instead of modifying his expectations and changing his behavior, he insists that it is others who err, not he. His pride is such that he adamantly refuses to acknowledge his own fallibility. Unyielding, uncompromising, and unforgiving, his attitude is 'I'm going to hold my ground if it costs me everything.'"[117]

6

COLLEGE SHOOTERS

Random and Ambiguous Attacks

The targeted college shooters presented in the previous chapter had long-standing grievances with their universities and targeted specific people in their attacks. In contrast, the shooters presented in this chapter committed random or ambiguous attacks. The targeted attacks were heinous acts, but they were responses to real situations. The rationales for the random attacks are much less tangible. Charles Whitman, for example, had no quarrel with his university; he had an intense, long-standing quarrel with himself.

RANDOM ATTACKS BY PSYCHOPATHIC SHOOTERS

Charles Whitman

"As I look back over my past few adult years they seem so wasted. Will I ever accomplish anything I set out to do?"

Date: August 1, 1966
Age: 25
School: University of Texas
Location: Austin, TX

Killed: 16
Wounded: 32
Outcome: Shot and killed by police

During his time in the marines, Charles Whitman trained as a sharp-shooter and became an outstanding marksman. This was not his first exposure to guns, however. A photograph shows him at two years of age holding two rifles, both taller than he was. His father said, "I'm a fanatic about guns. I raised my boys to know how to handle guns."[1]

Whitman's father loomed large in his life. "A self-made man and proud of it, he used his money to buy what he wanted, unapologetically. Some acquaintances, however, found his pride to be monumental ego-tism; he provided very well for his family—and never let them forget it."[2] Mr. Whitman gave his kids everything he could and then com-plained that they were "spoiled rotten."[3] He indulged his children and yet was also strict and punitive, spanking them with a belt and a paddle. Mr. Whitman also beat his wife, so the children may have witnessed domestic violence. The family environment was an odd mix of prosper-ity and punishment.

Years later, when he was a student at the University of Texas, Whit-man told a professor, "I just despise my father. I hate him. If my father walked through that door, I'd kill him." When his professor said that Whitman didn't really mean that, Whitman replied, "I certainly do."[4] Whitman, however, seemed less bothered by the domestic violence than his inability to surpass his father's accomplishments. During a session with the campus psychiatrist, Whitman "readily admitted that he lived for the day when he could consider himself his father's superi-or."[5]

Whitman was a show-off and a daredevil who got into various kinds of trouble. He poached a deer, took it to his dormitory, and was skin-ning it in the shower when he was caught and arrested. He had fre-quent car accidents and five traffic violations in just over two years. Once, while in a car with friends, he pointed a gun at a pedestrian. When the man appeared to reach for his own gun, they sped off in their car, with Whitman laughing.

He also laughed over a cruel practical joke he pulled with a friend. After they were in a car accident, he went to the dormitory looking bloody and ragged and reported that his friend had been killed. Their buddies were horrified; they even called the friend's girlfriend in the middle of the night and told her the bad news. When the supposedly dead man walked into the dormitory, Whitman rolled on the floor with laughter. As noted by his biographer, Whitman "seemed to enjoy watching others squirm,"[6] finding sadistic pleasure in their distress.

Whitman's most serious misconduct, however, occurred in the ma-rines. He was caught gambling and threatened to kick out the teeth of another soldier for refusing to pay a $30 debt with $15 interest. Whitman was demoted from lance corporal to private and given thirty days' confinement and ninety days' hard labor. In another gambling incident, Whitman bounced a check for a debt he owed. When the man demanded payment, Whitman—who towered over the man—intimidated him, then promised he would pay the debt, but never did.

Whitman earned a military scholarship for college. Although intellectually gifted, he did not apply himself and lost the scholarship. He struggled academically and could not settle on a career path: "Within a period of less than five years, his plans shifted from mechanical engineer to career marine officer to architectural engineer to real estate agent and finally to lawyer."[7] He wanted desperately to make a lot of money but couldn't even finish a degree, instead settling for a series of menial jobs.

Not only did Whitman fail to outachieve his father, he was financially dependent on his wife, who sailed through college and quickly established herself as a teacher. His sense of failure compared to his father and wife apparently damaged his sense of himself as a man. According to his biographer, the notes Whitman left after killing his mother and wife indicate that, "The fact that he had never been financially independent bothered him more than the murders he had committed."[8] A further blow to his manhood was his fear that he was sterile; this may have been related to the testicular surgery he'd had in eleventh grade.

Though Whitman professed to love his wife, he beat her on multiple occasions. He must have been fierce, because his wife told her parents she believed Whitman was capable of killing her—a perception that was all too true. At times, the couple talked of separation and divorce.

Despite Whitman's dark side, his public persona was remarkable. A professor noted that Whitman deserved "all the standard appellations of a high school yearbook. He was easily the 'Best Looking,' 'Friendliest,' and 'Most Mature.'"[9] Whitman's psychiatrist said that despite Whitman's hostility, "There was something about him that suggested and expressed the all-American boy."[10] The day before committing mass murder, when Whitman bought supplies for his attack, the clerk did not ask him for identification because he seemed like "such a nice young man."[11] Whitman was clearly good at impression management. His biographer described him as "a consummate actor."[12]

Whitman was shocked when his mother decided to leave his father. After years of abuse, Mrs. Whitman had had enough. On March 2, 1966, Whitman drove from Texas to Florida to pick up his mother. He brought her to Austin, where she found an apartment. Whitman's father called repeatedly, trying to salvage his marriage. The stress of dealing with the breakup of his family left Whitman depressed and agitated. He decided to quit college and leave his wife, saying she'd be better off without him. When one of his instructors—also an ex-marine—ordered him to continue his studies, Whitman acquiesced. He also decided to stay with his wife.

Eventually, however, Whitman decided to end his life amid a massive bloodbath. He carried out the murders of his mother and wife with remarkable calmness. He apparently killed his mother in her apartment by first strangling her, then bashing her head with a blunt object, and finally stabbing her in the chest with a large hunting knife. He then returned home where his wife was sleeping and stabbed her in the chest five times. Later that day, he bought his final supplies for his attack, went to campus, ascended the campus clock tower, and rained death on innocent people.

What motivated Whitman? He hated his father and claimed to love his wife and mother, but he murdered the two women closest to him and made no effort to kill his father. Rage percolated in him for a long time, but it is hard to understand why it took the form it did. Two external events may have influenced Whitman. First, Truman Capote's true-crime book *In Cold Blood*, about a mass murder, was reportedly the most talked about book of 1966. Then, on July 14, 1966, Richard Speck raped and killed eight student nurses in what was called "the crime of the century." Gary Lavergne commented, "The power of mass murder to capture the attention of, to shock, and to break the heart of a nation could not have escaped Charlie."[13]

Of course, Whitman had talked about shooting people from the tower before Speck had committed his murders. He'd told his psychiatrist about this idea back in March 1966 and had also mentioned it to friends. Perhaps *In Cold Blood* and Speck's crime broke whatever barrier had been keeping Whitman's rage in check. Or maybe it was more personal. In 1963 Whitman wrote, "As I look back over my past few adult years they seem so wasted. Will I ever accomplish anything I set out to do?"[14] Three years later, he still had nothing to show for himself. He was a wife batterer, just like the father he despised. He worked at menial jobs and couldn't settle on a career. He was financially dependent on his wife. He feared he was sterile. He saw no future for himself. In the words of his biographer, "He climbed the Tower because he wanted to die in a big way; not by suicide, but by taking others with him and making the headlines. He died while engaging in the only activity in which he truly excelled—shooting."[15]

✵ ✵ ✵

Charles Whitman suffered from failed narcissism. He'd had big dreams that never materialized. He was a powerful, charismatic ex-marine, but he was dependent on his wife. He wanted to surpass his father in material success but couldn't even finish a college degree. Eventually he found a way to make the world take notice of him. His psychopathic traits include his chronic disregard for laws and regulations, his lack of empathy, his impression management, and his sadistic pleasure in making others squirm.

After his death, an autopsy found that he had a brain tumor. Based on the autopsy, a subsequent investigation, and the opinions of numerous experts over the years, the consensus is that the tumor does not account for his rampage.[16]

Whitman may best be classified as an *explosive psychopath*. These are psychopaths who are "deeply frustrated by the futility and hopelessness of their lives."[17] Rather than being chronically abrasive, they have discrete episodes in which their frustration and rage comes pouring out. They often abuse "safe partners," people who come to symbolize their failures and serve as outlets for their rage. In Whitman's case, his wife appears to have served this function. As Millon and Davis commented, "Because they are unable to resolve the real sources of their resentment and frustration, they come to feel that these symbols of futility and hopelessness must be removed from the scene."[18] Also, for these psychopaths, "impotence and personal failure become the source of these aggressive acts."[19] This fits Whitman.

Wayne Lo

"I have the power to bring the whole school down to its knees."

Date: December 14, 1992
Age: 18
School: Simon's Rock College
Location: Great Barrington, MA

Killed: 2
Wounded: 4
Outcome: Called police to report himself. Prison

Wayne Lo was born in Taiwan and moved to the United States when he was twelve. He lived with his parents and younger brother in Montana. Lo's father had been a pilot in the Nationalist China Air Force but had since left the military. After immigrating, his father opened a Chinese restaurant. Mr. Lo was a strict disciplinarian and "would beat Wayne with a riding crop when he disobeyed an order."[20] Lo sometimes held out his hands and said, "Punish me."[21] During his evaluation after the attack, Lo reportedly took pride in what he'd endured as a child, seeming grateful for his father's strictness.[22]

Lo was bright and respected at school. He was also, however, narcissistic, "sometimes stubborn and arrogant, disagreeing with teachers whom he took to be intellectual inferiors, and refusing to complete assignments which he considered pointless."[23] He could also be manipulative and deceitful. He once hinted to a teacher that he was suicidal, but instead of killing himself, he stole his mother's car and drove out of state to spend five days with a girl.[24]

When Lo attended Simon's Rock College, he became known for his bigotry. Extreme prejudice is often seen in people with sadistic personalities who enjoy being hostile toward minority groups. For example, Eric Harris admired Hitler and made racist, misogynistic, anti-Semitic, and homophobic comments. Similarly, Lo and his friends made public comments against African Americans, Jews, and gays.[25]

Lo also made frequent comments about wanting to kill people at school. A peer said, "It's not like we haven't been afraid of Wayne and his friends. . . . My friends and I had been talking daily about how scary he is."[26] A friend of Lo's said, "Wayne often spoke about getting an automatic weapon and going into the cafeteria and shooting people at random."[27] Lo also gave a female student unwanted attention, to the point that she told her faculty adviser and Lo was told to leave the woman alone.[28] Overall, "The students at Simon's Rock disliked him and feared him. Girls felt stalked and harassed by him."[29]

Eventually, Lo did what he had talked about—he committed a rampage attack. During the assault, his gun, however, kept jamming; if it hadn't, the number of victims could have been much higher.[30] After shooting multiple people, Lo called the police and announced that he was the shooter. He said, "the people at Simon's Rock needed to be taught a lesson."[31] When apprehended, "The officers were surprised by Wayne's calm manner and polite attitude. He wasn't sweating, shaking, or hyperventilating."[32] This lack of emotional arousal in the wake of murder is striking.

Lo claimed that during his attack he believed he was on a mission from God. This, however, appears to have been a lie. The night before the shooting, he told a friend that he was writing out the Book of Revelation to give people the impression that he was crazy.[33] In addition, Lo called the police after his rampage, demonstrating that he knew he had committed a crime; if he truly believed he was on a mission from God, why call the police? Furthermore, while in prison, Lo exhibited a narcissistic delight in fame and a psychopathic interest in deception. According to court documents, "the defendant talked about the killings with other inmates and told them that he was excited that he was getting attention from the news media and that he hoped to be on television or have a movie made about what happened. The defendant also discussed the insanity plea and asked the inmates 'if there was any way to fool . . . the shrink.'"[34] A reporter for the *New York Times* who interviewed Lo seven years after the attack was struck by Lo's remarkably smooth presentation, noting he "often spoke with disarming frankness. He was also manipulative, controlling and so eager to portray himself in a positive light that it was sometimes impossible to believe he thought he was telling the truth."[35]

Why did Lo go on a rampage? Maybe he was trying to prove something. He was on the short side at 5'5" and, according to a friend, Lo was very sensitive about it.[36] It seemed vitally important for Lo to be seen as masculine. His friends used to joke with him: "We'd be like, 'How tough *are* you Wayne?' And he'd say, 'I'm tough.' . . . It was just ridiculous."[37] After the attack, one of his friends said, "This is a terrible thing to say, but it was almost as if Wayne did those shootings to impress his friends."[38]

Was there a triggering event for Lo's rampage? He had no long-standing grievance against the school, but he did have a run-in with the administration shortly before his attack. Over Thanksgiving break, all the students who stayed on campus were moved to a single residence hall. Lo complied but then moved back to his regular dorm room without permission.[39] He was fined for this, but there were no serious consequences. Nonetheless, Lo's response to the fine was startling: "If I'd known you were going to throw the whole book at me, I would have gotten my money's worth. I have the power to bring the whole school down to its knees."[40] Approximately two weeks later, he did just that.

* * *

Wayne Lo had a belligerent, intimidating presence, but not in all settings. There were no reports of disruptive and disrespectful behavior in class, as there were with Robert Flores. Apparently, Lo was skilled enough in impression management to control himself to fit the setting. His comments about faking mental illness and his ability to succeed in doing so with mental health examiners after his attack provide further evidence of impression management. In addition, he was sensitive about being small and eager to prove how tough he was. He was also angry about school personnel exercising power over him.

These factors suggest that Lo was a *reputation-defending antisocial*. Such people are extremely sensitive to slights to their social standing and "need to be thought of as invincible and formidable persons."[41] To prove how tough they are "may require acts of aggressive leadership or risk-taking behaviors, often of a violent or criminal nature."[42] Lo also showed signs of being an *unprincipled psychopath* in his deceitfulness and manipulation of people.

COMMENTS

Unlike the targeted attackers, Charles Whitman and Wayne Lo were not chronically abrasive people who made enemies wherever they went. Whitman generally presented well, with no reports of disrespectful or disruptive behavior in class. Though Lo was belligerent with peers, he presented well elsewhere. He also demonstrated his impression-management skills after the attack, both with mental health professionals and reporters. Whitman's and Lo's ability to deceive people distinguishes them from the *abrasive psychopaths* who engaged in targeted attacks.

Finally, both Whitman and Lo experienced violence in the home that may have been traumatic, though neither shooter accused his father of abuse. Nonetheless, although they were psychopathic, they may also have had at least one aspect of the traumatized shooters: physical abuse. Unlike the traumatized shooters, however, Whitman and Lo neither grew up in poverty or squalor nor with criminal or substance-abusing parents. Neither did they come from broken homes or have changing caregivers. Thus, even if they had been abused, their histories do not match those of the traumatized shooters.

RANDOM ATTACKS BY PSYCHOTIC SHOOTERS

Seung Hui Cho

"Oh the happiness I could have had mingling among you hedonists, being counted as one of you."

Date: April 16, 2007   **Killed**: 32
Age: 23   **Wounded**: 17
School: Virginia Polytechnic   **Outcome**: Suicide
Institute and State University
Location: Blacksburg, VA

With all shooters, we seek to answer the questions of who they were and why they killed. These questions are particularly challenging with Seung Hui Cho. Why did he go on a rampage against random people? His advances had been rejected by three women, two of whom reported him to the campus police for harassment; the officers told Cho to leave the women alone.[43] He could have targeted these women or the officers involved, but he didn't. Similarly, Cho had been removed from a poetry-writing class because his behavior had unnerved the students and professor.[44] He could have targeted his classmates or the instructor, but he didn't. In yet another incident, Cho had become enraged during a meeting with Professor Carl Bean, his instructor in technical writing, who had suggested Cho drop the class.[45] Cho could have killed Professor Bean, but he didn't. Instead, he killed strangers. He first murdered two students in a residence hall and then attacked random students and professors in another building. Why? To answer this question, we have to look not only at who Cho was but also at who he believed he was.

The day of his rampage Cho mailed a letter to the English department that was signed "Ax Ishmael."[46] He also sent a manifesto to MSNBC, in which he wrote, "I am Ax Ishmael. I am the Anti-Terrorist of America."[47] When his dead body was found, the words *Ax Ishmael* were discovered in red ink on his arm.[48] It appears that Cho committed his attack as Ax Ishmael, the Anti-Terrorist of America.

Was this a name he consciously adopted, or did he really believe he was somebody else? It is my opinion that he likely believed he truly was somebody else. Evidence suggests that Cho was out of touch with reality and struggled with his identity: when he contacted a female student anonymously and she asked him who he was, he wrote back, "I do not know who I am."[49] Later on, he left a Shakespeare quotation on the whiteboard on this student's dorm room that included the line, "I know not how to tell thee who I am."[50]

In fact, Cho became known as "Question Mark." He signed in to class with a question mark instead of his name,[51] his Facebook name was "?"[52] and sometimes he "introduced himself as 'Question Mark,' saying it was the persona of a man who lived on Mars and journeyed to Jupiter."[53] On other occasions, he introduced himself as Cho's nonexistent twin brother, "Question Mark," and asked to speak to Cho.[54] Perhaps this could be viewed as a prank, but by all accounts Cho was without a sense of humor.

Cho claimed he had a supermodel girlfriend named Jelly who lived in outer space and called him Spanky. He occasionally asked his roommates to stay away because Jelly was visiting.[55] For a writing class, he wrote a short story called "The Adventure of Spanky" and signed it "Spanky I.," with "Seung Cho" underneath in parentheses.[56] Maybe he thought he was Spanky, maybe he knew he wasn't, or maybe he wasn't sure. Interestingly, in the story, Jelly tells him that they cuddled and made out the day before, but Spanky has no memory of this and is very confused. He cannot tell what is real and what isn't. Perhaps this expressed Cho's own confusion about reality.

Whoever Cho believed he was by the time of his attack, his manifesto reveals his delusions of grandeur: "Like Moses, I spread the sea and lead my people—the Weak, the Defenseless, and the Innocent Children of all ages that you fucked and will always try to fuck—to eternal freedom."[57] Cho also compared himself to Jesus: "Thanks to you, I die, like Jesus Christ, to inspire generations of the Weak and Defenseless people."[58]

Furthermore, Cho envisioned a global revolution in the wake of his attack, writing, "the vendetta you have witnessed today will reverberate throughout every home and every soul in America and will inspire the Innocent kids that you have fucked to start a war of vendetta. We will raise hell on earth that the world has never witnessed. Millions of deaths and millions of gallons of blood on the streets will not quench the avenging phoenix that you have caused us to unleash."[59]

Besides grandiosity, the manifesto reveals Cho's extreme paranoia. He believed he was facing annihilation, writing, "Don't you just wish you finished me off when you had the chance? Don't you just wish you killed me? You had a hundred billion chances and ways to have avoided today, but you decided to spill my blood. You forced me into a corner and gave me only one option."[60] Another prominent theme in Cho's writing is the extraordinary sense of victimization he described. He wrote about being fucked, raped, crucified, buried alive, vandalized, emotionally sodomized, and destroyed. What he meant by all this is unclear. His most upsetting experience at Virginia Tech appears to have been his meeting with Professor Bean. No one was torturing him or trying to harm him. It was all in his head, but was no less real to him for all that.

The manifesto also contains references to hedonism. On the one hand, he was bitterly contemptuous of hedonists. On the other hand, the first sentence says, "Oh the happiness I could have had mingling among you hedonists, being counted as one of you."[61] He hated them, but he wanted to be one of them, perhaps hating them because he knew he couldn't be one of them.

So who was he, and why did he kill people? It appears that he thought he was Ax Ishmael, the Anti-Terrorist of America, and that he was avenging all the horrible wrongs that he and other weak and innocent people have endured, that he was leading a global uprising of the oppressed. The reality is that instead of protecting innocent people, he gunned them down in cold blood. He was the killer, the annihilator.

Who was he really—not as Ax Ishmael but as Seung Hui Cho? He was a profoundly shy, scared, inhibited young man who could not function socially. He struggled with women, failing in his attempts at finding a girlfriend and being twice told by campus police to stop harassing women. Shortly before his attack, he hired a woman from an escort service who met him in a motel room. She danced for him briefly before he tried to force himself on her, but she pushed him off and left.[62] Even with a hired woman he was a failure.

His sense of self may have also been hurt by his older sister's outstanding abilities. She was accepted into both Yale and Princeton, graduated from Princeton, and was hired by the State Department. She was the epitome of success, and he was a "loser."

Cho was the outsider looking in on everyone else living happy lives. He expressed this in a short story about a student named Bud who planned a school shooting. Bud looked into a classroom where "everyone is smiling and laughing as if they're in heaven-on-earth, something magical and enchanting about all the people's intrinsic nature that Bud will never experience."[63] Cho wrote a poem called "Loser" in which he laments his inability to have a life like other people:

> In his dream, he lives two lives,
> because in this world he has no life . . .
> Only if LOSER could live his lives.
> Something LOSER can't ever do!—live those lives
> and be normal and actually have a life.[64]

In a piece of writing found in his room after the attack, Cho had written, "Kill yourselves or you will never know how the dorky kid that [you] publicly humiliated and spat on will come behind you and slash your throats."[65] How did Cho see himself? As a loser, a dorky kid who could never live a normal life like everybody around him.

Was there a triggering event for Cho's attack? Perhaps. In fact, the same event that seems to have most enraged him may also have determined the date of his rampage. The previous year, on April 17, 2006, Cho had a disturbing episode with Professor Bean. Cho, who usually stayed silent or spoke so softly that he was barely audible, actually yelled when Bean recommended that he drop his class.[66] Of note is that Bean had a particular interest in the Holocaust. A year later, the day of Cho's attack, Cho mailed a letter to the English department complaining about his treatment by Bean. Cho said five times said that Bean "went on a holocaust on me." The letter indicates the significance of the incident to Cho and demonstrates how his paranoia distorted reality. "When he realized that I'm a weak and defenseless kid," Cho wrote, "the color of his face changed and his eyes and lips turned Satanic. Impulsively, he viciously tore me apart like a beast, wickedly laughed in my face, completely desecrated me over and over in multiple ways and tried to smother me out. He went on a holocaust on me, and he seemed to enjoy every moment of it."[67] This incident occurred on April 17, 2006; Cho's attack was on April 16, 2007—one day short of the one-year anniversary. Why one day away? Why not on April 17? Perhaps because the incident with Bean was on a Monday and Cho wanted his counter-attack to be a year later to the day. Or perhaps, more importantly, April 16, 2007, was Holocaust Remembrance Day. Bean was interested in the Holocaust, and having felt like he was a victim of Bean's committing "a holocaust on him," perhaps Cho timed his own holocaust accordingly.

※ ※ ※

Though Cho was never diagnosed as schizophrenic during his lifetime, the severity of his psychosis suggests that he was schizophrenic. His paranoia inflated negative events into experiences of crucifixion, rape, and murderous attempts to annihilate him. As with several other psychotic shooters, Cho created an ideology that supported his attack. He even created a new identity for himself: Ax Ishmael, the Anti-Terrorist of America.

Steven Kazmierczak

"You can write a book about me someday."

Date: February 14, 2008   **Killed**: 5
Age: 27   **Wounded**: 17
School: Northern Illinois   **Outcome**: Suicide
University
Location: DeKalb, IL

Steven Kazmierczak was an outstanding student in sociology—the golden boy of the department. He impressed his professors as a rising star with a great future in the field. So how did he go from golden boy to mass murderer?[68]

Kazmierczak was an enigmatic person with an unusual life history. By the time he was eighteen years old, he had been hospitalized nine times for suicide risk or attempts. In addition to the hospitalizations, he was in and out of residential treatment programs due to his chronic depression and psychotic symptoms. Eight years before his attack, "Steven acknowledged that he was paranoid and claimed to have 'special powers.' He claimed to hear voices that continually commented about what he was thinking and how he behaved. It was reported that Steven suffered auditory hallucinations and on at least one occasion had a visual hallucination."[69] Kazmierczak reported that he could "see" a former girlfriend and that he could read minds. He said he had always had this ability but that it had become stronger with age.

Despite his mental health problems, Kazmierczak completely turned his life around, becoming an academic success at Northern Illinois University (NIU). He impressed the faculty not only with his intellectual ability but with his personal qualities, too. "He was exceptional as a student, one of those who was definitely a standout," the postattack report says. "He was every professor's and advisor's dream come true, a very respectful student who was polite and so dedicated and conscientious. Nobody had anything bad to say about him."[70] This was an astonishing recovery from suicide attempts and psychosis.

Though his professors described him in glowing terms, his peers saw him differently. He talked obsessively about Ted Bundy, Jeffrey Dahmer, Hitler, and the rampage at Columbine. His preoccupation with serial killers and other murderers apparently alienated people, and he was given nicknames such as "Strange Steve" and "Psycho."

Kazmierczak had an older sister, Susan, who reportedly was "more compliant, better behaved, and more successful academically than her brother."[71] Kazmierczak did not get along with her, and in eighth grade he once chased her from the house with a knife. Following the shooting at Northern Illinois University, Susan expressed surprise that Kazmierczak had not tried to kill her instead of students he didn't even know.

Kazmierczak had an erratic work history. He was fired several times due to behavior problems, poor attendance, or both. On September 20, 2001, Kazmierczak joined the US Army. To get in, however, he'd provided false information and did not report his extensive history of mental health treatment. This was discovered, and he was discharged on February 13, 2002.

Kazmierczak graduated from NIU in May 2006 and began graduate school in sociology there the following fall. When the department underwent changes, however, he transferred to the University of Illinois. Things seemed to fall apart for him at this time. His mother died in September 2006, he didn't handle the transition to a new school well, and he had difficulties with his girlfriend. Kazmierczak's functioning further deteriorated over 2007, and during the early weeks of 2008, he became less social, isolating himself more and more. Then, on February 14, 2008, he returned to the building where he'd had his first class at NIU and gunned down strangers.

As always, the question *Why?* demands an answer. Kazmierczak complained that at NIU there were "a lot of well-to-do and uppity people."[72] He reportedly had a preoccupation with, and intolerance of, people he considered overprivileged. Was this an issue of status and envy? Did he strike out against those he felt threatened by?

Kazmierczak left no messages about his attack. We don't know what reasons he thought he had for doing what he did or why he chose the place he did. Because he had transferred to the University of Illinois, he had to travel three hours to get back to NIU. Thus, it was not a location of convenience. He not only traveled to NIU but went to the lecture hall where he'd had his first class and many of his subsequent sociology classes. This was the place where he had turned his life around, where he had recovered from his mental health problems and established himself as the star student in the sociology department. Since then, however, his life had gone downhill. He was in a new school, he was no longer the star, and it probably seemed like his life was unraveling. Maybe he envied those who were on the same path he had been on, so he went back to his beginnings at NIU to kill those who were following in his footsteps and were likely to succeed where he had failed.

❄ ❄ ❄

Steven Kazmierczak left no manifesto or evidence that his attack was driven by ideology. He was, however, attracted to ideologies, including the Nazis and Nietzsche. (As a teenager, Kazmierczak had a business card from the KKK and drew swastikas with spray paint.) He also was fascinated by role models for violence, including Jeffrey Dahmer, Ted Bundy, Hitler, Harris and Klebold, and Seung Hui Cho. He had a history of psychotic symptoms, but it is not clear that his psychosis drove his rampage. His symptoms were significant enough to suggest schizophrenia, but if he were schizophrenic, the symptoms were episodic, not chronic. Like other shooters, status seemed to be a concern. Also, as seen among other psychotic shooters, he had an older sister who outperformed him and whom he hated.

Matti Saari

"You'll be sorry."

Date: September 23, 2008   **Killed**: 10
Age: 22   **Wounded**: 1
School: Seinajoki University   **Outcome**: Suicide
Location: Kauhajoki, Finland

Less than a year after Pekka-Eric Auvinen's rampage, Finland was again shocked by a school shooting. Matti Saari followed in Auvinen's footsteps—not just by committing a school attack, but by deliberately modeling himself on Auvinen.[73]

Saari got off to a rough start in life. As a toddler, his growth and development were slow, and he had frequent illnesses and hospitalizations. Physically, "his height-weight curve was lower than expected. He remained slight in build for a long time but later gained weight. His height was below the average for Finnish males."[74]

In terms of temperament, "He has been described as lively and happy as a baby but shy, withdrawn, and quiet as a child and later in his life."[75] Saari's parents separated when he was a year old. He had an older brother who suffered from a congenital illness and died when Saari was seventeen, which reportedly was a devastating loss for him. The family relocated twelve times due to the father's work, resulting in six school changes for Saari in nine years of primary and secondary schooling.

In school, his peers reportedly assaulted him, threatened to break his moped, spit in his face, and drew caricatures of him on the blackboard.[76] His mental health records begin at age thirteen and indicate problems with anxiety and panic attacks, as well as depression and suicidal thoughts. In 2007 he had an episode of depression or psychosis in which "he lay motionless and apathetic in his bed, refusing to eat or drink anything."[77]

Long before this, however, he had thought about murder. According to a friend, in 2005 Saari had talked about "going on a shooting spree in a restaurant in his former hometown."[78] This means that Saari was fantasizing about a rampage two years before Auvinen's attack.

Saari joined the military, but he struggled to fit in and was picked on. His fellow soldiers described him as "weird and silent."[79] He lasted less than two months. Saari also had an erratic educational history as a young adult. He dropped out of upper secondary school, a vocational school, and yet another school.[80] He eventually attended the culinary-

arts program at Kauhajoki Polytechnic where he completed the first
year satisfactorily and began his second year in September 2008.

In Saari's later school years, he got involved with "petty theft and
intoxicants."[81] His behavior seemed to become increasingly odd, and he
disturbed people by the way he played with a knife. He also made
reference to suicide and expressed admiration for Auvinen's shooting in
Jokela the previous autumn.

His drinking became more problematic, and "His intoxication was
occasionally accompanied by aggressive behavior, fisticuffs, and language his friends considered frightening."[82] While drunk at a party in a
restaurant, he talked about school shootings with women he was trying
to pick up; when rejected, he commented, "You'll be sorry."[83] When an
employee of the restaurant intervened, Saari reportedly seemed
"strange," did not make eye contact, and did not respond to the employee. Similarly, he did not make eye contact when he met with a nurse
specialist about his depression. In the summer of 2008 there was an
unexplained incident on a ship where Saari was "imprisoned" because
he had become violent toward a friend.

His friends noticed a change in his behavior. Though some people
saw Saari as a typical young man, others thought he was "abnormal."[84]
He became obsessed with guns and school shootings. Shortly before the
attack, a brief relationship with a girlfriend ended. Also, several acquaintances of his were killed in a car accident. The impact of these
events is unknown.

In Finland, people must be interviewed to get permission to buy
firearms and then must present the weapon to the police before they
are allowed to use it. Saari's behavior when he presented his gun to the
police on September 2, 2008, was noteworthy. According to the postattack report, "The policeman was bothered . . . by the perpetrator's
[Saari's] odd behaviour. For example, he had been giggling and snuf-
fling while presenting the gun. . . . The policeman who had performed
the inspection did take the matter up in the police department later that
day, saying that he hoped this was not the next school killer."[85]

On September 19, it came to someone's attention that Saari had
posted videos online about shooting. On September 22, the police
interviewed Saari, who stated that there were lots of videos online about
shooting. The officers did not confiscate his gun or conduct any further
evaluation. The next day, he committed his attack.

While Saari did not leave a manifesto, he did leave behind a note
saying that the attack was due to his hatred of humanity and was also
revenge for bullying. As retaliation for bullying, however, the attack did
not make sense, as "There are no records or references indicating that
the perpetrator had been discriminated against or bullied at Kauhajoki

Polytechnic. His studies went well there. The perpetrator had told his mother and friends that he liked it in Kauhajoki. He also had a few friends at the polytechnic, with whom he spent some of his leisure time."[86] The official report concluded, "There is no indication of the act being an act of revenge."[87] Also, as noted above, three years earlier he had talking about committing a rampage attack at a restaurant; considering this, revenge for mistreatment at school was not the motive.

Saari, like Auvinen, admired Harris and Klebold. He also admired Auvinen. He traveled to Jokela and took photographs of the school where Auvinen committed his rampage. He bought guns from the same company as Auvinen. And, like Auvinen, he not only shot people but set fires in the school as well. On the day of his attack, Auvinen wore a shirt that said, "Humanity is overrated." Several days before his attack, Saari got drunk and said to people, "Humanity is overrated." Furthermore, Saari's "hair and dressing style had undergone a change during the summer preceding the incident. He now combed his hair back and wore a black leather jacket, which attracted attention. His new style was reminiscent of that of the Jokela school killer"—Auvinen.[88] Though Saari left no manifesto like Auvinen's, he did leave two suicide notes that resembled Auvinen's writings, including the comments, "I hate the human race, I hate mankind, I hate the whole world, and I want to kill as many people as possible."[89]

❊ ❊ ❊

Matti Saari, like Auvinen, appears to have had an avoidant personality that evolved into schizotypal personality disorder. Identifying Saari as psychotic is tentative due to insufficient information. Nonetheless, as is common among schizotypals, he behaved in strange ways and struck people as odd. In addition, schizotypals frequently exhibit inappropriate affect, as Saari did when he presented his gun to the police. He also did not make eye contact the way most people do. He was anxious, depressed, and unable to function socially. Like other psychotic shooters, he seems to have used Auvinen, Harris, and Klebold as figures he could mentally attach himself to and imitate, thereby experiencing a sense of power.

COMMENTS

Seung Hui Cho, Steven Kazmierczak, and Matti Saari differed from the psychotic shooters who engaged in targeted attacks. Those shooters, in addition to their psychotic symptoms, exhibited narcissistic, demanding, and abrasive behavior. Cho was clearly an odd young man, but he did not act entitled or demanding. He was profoundly shy and anxious, not arrogant and abrasive. Similarly, Saari was a shy, anxious young man who struck people as odd, but he was not chronically rude, condescending, or obnoxious. In contrast, Kazmierczak's professors saw him as a model student and a wonderful young man.

In comparing the targeted and random college attackers, some generalizations can be made. The shooters who carried out targeted attacks had belligerent personalities that alienated and frightened people around them. This is true of both the psychopathic and psychotic-psychopathic shooters.

The targeted attacks were the culmination of long battles between the perpetrators and their universities. In contrast, the random shooters had no long-brewing battles with professors or departments, no e-mail campaigns about grievances, and no lawsuits against their universities. Cho wrote a manifesto, but the content had nothing to do with Virginia Tech. Whereas the targeted shooters could point to external events that in their minds warranted a violent response, the random shooters seemed to be driven more by their own internal dynamics. There were, of course, external stresses, such as Whitman's parents' separation or Cho's conflict with Professor Bean, but there is no logical connection between these events and their rampages.

The external situations of the targeted shooters were more desperate than those of the random shooters. Lu was unemployed despite sending résumés all over the country; he was poor and pessimistic about his prospects. Fabrikant was fighting for tenure, and if he failed his career would be in serious trouble. Flores was struggling financially, his wife had left him, and his academic failures devastated his economic and career prospects. Odighizuwa's wife had left him, and he was desperately poor, a law school dropout with student loans to repay. Bishop had lost her fight for tenure, sending her career and entire identity into a tailspin. Halder was poor, isolated, and without prospects.

In contrast, Whitman was being supported by his wife. Both Lo and Cho were supported by their parents. Saari was doing well in school and had no known financial concerns. Kazmierczak had a brilliant academic career. None of the random shooters had children, whereas four out of six of the targeted shooters did, which resulted in added financial strain. Overall, the targeted shooters had greater responsibilities and more significant life stressors to deal with than the random shooters.

AMBIGUOUS ATTACKS

Edward Allaway

"They had control of my being. They were giving commands."

Date: July 12, 1976   **Killed**: 7
Age: 37   **Wounded**: 2
School: California State   **Outcome**: Called police,
University   turned himself in.
Location: Fullerton, CA   Prison

Edward Allaway accused his first wife, Carol, of being unfaithful. He believed that men entered his bed while he slept and had sex with her. To prevent this, Allaway put a lock on the bedroom door and kept two loaded guns under the bed.[90] His wife convinced him to get inpatient psychiatric treatment, so he spent time in Oakwood Hospital in Dearborn, Michigan. Despite his mental health treatment, Carol divorced him, and Allaway moved to California.[91]

Allaway then married a woman named Bonnie. He threatened to slice her face with a penknife if she ever cheated on him.[92] Eventually, however, he believed that Bonnie, too, was having affairs. He also thought she appeared in pornographic movies that were filmed in the building where he worked as a custodian at California State University.[93] Allaway believed that his coworkers forced Bonnie to participate in pornography and then tortured her.[94] Some employees did watch pornographic films at work, but there is no evidence they ever made any, with or without Bonnie.[95]

The sexual focus of Allaway's delusions is interesting in light of other facts. He was severely upset by obscene graffiti in the restrooms he cleaned. Additionally, he said that sometimes men had homosexual encounters in the bathrooms and even invited him to join them—perhaps seriously, perhaps teasingly.[96] Furthermore, Allaway said he was dishonorably discharged from the marines because he contracted venereal diseases three times.[97] Assuming this is true, it suggests that he visited prostitutes, which makes his report of feeling disturbed by sexual graffiti seem odd. Perhaps he had profound guilt or distress related to sex that was exacerbated by his psychosis.

Not much information is available about Allaway's early life. He was the youngest of four children, with three older sisters. He had a "rocky relationship with his father, an alcoholic factory worker."[98] He reportedly attempted suicide, but no details are known.[99]

Allaway had an erratic work history, with numerous jobs that didn't last long. In some cases he was fired for fighting with his coworkers.[100] A tense situation developed at the University of California, where Allaway had a hostile attitude and angry outbursts. Though some people became afraid of him, his paranoia caused him to be afraid of others.[101]

His marriage to Bonnie went well at first, but one night neighbors heard such screaming from their apartment that someone called the police. The couple separated over Memorial Day weekend, 1976, just six weeks before Allaway's rampage.[102]

Besides his delusions about his wife's affairs, Allaway reported auditory and visual hallucinations. He believed that certain men "urinated on Bonnie and sodomized her. They used her as their whore."[103] He began having bizarre experiences:

> One night he claimed he saw a woman standing in the doorway outside his apartment. She cupped her hands to her mouth and blew, instructing Allaway to breathe in. When he did, Allaway became disoriented and stumbled back inside.
>
> Then a man crashed through the apartment window. Allaway thought he heard Bonnie screaming for help. The mysterious assailant lunged toward Allaway, forcing him to say he wanted Bonnie to suffer. Allaway heard voices outside the door ask if Bonnie's nipples should be cut off. Allaway, under pressure, agreed to let them "just cut one."[104]

On July 12, 1976, Allaway went to the university library where he worked and gunned people down at close range. A fellow custodian heard Allaway mutter, "I'm going to kill all these SOBs for messing around with my wife."[105] He shot a photographer, a media assistant, a graphic artist, and a retired professor. He also shot two fellow custodians who were said to have been among his few friends at the university. One of these was Deborah Paulsen, a woman he wanted to marry or move in with. She reportedly liked Allaway initially but eventually rejected him.[106] This could have been a motivating factor in the attack, but nothing Allaway said before, during, or since his rampage has confirmed this. Ten years after the rampage, Allaway insisted that there was nothing connecting his victims. He blamed the voices he heard, stating, "They had control of my being. . . . They were giving commands, and I was being punished."[107]

After his attack, Allaway fled in his car, seeking out his wife at the hotel where she worked. From there he called the police and said, "I went berserk at Cal State Fullerton, and I committed some terrible act. I'd appreciate it if you people would come down and pick me up. I'm unarmed, and I'm giving myself up to you."[108]

✻ ✻ ✻

Edward Allaway was diagnosed as paranoid schizophrenic;[109] this appears to be an accurate diagnosis. He had both hallucinations and delusions. He also developed an extreme sensitivity to sexuality reminiscent of Alvaro Castillo's severe discomfort with sex. The timing of Allaway's attack appears to have been related to his life circumstances, coming six weeks after he and his wife separated. He also was unhappy at work and wanted to transfer to a new position. His rampage, however, appears to have been a direct result of his psychosis.

The attack is considered ambiguous for several reasons. First, he made a comment about killing the "SOBs" whom he believed were having sex with his wife. Whether or not he had specific people in mind is unknown. Second, he claimed years later that he was shooting people randomly. Despite this, he did not go to a random place at the university but instead chose the building where he worked and knew people. And finally, shooting the woman who rejected him may not have been random.

One Goh

"My entire life, I cannot do things other people do."

Date: April 2, 2012   **Killed**: 7
Age: 43   **Wounded**: 3
School: Oikos University   **Outcome**: Fled scene.
Location: Oakland, CA   Picked up at supermarket.
                                  Prison

One Goh's life was a series of financial and familial losses and failures.[110] Goh came to the United States from South Korea, arriving at a young age with his parents and two older brothers. His brothers made successful transitions to their new country; Goh did not.

Goh had a series of jobs but was never financially stable. He had federal tax liens against him totaling more than $23,000.[111] He owed $10,377 to a bank, had been sued over a credit card debt, and had been evicted from an apartment for failing to pay his rent.[112] In Virginia, Goh owned a construction company that failed. He also had a failed marriage, leaving behind an ex-wife and twelve-year-old daughter when he relocated to the West Coast.[113] In California, Goh was fired from his job as a food deliveryman because of his hot temper.[114] He also had several run-ins with law enforcement, most commonly due to traffic violations, but with at least one arrest for misdemeanor assault and battery in 1993.[115]

Besides lost jobs, lost money, and the loss of his relationships with his ex-wife and daughter, Goh lost a brother and his mother. Just over a year before Goh's attack, his brother, who was a decorated US Army veteran, was killed in a car crash.[116] Not long after that, Goh's mother, who had returned to Korea, died.[117] At age forty-three, Goh apparently was without friends, without a girlfriend or wife, living with his father, and attending Oikos University where he studied nursing.

Though Goh complained that his classmates made fun of his poor English skills, a university administrator challenged this and pointed out that most of the students—who are immigrants from around the world—do not speak English well.[118] Also, though some reports in the aftermath of the attack stated that Goh had been expelled from the school, he apparently withdrew voluntarily.[119]

What, then, was the trigger for his attack? Goh's biggest issue with the university was financial. When he withdrew from his classes in November 2011 he sought to get his tuition reimbursed. He had a series of meetings with administrators in which he demanded his full tuition back, and when they refused, he became angry.[120]

After his attack, Goh revealed that his primary target had been Won-ja Kim, who had been the assistant director of the nursing program. By April 2012, however, she was no longer employed at the university.[121] Goh did not know this and during his attack searched for her in order to kill her. Not able to find her, he unleashed his rage on ten people he did not know; he later told police that he wanted to kill as many people as he could.[122] He then fled the scene, called his father from a supermarket, and said he had done "very bad things."[123] A clerk overheard this conversation and notified store security, who detained Goh and contacted the police.

What was wrong with Goh? After his attack, two psychiatric evaluations concluded that he had paranoid schizophrenia.[124] He reportedly had both hallucinations and delusions. His hallucinations included voices talking to him and seeing faces in mirrors. His delusions involved "the battle between God and Satan and his role in that battle."[125] Goh's symptoms were severe enough that a judge ruled him to be mentally unfit to stand trial.[126]

✽ ✽ ✽

One Goh's attack was ambiguous because he reportedly was after one specific target but, not finding her, shot people indiscriminately. Even if he had found his target, he may still have shot random people. Also, he reportedly disclosed that he had intended to kill as many people as possible.[127] If true, then he intended to commit a mixed attack involving one specific target and multiple random targets.

COMMENTS

Both Allaway and Goh were psychotic. Both were the youngest children in their families and apparently the only ones who struggled with mental illness. They both had failed marriages and problematic work histories. They both fled the scenes of their attacks and telephoned people to confess what they had done; Allaway called the police and Goh, his father. Finally, both were picked up by police without a struggle.

The trigger for Goh's attack apparently was his financial dispute with the university. Thus, like the college shooters who engaged in targeted attacks, money was a key issue. Allaway's attack appears to have been driven by his psychosis, though he was also unhappy with his work situation and was looking to leave it, which may have contributed to the stress that led to his attack.

7

ABERRANT ADULT SHOOTERS

Why would a grown man or woman shoot little children in an elementary school? What makes young adults commit attacks at colleges they do not attend? What motivates men in their twenties and thirties to return to schools they attended years earlier and gun down people they do not know? The shooters presented in this chapter are perhaps the hardest to understand because of their lack of connection to the schools they attacked. This chapter explores the lives of ten perpetrators I call *aberrant adult shooters*. The eleventh case in this chapter does not resemble the others but was aberrant in terms of the setting where his rampage occurred.

YOUNG ADULTS WHO ATTACKED COLLEGES THEY DID NOT ATTEND

Marc Lépine

> *"I have decided to send the feminists, who have always ruined my life, to their Maker."*

Date: December 6, 1989
Age: 25
School: École Polytechnique
Location: Montreal, Canada

Killed: 14
Wounded: 14
Outcome: Suicide

Marc Lépine hated his father—and with reason. Liess Gharbi was controlling and bad-tempered. He frequently swatted his wife, son, and daughter on the back of the head.[1] He once struck Lépine in the face so hard that the marks lasted a week, after which Mrs. Lépine filed for divorce and the family separated into two households.[2]

Lépine's sister, Nadia, was three years younger but more assertive and dominant. She taunted him and put him down in front of his friends. When she saw him kiss a girl, she burst out laughing, and he felt humiliated. When he didn't have a girlfriend, she made fun of him and called him "gay."[3] When Lépine was twelve or thirteen years old he was so enraged by Nadia that he made a mock grave for her in the backyard, with her name and photograph on the gravestone.[4] Mrs. Lépine commented, "I thought it was strange behavior. . . . But Marc was different than other boys."[5]

As an adolescent and young adult, Lépine was extremely shy, anxious, and socially awkward. A couple of male friends noted that he was socially immature—at age twenty he seemed much younger. His behavior struck people as strange—perhaps he laughed too loud or argued too much.[6] Mrs. Lépine described him as "enigmatic" and said some of his behavior "just wasn't normal."[7] One abnormality was that he was "a fervent admirer of Adolf Hitler."[8]

Although intelligent, Lépine pursued a circuitous route through college, taking courses in one field, switching to another field, failing classes, and dropping out of courses. He had a series of menial jobs that never lasted long. His goal was to attend the École Polytechnique and become an engineer; he applied to the school twice and was rejected both times. He also tried to join the military but was rejected there, too.[9]

Lépine became obsessed with feminists, and in his suicide note he blamed them for ruining his life.[10] His note expressed particular contempt for women in the military. During his rampage, he shouted, "You're women, you're going to be engineers. You're all a bunch of feminists. . . . And I hate feminists!"[11] His belief that feminists ruined his life was paranoid.

Not only was Lépine paranoid, but a friend of his recalled "in the early 1980s" when "Marc was taking a computer-programming course in the downtown building where I worked. One day I came upon him in a crowded elevator. I scarcely recognized him; he seemed completely out of it and was mumbling what sounded like German words. And then, right there in the midst of all those office workers, he raised his right arm in a Nazi salute. I could have died! Everyone stared at him as though he was nuts."[12] This behavior suggests psychosis.

Lépine's rage and contempt were directed at three groups of women: police officers, soldiers, and engineers. Why them? These women were functioning in traditionally male roles, two of them being roles that he had pursued and failed to achieve. He was rejected by the military, and he was rejected by École Polytechnique where he had aspired to study engineering. He didn't commit mass murder at a mall, restaurant, or a randomly chosen street corner. He committed murder at the school that rejected him, where women were succeeding in the career he aspired to. His rampage was most likely an attempt to destroy threats to his identity as a male.

❄ ❄ ❄

Though he was not diagnosed while alive, Lépine appears to have had schizotypal personality disorder: his mother and friends found him to be odd and enigmatic, and he had the delusion that feminists had ruined his life. Also, he was a bright young man but ended up not working, not attending school, and with virtually no social life. This lack of accomplishment is common among schizotypals. Like other psychotic shooters, Lépine was attracted to Nazism. He apparently had a severely damaged masculine identity and resented women who outperformed him.

Jillian Robbins

"When I woke up that day, I decided I was going to die."

Date: September 17, 1996   **Killed**: 1
Age: 19   **Wounded**: 1
School: Pennsylvania State   **Outcome**: Overpowered.
University   In prison
Location: University Park, PA

When Jillian Robbins was eleven years old, she told her mother, "I want to die." Mrs. Robbins could not understand her daughter's depression: "She had always been happy and wonderful and bouncy and never cried and just nothing but joy. . . . And something started changing in early puberty."[13]

The family faced several upheavals over the years. Robbins was five when her parents divorced. A few years later her mother remarried, then divorced again. Then she married her second husband a second time, but again they divorced.[14] Robbins's father also remarried. Though these changes were presumably stressful for Robbins, there is no evidence of parental alcoholism, child abuse, or other traumas.

Robbins bounced back and forth between her parents' homes during adolescence.[15] Her mother attended a graduate program at Penn State in University Park, Pennsylvania, and then worked there as an administrator. When Mrs. Robbins relocated to the university's Harrisburg campus, her daughter stayed back at University Park. Robbins's father, whom she reportedly idolized, was an administrator for the army reserve.[16]

Apparently following in her father's footsteps, Robbins joined the army reserve as a junior in high school. She attended basic training in the summer of 1994 but dropped out of high school. Then, because she did not have sufficient high school credits, the army reserve kicked her out.[17]

Robbins worked at a diner, and at eighteen she married a coworker she had not known for long. After six months, she moved out.[18] No details about the marriage have come to light. The following summer, she had an inpatient stay in a psychiatric hospital.[19]

Though Robbins found a new boyfriend, the relationship was unstable. On September 16, 1996, they had a big fight.[20] The next morning, Robbins took the rifle her father had given her to the Penn State campus and opened fire. She killed one person and wounded another. Two other students were nearly hit; they found bullet fragments in their backpacks.[21] A student wrestled Robbins to the ground before she could shoot anyone else.

What was wrong with Robbins? She had a long history of depression and psychiatric hospitalizations and had attempted suicide several weeks before the shooting.[22] She also had symptoms of schizophrenia. Robbins reported that as early as tenth grade she had both auditory and visual hallucinations. She heard voices and saw "tall, dark people with dark coats and no eyes." She said, "I could not handle the stresses of life. I could not handle the hallucinations, the delusions any more."[23] The nature of her delusions remains unknown. Her peers observed her oddness. A coworker said, "Everybody that worked there said the same thing: She did act strange and weird."[24] She was given the nickname "Crazy Jill."[25]

The district attorney sought a plea agreement to avoid a trial that would allow Robbins to enter an insanity plea. He commented, "It was a solid claim for an insanity defense."[26] Insanity pleas are rarely successful; for the district attorney to admit that Robbins had a solid claim suggests there was compelling evidence that she was psychotic.

But why did she shoot college students? Robbins could not explain this, saying she just wanted to die. Friends reported, however, that she did not like "preppy" people.[27] Perhaps as a high school dropout she envied college students.

✿ ✿ ✿

Jillian Robbins and Brenda Spencer had several things in common. They both had fathers who served in the military and gave them rifles as gifts. Both were expert sharpshooters—Spencer trained by her father, Robbins by the army. Both had parents who worked in universities. Both were described as tomboys with no interest in traditional femininity. Also, both sets of parents were divorced. They differed significantly, however, in personality. Spencer was fully grounded in reality, upbeat and fun-loving, and found sadistic pleasure in killing; Robbins was depressed, suicidal, and psychotic.

Kimveer Gill

"Let the blood flow, Let the streets run red with blood,
Blood of mine enemies."

Date: September 13, 2006 **Killed**: 1
Age: 25 **Wounded**: 19
School: Dawson College **Outcome**: Hit by police
Location: Montreal, Canada gunfire. Suicide

At age twenty-five, Kimveer Gill was not in school, had no job, didn't hang out with friends, and wasn't dating. He stayed in his room, played video games, and posted messages on VampireFreaks.com. He had not always been like this.

Gill had been a normal child who was "quiet, nice, sensitive and generous."[28] At age nine he received a certificate for outstanding effort at school and the following year was given a Citizenship Award.[29] He enjoyed playing floor hockey, basketball, and tennis. In sixth grade, his goal was to become a lawyer and "make people go to jail."[30] He received certificates of merit for good conduct two consecutive years in high school. Gill was a well-liked boy who was not ostracized or bullied. As a classmate stated, "He wasn't a guy that got picked on, not at all—who picks on a tall, big guy who could kick your ass if you picked on him?"[31] Despite his size, Gill was repeatedly described as gentle.

Gill attended Vanier College with several high school friends. After one semester, however, he dropped out and joined the Canadian Army. Just one month later, he was "honorably released." This reportedly could mean he didn't meet the military's standards, left voluntarily, or was discharged due to medical reasons. His mother said he left because he missed home. Two of Gill's fellow recruits, however, said he was discharged because he didn't meet military standards of behavior.[32]

Gill found work but was laid off in 2001. This reportedly was a serious blow. He then had several odd jobs and took six months of coursework in industrial drafting at Rosemont Technology Centre. His friends noted that Gill was not moving ahead in life as they were, commenting that it seemed like he was mentally still in high school.[33] (Marc Lépine's friends had made essentially the same observation about him.)

Through his early twenties, Gill did not progress academically, occupationally, or socially. He began to drink. He increasingly isolated himself. He also began spending more time with an old friend, Rajiv Rajan. According to Mrs. Gill, "Rajiv said that it was very easy to manipulate Kimveer because he's too honest and too trusting."[34] This raises the question of what Rajan was manipulating Gill to do.

Rajan's influence is important, because in January 2006 he and Gill took photographs of themselves posing with one of Gill's firearms—the same one Gill later used at Dawson College. In fact, after Gill's rampage, Rajan reportedly vowed to follow in Gill's footsteps by carrying out another school shooting.[35] Whether the two men discussed committing a rampage attack is unknown, but it would not be surprising.

As 2006 progressed, Gill became increasingly isolated. A neighbor commented, "He never had friends with him. He was always alone."[36] Gill's mother noticed he was becoming more and more withdrawn.[37]

Gill posted messages and information about himself on Vampire-Freaks.com, where he expressed admiration for Eric Harris and Dylan Klebold and imitated Harris's writing. For example, Harris liked to write "*Ich bin Gott*," German for *I am God*. Gill also wrote "Ich bin Gott" and "I am God."[38] Gill's postings suggest he had delusions of grandeur. He wrote,

> Stop praying to your imaginary gods little monkeys
> Because I'm the only god you need to pray to
> I AM GOD.[39]

On September 10, just three days before his rampage, Gill wrote, "God, you humans are so inferior."[40] He also appears to have been paranoid. For example, though he was not under surveillance, Gill believed the police were watching him. He wrote, "I wonder why my household has been under surveillance by law enforcement for six years now?"[41]

Gill's online writings said nothing about his impending attack. It is perhaps noteworthy, however, that three days before his attack he wrote of the video game *Postal*, "I want them to make a game so realistic that it looks and feels like it's actually happening. . . . You gotta bring Postal into the mainstream. I want more people to see what I see. . . . Postal Dude was sad before he became angry and psychotic. . . . He was normal, but the world made him the way he became."[42] This suggests Gill identified with "Postal dude."

Why did he attack Dawson College? Gill had never attended the school, or even applied to it.[43] Why did he attack people at a college he had no connection to? Gill may have had the same feelings as Lépine toward students in college—that they were living the life he wanted to live. He could have chosen anywhere, but he chose a college. The kind of school he could have—perhaps felt he should have—been attending. The kind of school he started but left. It apparently was an attack against people who were doing what he was not—moving ahead in life.

Envy is a powerful force. Of those with higher status than he, Gill wrote, "Why does society applaud jocks? I don't understand. They are the worse kind of people on earth. And the preps are no better, they think they are better than others………..but they're not."[44] Gill, in the lonely isolation of his room, viewed jocks and preps as society's favorites. But he, like other envious shooters, found a way to elevate himself: "I love guns. I really do. The great equalizer."[45]

✿ ✿ ✿

Kimveer Gill was not diagnosed as psychotic during his lifetime, but his online postings suggest both paranoid delusions and delusions of grandeur. Whereas many psychotic shooters struggled socially and emotionally throughout their lives, Gill was a high-functioning young man all the way through high school. He appeared to be destined for success until he reached early adulthood. Whereas Lépine apparently had schizotypal personality disorder, Gill appears to have had adult-onset schizophrenia. Within a few years, this bright, capable young man collapsed into a nonfunctioning, isolated loner.

Besides his psychosis, Gill may have had peer support for his attack through his friend Rajiv Rajan. His attack was perhaps primarily driven by envy, which may have been particularly strong because his father was a college professor who wanted him to continue his education.[46] This may explain why Gill chose to attack a college rather than any other setting. He was gunning down those who were succeeding in the area in which he had not only failed himself but failed his family.

COMMENTS

These three shooters—Lépine, Robbins, and Gill—had several things in common. First, they were all psychotic. In addition, they were all within the age range of traditional undergraduate or graduate students—twenty-five, nineteen, and twenty-five, respectively. They all had at least one immigrant parent—Lépine's father from Algeria, Robbins's mother from Finland, Gill's mother and father from India. They all had family members who served in the military, they all had military aspirations of their own, and they all failed in these aspirations. Robbins and Gill had family members involved in higher education, and if we count Lépine's mother, who had been a university student, so did he. Also, none of them were attending college or had completed a degree. Thus, they all failed in both their military careers and their educations.

ADULTS WHO ATTACKED SCHOOLS THEY HAD ATTENDED YEARS BEFORE

Patrick Purdy

"I guess I'm just not good enough."

Date: January 17, 1989
Age: 24
School: Cleveland Elementary School
Location: Stockton, CA

Killed: 5
Wounded: 31
Outcome: Suicide

Patrick Purdy came from a broken home, lived on the streets of Los Angeles as a teenager, started prostituting himself to men when he was somewhere between thirteen and fifteen, became an alcoholic and drug addict, and drifted around the country, going from job to job.[47]

Purdy's parents separated after his father threatened his mother with a gun.[48] The parents divorced, and his father abandoned the family. Purdy's mother married and divorced three times. She struggled with alcoholism, and several charges of neglect were filed against her.[49] A neighbor recalled that in winter, Purdy and his siblings "wouldn't have jackets on. It would be cold. They were locked out of the house. No kind of supervision, no guidance."[50] According to one report, his mother threatened to kill Purdy.[51]

When Purdy was nine, he and his siblings were removed from the home. At some point he returned to his mother's care, but she kicked him out of the house when he was thirteen after he hit her. He lived on the streets, staying with whomever he could find, and spent some time with his father. When he was fifteen, he said he hated his mother and "could chop her head off."[52] He called her a "bitch, liar, thief, asshole, witch, cruel, torturer, mean, low down, evil, black whore, child abuser, inflicter of cruel and unusual punishment."[53] He said he "preferred living under bridges, eating off garbage dumpsters, and prostituting myself to living with the slave driver mother dearest."[54]

Purdy drifted between Florida, Oregon, and Connecticut, picking up jobs when he could, never lasting long in one position. Substance abuse was likely his biggest obstacle to staying employed. He was alcoholic from the age of twelve and used "LSD and other hallucinogens, modeling glue, PCP, amphetamines, heroin, and cocaine."[55] Despite his chronic substance use, Purdy was clean and sober when he carried out his attack.

At fifteen, Purdy was arrested for soliciting sex from an undercover police officer. He went on to be arrested many times for drugs, traffic violations, vandalism, attempted theft, and other charges.

Purdy complained that people taunted him because he was gay. He was often depressed and at thirteen attempted suicide by overdosing on drugs and alcohol. When he reported this during a disability evaluation, the psychologist got the impression that Purdy saw himself as failure in everything, even suicide. He demonstrated self-awareness, commenting, "I have never been able to get along with others or act in a socially appropriate manner."[56] At twenty-three, he was living out of his car, feeling "lonely and unloved."[57]

Near the end of his life, Purdy became prejudiced toward Southeast Asians, a group that had moved into his hometown in significant numbers since he was a child. It was also reported, however, that he didn't like whites and hated authorities. On the day of his attack, he wore a flakjacket on which he had written "Freedom," "PLO," "Hezbollah," and "Death to the Great Satin [sic]."[58] The Great Satan was the United States. Purdy had also drawn an American flag inside a circle with a slash through the flag. He apparently hated both the United States and immigrants.

Why did he attack Cleveland Elementary? He attended the school from kindergarten through third grade. In the intervening years, the student population had become 70 percent Asian. Maybe he choose that school as a way to express his opposition to "foreigners" coming to this country and taking jobs away from him, which had been one of his complaints. Alternatively, because of the misery and trauma he experienced as a child, perhaps he was envious of the happy children he saw playing at recess. A third possibility is that the attack served as misplaced revenge for having been teased by rich kids at that school, or perhaps envy that the Asian students had nicer clothes than he did.[59]

Purdy apparently considered attacking other schools before deciding on Cleveland Elementary. He was seen stalking a local middle school and a high school shortly before his attack. Maybe he chose Cleveland Elementary because he felt too inadequate to successfully attack teenagers, deciding instead to unleash his rage on the most vulnerable students he could find.

Though Purdy committed his rampage alone, he and his half-brother, Albert, had often talked about killing people, usually police officers. A few days before the attack, they discussed killing people. When Purdy said, "Let's do it," Albert told him, "You're not ready," and added, "they're not worth it."[60] It is unclear who "they" referred to—cops, children, or some other targets. A month after Purdy's attack, Albert was arrested for possessing explosive devices. What he intended to do with them remains unknown.

* * *

Patrick Purdy was a traumatized shooter. He had a highly dysfunctional and violent family that physically and emotionally abused him. He was kicked out of his home at age thirteen and lived on the streets where he experienced sexual abuse in the form of homosexual prostitution with men. Aside from this, we have no idea what other traumas may have occurred while Purdy was on his own. Being homeless in Los Angeles exposed Purdy to danger at a very young age, and he may have experienced any number of hardships.

Also, Purdy resembled other traumatized shooters in having a peer (his half-brother) who supported his violent intentions. He also had a family role model for the misuse of firearms in his father, who threatened Purdy's mother with a gun. No other traumatized shooter had a history of severe substance abuse as long as Purdy's. He also differed from most traumatized shooters in having political beliefs that may have influenced his attack.

Bruco Eastwood

"They have me suffering, alive but in pain."

Date: February 23, 2010   **Killed**: 0
Age: 32   **Wounded**: 2
School: Deer Creek   **Outcome**: Prison
Middle School
Location: Littleton, CO

By the time Bruco Eastwood shot two students at his former middle school, he was severely psychotic. He not only heard voices talking to him but also engaged in loud conversations and arguments with them, even in front of his father.[61] Sometimes Eastwood threw punches and kicks at nonexistent enemies.[62] During his trial, "Eastwood occasionally made gestures during the hearing, appearing to grab invisible objects around his head and torso, throwing them over his shoulder or to his side."[63]

Eastwood also had multiple delusions. He believed there were "mutants or transformers that were taking over his body."[64] He also believed that creatures stole food from his stomach and that a Nielsen Ratings box attached to his television was projecting voices into his head.[65] Besides his psychotic symptoms, Eastwood had a long history of violent behavior, alcoholism, and arrests.[66]

Not much is known about Eastwood's childhood. His father was Apache, and his mother was Irish.[67] His parents separated and eventually divorced,[68] with Eastwood living with his mother. The separation occurred when Eastwood was approximately twelve years old—about the time that he attended Deer Creek Middle School. Eastwood reportedly did not have a good time at Deer Creek;[69] he was poor and resented the richer kids who allegedly picked on him.[70]

Five years before his attack, Eastwood lost his job at a grocery store and went to live with his father, where he helped out on the ranch.[71] He never graduated from high school but worked on getting his GED for two years, in the end failing to pass the test.[72] He had a lifelong dream of being an astronaut but never came close to achieving it.[73]

The day of his attack, Eastwood entered the school, said he was a former student, talked with a couple of teachers, and then left.[74] He opened fire outside the school, wounding two students before being tackled by a teacher and held until the police arrived.[75]

* * *

Eastwood was a psychotic shooter with a long history of hallucinations and delusions. His psychosis was significant enough that he was found not guilty by reason of insanity.[76] He reportedly sought revenge for his alleged mistreatment at the school, but shooting kids who hadn't even been born when he attended Deer Creek was not revenge. Why commit such an attack twenty years later? Perhaps his failure to obtain his GED resulted in resentment toward other students who presumably would succeed where he had failed. Also, his psychosis was severe, and he may have had hallucinations or delusions that drove him to violence.

Wellington de Oliveira

"Our fight is against cruel, cowardly people."

Date: April 7, 2011   **Killed**: 12
Age: 23   **Wounded**: 12
School: Tasso de Silveira   **Outcome**: Suicide
Municipal School
Location: Rio de Janeiro,
Brazil

Wellington de Oliveira was adopted from a schizophrenic woman. His mental health issues were severe, and a psychiatrist concluded (after the shooting) that de Oliveira was schizophrenic as well.[77] De Oliveira committed his attack at the school he had attended from 1999 to 2002. He was twenty-three years old at the time he gunned down children twelve to fifteen years of age.[78]

De Oliveira's adoptive siblings said, "He was very alone, absent, closed up"[79] and never had friends.[80] When there was a party in the house, he stayed in his bedroom. He watched other kids play soccer but did not join in. When directed to participate in group projects at school, de Oliveira refused and asked to work independently.[81]

According to peers and teachers, "he was routinely bullied at school, rejected and taunted by girls in class, and forced to endure 'constant humiliation' including being thrown into a school garbage can."[82] Because he walked with a limp, peers taunted him and nicknamed him "Swing."

When the World Trade Center was destroyed on September 11, 2001, de Oliveira became fascinated with terrorists. He studied terrorist attacks and began calling himself "Bomberman," meaning a suicide bomber. He said that someday he would blow up his school.[83] His nickname was reportedly "Al Qaeda."[84] De Oliveira talked about imitating the attack on the World Trade Center by crashing a plane into the giant statue of Christ the Redeemer in Rio de Janeiro.[85]

De Oliveira's mental health deteriorated in the last few years of his life. His adoptive father died in 2008; eight months before the attack, his adoptive mother died.[86] She apparently had been the only person with whom he had any meaningful connection. After this, he withdrew even more. He'd held the same job since 2008, but when assigned new responsibilities requiring more social interaction than he could manage, he quit. Shortly before the attack his appearance and behavior changed; he became disheveled and said strange things.[87] His sister said that his comments often made no sense,[88] suggesting disorganized thoughts, which are symptomatic of schizophrenia.

His interest in Muslim terrorists led him to study Islam. He talked to his sister about Islam and read the Quran four hours a day.[89] He grew a beard and told people he was Osama bin Laden.[90] Besides bin Laden, his heroes were Seung Hui Cho, whom he referred to as "a brother," and a Brazilian named Edmar Aparecido Freitas, who in 2003 had shot eight people at his former school.[91] Like Cho, de Oliveira framed his attack within an ideology that justified his violence. He said, "Our fight is against cruel, cowardly people who take advantage of the kindness, the innocence, the weakness of people who are incapable of defending themselves."[92] As with Cho, however, there was no connection between his ideology and his actions. Instead of acting on behalf of the weak and the innocent, he murdered them.

De Oliveira left an odd suicide note in which he wrote, "You should first know that the impure cannot touch me without gloves, only the chaste or those who lost their chastity after marriage and were not involved in adultery can touch me without gloves . . . nothing impure can have direct contact with a virgin without his permission."[93]

His preoccupation with sexual purity is reminiscent of Alvaro Castillo's obsession with lust, sin, and sexuality. Castillo wanted to die a virgin and avoid the sinfulness of sex. One of the students who survived the attack said that de Oliveira singled out girls for killing.[94] In fact, ten of the twelve fatalities were girls. Perhaps his focus on killing girls was related to his bizarre ideas about sex.

* * *

Wellington de Oliveira presented with multiple symptoms of schizophrenia: severely impaired social functioning, poor grooming, strange talk, bizarre preoccupations, and a grandiose delusion of himself as the defender of the weak, even as he killed them. He had role models for violence and an ideology that supported his action. The bullying he endured may have been worse than that endured by any other psychotic shooter.

Adam Lanza

"........."

Date: December 14, 2012   **Killed**: 27
Age: 20   **Wounded**: 2
School: Sandy Hook   **Outcome**: Suicide
Elementary School
Location: Newtown, CT

Though Adam Lanza was bright, he struggled with profound impairments all his life. He barely functioned socially, rarely spoke, could not tolerate being touched, and had periods of total withdrawal in which he became unresponsive. He was hypersensitive to light and sound, and yet he had a blunted sense of pain.[95] Lanza struggled emotionally in academic settings and as a young adult wondered why he was "such a loser."[96]

Lanza's parents separated in 2001, when he was nine years old. He lived with his mother and maintained contact with his father until 2010. At that point, Mr. Lanza had reportedly begun seeing another woman, and Lanza cut off contact with both his father and older brother.[97]

Lanza's uncle served in the military and then as a police officer.[98] Lanza admired him and was obsessed with the military. He covered the walls of his basement with military posters and played military video games for hours.[99] He even wanted to join the marines. Though his mother took him target shooting, she dissuaded him from applying to the military.[100] Why did he want to join the marines? Perhaps because that would transform him from a nobody into a somebody. As described by reporter Matthew Lysiak, Lanza created an alter ego as his online persona: "The skinny and frail teenager chose to create an imposing, bulky, muscle-bound soldier dressed in desert camouflage."[101] No one can argue with the manliness of a marine.

Perhaps Lanza's need to feel powerful was also behind his interest in Satanism. A classmate said Lanza created a Satanic website with "the word *Devil* on it in red Gothic-style letters against a black background. It gave me the chills."[102] Lanza was also fascinated by mass murderers.[103] A search of his home revealed a remarkable spreadsheet, seven feet by four feet, covered in nine-point type, with Lanza's collection of data about five hundred mass murderers.[104]

Lanza was not merely shy—he struck people as very odd. One person recalled, "There was a weirdness about him."[105] Another said, "I don't even think withdrawn is the right word. Removed."[106] Someone else stated, "He was like a ghost."[107]

In 2005, Lanza was diagnosed with Asperger's Disorder.[108] This is a "pervasive developmental disorder" (PDD), which is in the same category that includes autism. Though Lanza's symptoms could be accounted for by a PDD, they could also indicate schizophrenia. Alternatively, perhaps as a child he was on the autistic spectrum but as an adult went on to develop schizophrenia. His mother suspected that he wasn't simply autistic, wondering "whether her son had outgrown what had previously been diagnosed as borderline autism into something much more extreme."[109] Similarly, Lanza's father questioned the diagnosis of Asperger's: "I was thinking it [the Asperger's diagnosis] could mask schizophrenia."[110]

As a child, Lanza played the saxophone, performed in theater, and was active in a technology club at school. As he grew older, however, he withdrew from these activities, and his functioning declined.[111] This deterioration, as well as his profound social impairment and inability to converse, suggest schizophrenia. Schizophrenics often have "poverty of speech," meaning they fail to engage in normal conversation and may barely speak at all. Lanza's periods of withdrawal and nonresponsiveness may have been catatonic episodes. He also had blunted or flattened emotions, which is another symptom of schizophrenia. A former classmate commented, "If you looked at him, you couldn't see any emotions going through his head."[112]

Schizophrenia may also account for his sensory-integration problems: "Perceptual dysfunction is the most invariant feature of the early stage of schizophrenia."[113] As one schizophrenic commented, "noises all seem to be louder to me than they were before. It's as if someone had turned up the volume."[114] Another person said, "My eyes became markedly oversensitive to light. Ordinary colors appeared much too bright, and sunlight seemed dazzling in intensity."[115] The sense of touch can also be distorted: "It was terrible to be touched. . . . Once a nurse tried to cut my nails. The touch was such that I tried to bite her."[116] Not only Lanza's devastating social inhibition but also his sensory sensitivity and his inability to tolerate being touched were consistent with schizophrenia. The lack of pain sensation is also found in schizophrenia.[117]

It is not known if Lanza had hallucinations as an adult, though as a child he smelled odors that were not present.[118] Perceiving nonexistent smells constitutes what are called *olfactory hallucinations*. There is no clear evidence of delusions. An elementary-school peer remembered that Lanza talked about aliens;[119] whether or not this was a result of psychosis is unknown. Andrew Wurst, a psychotic shooter, believed he was an alien and had other delusions about aliens; the same may have been true of Lanza.

Like other young-adult psychotic shooters, Lanza had essentially withdrawn from life. He was twenty years old, living at home with no friends or significant other, without a job, and without pursuing his education. His world had largely shrunk to a room where he played video games and watched movies.

❀ ❀ ❀

Lanza shared significant similarities with Seung Hui Cho. Both were profoundly awkward in social situations. Both demonstrated poverty of speech and flattened affect. Neither could tolerate being touched. Each felt like "a loser." The main difference between the two is that Cho's manifesto gives us solid evidence of his delusions of grandeur and persecution.

Without such a document from Lanza, how do we make sense of his attack? He may have sought "revenge" for mistreatment at Sandy Hook, but there is no consensus regarding how much he was picked on. In addition, Lanza "indicated that he loved the school,"[120] his family remembered his years there as "the best times of his life,"[121] and his father stated, "Adam loved Sandy Hook."[122]

People have speculated that perhaps he was jealous of the students his mother volunteered with at the school. Another possibility is that he felt so impotent that he sought out the only targets he believed he could handle—first graders.

Yet another possibility has to do with Lanza's enigmatic sexuality. His computer contained "materials regarding the topic of pedophilia and advocating for rights for pedophiles."[123] He also owned a script and a movie that portrayed sexual relationships between children and adults. Was Lanza sexually attracted to children? Was his attack driven by sexual frustration, killing those he desired but could not have?

Even stranger still, Lanza's computer contained two fictional pieces about having to defend himself against babies who were attacking him. Did he have paranoid delusions about babies and children? Did Lanza murder children as an act of self-defense? As early as fifth grade, Lanza cowrote a story about a murderous character who said, "I like hurting people. . . . Especially children."[124]

COMMENTS

Patrick Purdy, Wellington de Oliveira, Bruco Eastwood, and Adam Lanza came from a variety of backgrounds. Three of them were psychotic, with only Purdy being traumatized. No shooter in this group was psychopathic. The attacks at their former schools may have been driven by envy, misplaced revenge for harassment, sexual issues, or psychosis.

ADULTS WHO ATTACKED ELEMENTARY SCHOOLS TO WHICH THEY HAD NO CONNECTION

Laurie Dann

"You don't have to change your phone number. . . .
That won't stop me from killing you."

Date: May 20, 1988
Age: 30
School: Hubbard Woods Elementary
Location: Winnetka, IL

Killed: 1
Wounded: 6
Outcome: Attempted to escape. Took hostages in house. Surrounded by police. Suicide

Laurie Dann was an injustice collector. She remembered every slight, every rejection, and every time anybody hurt her and was determined to get revenge. She was also psychotic, sometimes to the point of catatonia. She would sit and stare at nothing or engage in meaningless, repetitive behaviors for hours. She wore the same clothes for days without regard for hygiene and did some very strange things.[125]

Though my discussion of psychosis has focused on hallucinations and delusions, another symptom is relevant in this case: grossly disorganized behavior. This refers to behavior that is flagrantly socially inappropriate or simply bizarre. This describes Dann's behavior—but not always.

In fact, when Dann was not psychotic, she was highly calculating, resourceful, and methodical in getting back at people. She also relished her revenge with sadistic glee. The story of Laurie Dann is so strange and packed with dramatic incidents that perhaps more than any other shooter this brief summary can only suggest her complexity.

Dann was born into a prosperous and intact yet emotionally barren family. As a child she was extremely small, unattractive, and odd—"a reticent, funny-looking little girl with an oversized nose and sailboat ears. . . . The kids accepted her, for the most part, but it sometimes bothered them that she almost never smiled and every so often would fix them with a blank stare that seemed to come from a million miles away."[126] Dann had surgery on her ears at age ten and on her nose between tenth and eleventh grades. After the surgery, she was considered attractive.

As a teenager, Dann violated rules and social norms. She cheated in school, cheated on her time card at work, and cheated on her boyfriend. She told elaborate lies about herself, claiming college degrees she didn't have and falsifying her employment history. When she did get jobs, they never lasted long. Her behavior was strange, inappropriate, and unreliable.

Dann also developed behaviors that appear to be symptoms of obsessive-compulsive disorder but may have been delusional. While walking outdoors she sometimes had to touch every telephone pole and avoid cracks in the sidewalks. She was so afraid of germs that she was unable to open a door or use silverware with her bare hands. After she was married, her thinking became very strange. Of her husband she once said, "I'm afraid if I close the cabinets in the kitchen he's going to stop loving me."[127]

Dann also demonstrated an unusual combination of personality traits. She dated a boy for a couple of months in high school. When he ended the relationship, "she hated him for it. He was surprised that such a mousy girl was capable of showing such intense contempt with just her eyes."[128] The combination of "mousy" and "contemptuous" seems like a contradiction, but it expresses Dann's desperate insecurity and towering rage when thwarted.

After marrying Russell Dann, her behavior became increasingly strange: "She began scattering trash throughout the house and leaving money in the oven and the freezer, canned food in the dishwasher, and makeup in the microwave."[129] Her husband tried to take things in stride, but after several years he decided to end the marriage. Dann had been dumped by boyfriends, dropped by friends, and fired from jobs, and though she was bitter, she was able to go on. The loss of her husband, however, was a loss she could not endure. She was determined to make him suffer.

Once, after Dann had moved out, Russell was talking on the telephone and heard a suspicious noise. He searched the house and "found Laurie, who was supposedly living with her parents, crouched in a pile of birdseed in her old closet, huddled up to the cordless telephone."[130] She had broken into the house, waited for Russell to be on the telephone, and listened in so she could find out his plans and torment him.

She fabricated a police report that Russell had stuck a knife into her vagina. She broke into his house again, and while he was in bed she stabbed him with an ice pick and escaped. Not content with torturing Russell, Dann began harassing an old boyfriend. She called the man's wife and claimed she was carrying the man's baby. She sent a letter to the hospital where he worked and accused him of raping her. When he moved and got an unlisted number, Dann located him, found out his new number, and continued her harassment.

Interspersed with her vengeance seeking were periods of grossly disorganized behavior. When Dann lived on campus at Northwestern University she broke into other people's rooms, stole things, and hoarded raw meat. University staff decided to investigate: "When they opened up the refrigerator they reeled at the ghoulish sight and smell of thick, dripping cuts of spoiled meat stuffed into every corner."[131] After Dann was kicked out of the room, the maintenance supervisor "found garbage in all the cabinets about the kitchen sink. Her bed was so badly damaged by urine that he had to toss both the mattress and the platform board into the dumpster. He also saw urine stains on several spots on the carpet."[132]

After leaving Northwestern University, Dann enrolled at the University of Wisconsin. One day she was found in a stairwell "totally nude, opening and slamming the fire door."[133] Her room was in deplorable condition: "They found a stinking hovel, a toilet filled with excrement, a carpet soaked with urine, garbage everywhere."[134]

Besides harassing her ex-husband and former boyfriends, she began calling other people at all hours and hanging up as soon as they answered. She did this with many families who had hired her as a babysitter and then stopped using her after they found she had stolen from them, vandalized their home, or was simply too weird.

Eventually, however, she switched from hanging up to making death threats. She called her former boyfriend and told his wife, "You don't have to change your phone number. . . . That won't stop me from killing you. And you might as well take your little baby and throw him in the garbage can."[135]

She threatened not only people who had hurt her but also people whom she apparently envied. She saw an article about a ten-year-old boy named Jim who had won a spelling bee, called the boy's mother, and said, "I just wanted you to know that I'm going to kill Jim today."[136] She was not really going to kill Jim—she just enjoyed making happy people suffer. Years before she had told her therapist that she envied happy families.[137]

Laurie Dann planned one grand day of vengeance on May 20, 1988. She stole arsenic and made poisoned Rice Krispies treats and poisoned juice containers. She mailed the poisoned items to some people and dropped them off at other people's homes. She drove to the home of Marian Rushe, whose five children Dann had babysat. With the mother's permission, she picked up two of the kids under the pretense of taking them out for a special day. While in her car, she gave them poisoned milk to drink. She drove to Lavinia Elementary, where she lit a bag of chemicals to set the building aflame. She then brought the children home and used gasoline to start a fire, intending to burn down their house and kill the mother and children.

Dann then went to Hubbard Woods Elementary, apparently because two of the Rushe children were students there. They, however, were on a field trip that day. Dann got inside the school and shot six children, ages six to eight years old. She also tried to burn this school down. She left the school, apparently expecting to escape. She ended up leaving her car, fleeing on foot, entering a home, and holding hostages while police surrounded the house. She shot one of the hostages and eventually killed herself. It was a rampage of staggering proportions. By one analysis, "If she had been successful in all she wanted to do on May 20, she would have fatally poisoned at least fifty people, shot to death at least a dozen school children, incinerated three members of the Rushe family in their home, and burned down two schools with 440 children inside."[138] As it happened, no one died of poisoning, none of the fires killed anybody, and the only shooting death was one six-year-old boy. This was indeed tragic, but thankfully the massive loss of life Dann planned did not occur.

* * *

Laurie Dann differed from all other school shooters in her multifaceted plans for vengeance against such a wide variety of people. She was a case of contradictions. She was insecure and mousy but capable of frightening rage. She would not touch a doorknob but left raw meat rotting, wore the same clothes for weeks, urinated on herself, and left feces in the toilet. She had periods in which she rode elevators for hours in a stupor-like state but could be ruthlessly efficient in seeking vengeance.

Dann had elements of both psychotic and psychopathic shooters. She was not diagnosed as psychotic while alive, and the variability of her functioning makes a specific diagnosis difficult. Her social awkwardness, insecurity, and odd behavior suggest schizotypal personality disorder, yet her grossly disorganized behavior and apparently catatonic states suggest schizophrenia. Evidence of psychopathy includes her chronic lying and deception, her disregard for rules and laws, her incredible lack of empathy, and her sadistic delight in making others suffer.

Her most striking personality trait, however, was her masochistic obsession with her own victimization. She accumulated a lifetime of injustices, never forgot them, let them fester, and, ultimately, sought to kill those she believed had wronged her.

Perhaps envy was at the core of her behavior. She enjoyed tormenting a spelling-bee champion's mother. Why? She envied people who were happy, people who were successful, people who were everything she wasn't. She did not have a happy family life as a child and failed at establishing her own family, which appears to be why she wanted to kill the Rushe family. Unlike so many families for whom she babysat, they did not fire her. Why, then, did she single them out for destruction? Apparently, because they were a happy family. This was something she could not abide. This aspect of psychopathy has been called *primitive envy* and is defined as "the wish to destroy that which one most desires."[139]

Dann had features of the *covetous psychopath*. Such people feel "deprived of their rightful level of love, support, or material rewards"; in response, "they are driven by envy and a desire for retribution."[140] Such a person becomes obsessed with what she doesn't have and wants to take from others. Though she sometimes stole property, what Dann most tried to steal was people's happiness and sense of security—two things that were markedly absent from her life. Covetous psychopaths commit "acts of theft or destruction" in attempts to "compensate themselves for the emptiness of their own lives, dismissing with smug entitlement their violations of the social order."[141]

Dann presented with both psychotic and psychopathic features, a powerful blend of masochism and sadism, and a hatred born of envy.

James Wilson

"Would you live in a house with thirty bodies buried under it?"

Date: September 26, 1988
Age: 19
School: Oakland Elementary School
Location: Greenwood, SC

Killed: 2
Wounded: 9
Outcome: Surrendered. Prison

On June 6, 1988, *People* magazine published an article about Laurie Dann's bizarre day of vengeance.[142] A young man named James Wilson read the article and was so fascinated that he tore it out and read it daily for four months.[143] Then he went on his own rampage. Afterward he said of Dann, "I could understand where she was coming from. I think I may have copied her."[144]

Wilson's father was a violent man. He beat his son with a belt, hit him in the head with a can and a shoe, and repeatedly threatened to shoot him.[145] His mother and grandparents reportedly abused him as well. Family instability was nothing new: "Wilson was born into a family with an alarmingly high prevalence of mental illness, at least four generations of recorded psychiatric hospitalizations, violence, and drug abuse."[146]

Wilson was also mistreated at school. He reportedly was ridiculed for being overweight as well as for the way he dressed.[147] This harassment haunted Wilson. After his attack, he said, "I was thinking about all my experiences at school."[148]

During adolescence, Wilson became psychotic.[149] His grandmother reported that he once believed a candle was a bomb and yelled at her to throw it away. Wilson had other paranoid thoughts, including a vague belief that people were out to get him. In addition, he had auditory hallucinations, "hearing voices that were telling him to go into the school and shoot people."[150] Prior to the attack, his grandmother saw Wilson talking to people who were not present.

Rather than taking him for professional treatment, Wilson's family responded to his behavior problems by giving him various relatives' medication. He was dosed with "sedatives, painkillers, antidepressants, and antipsychotic drugs."[151] His behavior deteriorated, however, and he was hospitalized seven times from ages fourteen through eighteen.

Wilson did not have much of a social life. He dated a young woman he had met in a psychiatric hospital, but this relationship ended several months before his attack.[152] He also engaged in prostitution with a forty-two-year-old man, trading sex for drugs.[153]

Wilson was fascinated by true-crime stories. The night before his attack, he was reading a biography of John Wayne Gacy, who had killed at least thirty-three men and boys and buried many of them under his house. The next morning, Wilson asked his grandmother, "Would you live in a house with thirty bodies buried under it?"[154] Then he left for his rampage. For unknown reasons, Wilson did not attack a school he had attended but, rather, Oakland Elementary, a school with which he had no connection.[155]

In prison, Wilson's functioning deteriorated dramatically. He "shaved off all his head and body hair, telling his attorneys that this was so that he could receive 'special thoughts.'"[156] His ability to maintain basic hygiene vanished. He urinated and defecated in his clothes and "lost all but one of his teeth because he let them rot."[157]

※ ※ ※

James Wilson, like Laurie Dann, had features of two types of school shooters. In his case, however, the types were traumatized and psychotic. He had a long history of abuse by multiple family members. Though his psychosis was recognized by family members prior to his attack, he does not appear to have been diagnosed until he was in prison. He had paranoid delusions and auditory hallucinations and ultimately descended into a state of grossly disorganized behavior.

In addition, he apparently was influenced by Laurie Dann's rampage and possibly other criminals, such as John Wayne Gacy. And like several other traumatized shooters, he had an older male role model in the family for the misuse of firearms—his father, who repeatedly threatened to kill him with a gun.

Thomas Hamilton

"I turn to you as a last resort and am appealing for some kind of intervention in the hope that I may be able to regain my self-esteem in society."

Date: March 13, 1996   **Killed**: 17
Age: 43   **Wounded**: 15
School: Dunblane Primary   **Outcome**: Suicide
School
Location: Dunblane, Scotland

Thomas Hamilton was obsessed with young boys. For over fifteen years, he ran clubs and summer camps for boys ages seven to eleven. He insisted they wear black swim trunks and took thousands of photographs of them. When parents learned about this and other aspects of the camps, there were complaints, suspicions, and investigations. No criminal acts were uncovered, however, so no charges were ever pressed against Hamilton. Nonetheless, people were uneasy.[158]

Hamilton's parents had divorced shortly after his birth, and he and his mother moved in with her parents. Her parents officially adopted Hamilton, and for some reason he was raised to believe that his grandparents were his biological parents and his mother was his sister.[159] If, and when, he found out about this remains unknown. He apparently went through his school years and classes at a technical college without incident. He opened a do-it-yourself shop for home-improvement projects that ran for thirteen years. He was then unemployed and received government benefits.

In 1973 Hamilton was briefly involved with the official Scouting association of Scotland. Due to complaints about his poor leadership, though, the association asked him to resign. This led to two decades of acrimonious retaliation by Hamilton. He became convinced that there was a conspiracy between the Scouts and the police to discredit him. He fought back by filing grievances against the people in these organizations he believed had wronged him.

Starting in 1981 he organized overnight camps and boys' clubs that he largely ran single-handedly. There were complaints about poor planning, lack of supplies, and inadequate accommodations. More disturbing, he was known to hit the children, sometimes with his hand, sometimes with a wooden spoon. He forced them into activities they didn't want to do. When a child who had nearly drowned earlier in his life refused to jump from a boat into the lake, Hamilton pushed the boy into the water and later defended this as an appropriate way to help the boy overcome his fear. The child, however, was terrified.[160]

Hamilton was criticized as being too controlling and militaristic. He refused to let the boys call or write to their parents, claiming that such contact only made their homesickness worse. He reportedly was domineering and "seemed to enjoy pushing the boys about."[161] One woman commented, "He was in his glory when he got a child crying."[162]

Though some boys seemed to enjoy the camp activities, others felt uncomfortable and fearful and thought Hamilton was weird. He made videos of the boys taking deep breaths in their bathing suits, with "an overconcentration on parts of the boys' bodies, especially the naked upper parts along with long lingering shots of the area between the waist and the knees."[163]

Hamilton became defensive when people questioned his tactics and reportedly never admitted to making a mistake. He apparently had a grandiose sense of himself as an expert who knew more about children than anyone else. He harassed parents with letters and telephone calls when they withdrew their sons from his programs.

Though there was widespread concern that Hamilton was a pedophile, no one ever came forward as a victim. The closest was one boy who reported that Hamilton sat next to him and "rubbed him on the inside of the leg"[164] and asked about his interest in joining the club.

Hamilton had a long history of dishonesty. His advertisements about his programs were often misleading regarding activities, staff, and facilities. He sometimes claimed to have a group of adults as an advisory committee to his camps, but became evasive when questioned about them. He also told people that the photographs he took of the kids would be passed along to his contacts in professional soccer and could lead to careers as athletes.[165] Hamilton had no such contacts. One person said of Hamilton, "It is my opinion he is a scheming, devious, and deceitful individual who is not to be trusted."[166]

Hamilton made many people uncomfortable. One person said, "He just made my skin creep."[167] Others noted that his manner of speech was odd: "He unnerved me quite a bit. . . . He spoke very slowly, very clearly, precisely, but with no emotion or expression . . . there was just nothing, nothing in there."[168] Another witness stated that Hamilton "never sort of looked you in the eye."[169] He had a restricted range of emotion: "He didn't laugh at anything."[170] He reportedly was nervous around adults and particularly uncomfortable with women. He had no close friends, he did not date, and he had no occupation apart from his one-man clubs and camps.

Though his conversation typically was mundane, on rare occasions he talked about ghosts and paranormal experiences. He believed the house he grew up in was haunted and described what sound like hallucinations: "He said that he would wake up to feel very cold and could see something at the bottom of his bed. He said that it made noises."[171]

When interviewed about his complaints against the Scouts, Hamilton continued to insist he was the victim of a smear campaign. A casual acquaintance noticed that for seven or eight years Hamilton's conversation had been "all one way . . . he was antipolice, he was antiestablishment, he was anti- the education authority, he seemed anti- anybody who opposed his views on how the clubs should be run."[172]

Hamilton's campaign against the authorities culminated in his letter to Queen Elizabeth, in which he stated, "I turn to you as a last resort and am appealing for some kind of intervention in the hope that I may be able to regain my self-esteem in society."[173] It must be noted that although he complained for years about being mistreated by the police and the Scouts, he had never been charged with any crime and his camps and clubs had never been shut down.

On March 13, 1996, Hamilton committed a horrible attack at Dunblane Primary School, shooting primarily five-year-old children, along with several teachers. He killed seventeen people and wounded fifteen, devastating the community and sending shock waves through the United Kingdom.

Why did he attack Dunblane Primary? Though he had rented space in other local schools for his boys' clubs, he had never used this school. Hamilton was convinced, perhaps accurately, that teachers at Dunblane Primary had warned students against enrolling in his programs. He wrote in a letter, "At Dunblane Primary School where teachers have contaminated all of the older boys with this poison even former cleaners and dinner ladies have been told by teachers at school that I am a pervert."[174] The same letter, however, noted that such warnings were given to students at "primary schools across the Region."[175] Even if teachers had warned children to avoid Hamilton, why shoot the children rather than the teachers?

Hamilton left no message as to his motive. Perhaps he sought to cause the maximum suffering by killing the community's children. Alternatively, perhaps he felt so feeble that he targeted the easiest targets he could find, like a cowardly bully who feels tough when he beats up someone half his size.

As for the timing of the attack, his club enrollment had dwindled; in fact, only one boy had signed up for one club. Hamilton was in debt. He had no friends or life partner. Whatever the reason, he meticulously planned and prepared for a rampage, carrying it out with ruthless efficiency.

☼ ☼ ☼

Thomas Hamilton was never diagnosed. He appears, however, to have had schizotypal personality disorder. He was a strikingly odd person who gave people "the creeps," was socially awkward, suspicious, and paranoid, avoided eye contact, and had a strange manner of speaking. He demonstrated no sense of humor, had a limited range of emotional expression, was uncomfortable with adults, and had no close friends or intimate relationships. He believed in ghosts, sensed their presence, and reported paranormal experiences, which is common among schizotypals. He also had the paranoid delusion that the Scouts and the police conspired to defame and discredit him.

What distinguishes Hamilton from nonviolent schizotypals? Like Laurie Dann, he was remarkably masochistic. He perseverated for years about minor incidents. In this respect he resembled the targeted college shooters who had longstanding grievances against people in their departments. The difference is that Hamilton did not target Scout members or the police but, rather, five-year-old children who had nothing to do with his grievances.

One other trait is significant here: Hamilton gave people the impression that he enjoyed dominating the children in his camps and clubs. He liked to "lord it over them" and engaged in harsh discipline. He reportedly was "in his glory" when he made children cry. These incidents reveal a sadistic pleasure in having power over others. Hamilton had other psychopathic features: an inflated sense of self, a pattern of deceptive behavior, lack of empathy, preoccupation with being a victim, and a resentment of authority. Like Laurie Dann, he exhibited a combination of two of the types of school shooters: psychotic and psychopathic.

Several subtypes of psychopathy seem relevant in understanding Hamilton. One is the *disingenuous psychopath*. This is someone who tries to maintain a facade of friendliness but is highly deceptive and manipulative. This psychopath has shallow relationships and cannot admit wrongdoing, projecting blame on others. When challenged or crossed, he is easily angered, and "when the thin veneer of sociability is eroded, there may be momentary upsurges of abuse and rage."[176]

This aspect of his behavior also suggests the *reputation-defending antisocial personality*. People with this subtype "react with great intensity when their status and capabilities are questioned."[177] Neither of these subtypes, however, captures his sadistic streak. This is perhaps best understood as the *enforcing sadist*. This refers to people in positions of authority who derive satisfaction from controlling and punishing others. As noted by Millon, "Power has gone to their heads. Many begin to dehumanize their victims."[178]

COMMENTS

The attacks by Laurie Dann, James Wilson, and Thomas Hamilton are perhaps the hardest to comprehend. They all gunned down young children at schools with which they had no connection. Notably, they all had features of two types of shooters; no other aberrant adult shooters fit two types. Among the aberrant shooters, those with the *most aberrant attacks* were the *most aberrant people*.

Dann and Hamilton resemble the college shooters who engaged in targeted attacks. They had long-standing grievances that built up over years. They also had psychopathic traits, as did all of the targeted college shooters. They differed from these shooters, however, in that the people they shot had nothing to do with their grievances. Wilson differs from Dann and Hamilton not only because of his traumatic history but also because he was the only one to have a role model for murder—his primary role model was Dann, though his interest in serial killers may also have influenced him.

ADULT WHOSE ATTACK WAS IN AN ATYPICAL EDUCATIONAL SETTING

Jiverly Wong

> *"I am Jiverly Wong shooting the people."*

Date: April 3, 2009   **Killed**: 13
Age: 41   **Wounded**: 4
School: American Civic   **Outcome**: Suicide
Association
Location: Binghamton, NY

Jiverly Wong killed thirteen people, wounded four, and killed himself at the immigration center of the American Civic Association in Binghamton, New York.[179] At first glance, this may not seem like a school shooting, but Wong had taken English classes at the center and returned to his classroom for his attack. Despite the fact that Wong killed as many people as Harris and Klebold at Columbine, his attack has received little attention.

Wong came from Vietnam with his parents and siblings in 1990; he was twenty-two at the time.[180] He had a harder time adjusting to this country than other family members. His siblings learned English and established themselves, but Wong struggled with the language and had a series of low-level jobs. He lived alternately in the Los Angeles area and in Binghamton, and had at least five encounters with the police over the years. These involved passing a bad check, driving an uninspected vehicle, and other minor violations.[181]

While living in California, Wong married, but he kept this secret from most people, including his family. He and his wife separated in 2005 and divorced in 2006. There were varying reports regarding whether or not Wong had any children. One article declared there were no children;[182] a different article quoted a former colleague who said Wong told him he had a daughter;[183] a third article reported that Wong often talked about his wife and kids having left him.[184]

Wong returned to the Binghamton area in 2007 and moved in with his parents. He worked at a Shop-Vac factory but still struggled with

English. He enrolled in an English class at the American Civic Association in January 2009 but stopped attending in early March.[185]

Wong was an unusually reclusive and silent man. According to his father, he had no friends and barely spoke to anyone in the family, spending much of his time in his room.[186] Outside of the home, however, he spoke to people about his love of firearms. It appears that his primary activity was going to shooting ranges. He also talked about shooting politicians,[187] hating America, and killing the president.[188] His obsessive talk about guns and killing led coworkers to joke that Wong "would come in mad one day and shoot people,"[189] though his family was not even aware that he had guns or went shooting.[190]

Wong's withdrawal became even more severe two weeks before his attack. "Wong stopped eating dinner, stopped watching television, and rarely emerged from behind his bedroom door."[191] On March 18, 2009, he wrote a letter to a local television news show complaining of harassment by police and indicating his homicidal and suicidal thoughts. The letter, however, was not mailed until April 3—the day of his rampage.[192]

Though never diagnosed, Wong appears to have been schizophrenic. His family members had their only glimpse of his psychosis several months after arriving in the United States. Wong told his father that people were trying to kill him; he pointed in front of him and said, "They're in front of me and trying to capture me."[193] Wong's father said that this was the only time he was concerned about his son's sanity.

Wong's suicide letter revealed paranoid delusions regarding police. He accused them of tampering with things in his home, keeping him under surveillance, spreading rumors about him, making him lose his job, trying to cause him to have a collision while driving, breaking into his room thirteen times, stealing money from him, and more.[194]

As to why Wong attacked the American Civic Association, we can only speculate. As with Marc Lépine, Kimveer Gill, and Steven Kazmierczak, perhaps Wong's attack was essentially symbolic. He, who had lived in this country nearly twenty years, attended an English-language class with recent immigrants. They were learning the language and preparing to move on with their lives; after twenty years, he was back where he had started, and going nowhere. The other immigrants represented the success he would never achieve. He felt like a failure and lashed out against those he assumed would succeed.

✿ ✿ ✿

Jiverly Wong was a psychotic shooter. He differed from the other aberrant adult shooters in that he was an immigrant and thus struggled not only with schizophrenia but also with acculturation. Whereas Patrick Purdy had generalized anti-American and anti-immigrant attitudes, Wong talked about killing the president and other politicians. Unlike Purdy, however, Wong's political ideas appear to have had no connection to his rampage.

8

PATTERNS AMONG SCHOOL SHOOTERS

Patterns can be fascinating but tricky to interpret. They may identify crucial factors or simply be coincidences. For example, Robert Poulin, Wayne Lo, and Eric Harris all committed their attacks at age eighteen. All three had psychopathic personalities, and all had fathers who were retired air force pilots. What are the odds of this? Pushing the odds even further, Poulin and Harris both had chest deformities and were rejected by the military. In addition, Poulin and Lo had parents who were schoolteachers, Lo and Harris were disciplined by school administrators, and Poulin experienced academic failure. This microcosm of three shooters contains several patterns: family members in the military, rejection by the military, family members in education, school problems, and biological challenges. These patterns occur frequently enough in the lives of shooters to appear to be relevant pieces in understanding the puzzle of their actions.

THE SIGNIFICANCE OF THE BODY

For decades, researchers have studied the connection between biological problems and violent behavior. One study found that male murderers had more chronic illnesses and physical defects than their brothers who did not commit murder.[1] Multiple studies have linked birth complications and minor physical anomalies to violent behavior.[2] Researchers in Denmark found a correlation between low birth weight and childhood precursors of psychopathy.[3] The American Psychological Association's recent report on gun violence noted the relevance of developmental factors such as "low birth weight, birth complications, and injuries."[4] Interestingly, a surprising number of school shooters experienced biological challenges that may have affected their identities or added to their distress.

Besides medical problems, simply being short and weak can be devastating for males, particularly if they have other identity issues. Elliot Rodger (not covered in this book) wrote about himself at age nine, "I became extremely annoyed at how everyone was taller than me and how the tallest boys were automatically respected more. It instilled the first feelings of inferiority in me, and such feelings would only grow more volatile with time. I desperately wanted to get taller."[5] Rodger's desperation to grow was so great that he would lie on the ground "trying to stretch my body as much as I could."[6] He also became painfully aware that he was weaker and less athletic than his peers: "This vexed me to no end."[7] Throughout his life he felt inadequate as a male.

Table 8.1 lists the shooters and their medical problems or short statures (all of which were at or below the fifth percentile).

Among those shooters who fit solely into the psychopathic category, at least 75 percent (nine out of twelve) had body issues. Many of these physical characteristics had a direct bearing on perceived manliness, including short stature, thin build, chest deformity, and fear of sterility. In fact, this small sample contains two shooters with deformed chests and two with fears of sterility. What are the odds of this occurring? It certainly seems to be more than a coincidence. In fact, the high frequency of body issues among psychopathic shooters suggests a possible link between feeling weak or damaged and extreme narcissism. Maybe they overcompensated for their sense of inadequacy by seeking superiority via physical domination of others.

Yochelson and Samenow found that among criminal personalities "dissatisfaction with body build is exceedingly frequent. Even as strong, attractive youngsters, many regard themselves as weak and scrawny."[8] If psychopaths with good physiques often feel weak and scrawny, what must it feel like to actually have a physical shortcoming?

Although masculinity was not a relevant concern for females Brenda Spencer and Laurie Dann, body issues may still have been significant to their identities. In Dann's case, her "oversized nose and sailboat ears"[9] may have caused extreme self-consciousness. She was certainly aware of how small she was. Dann, whose maiden name was Wasserman, wrote a prophecy for her junior high yearbook; the prophecy simply said, "Laurie Wasserman grows."[10]

In contrast, reports about Brenda Spencer give no indication that she suffered poor self-esteem. Perhaps what Yochelson and Samenow found among young males with criminal personalities was also true for

Table 8.1: **Biological Issues Among School Shooters**

PSYCHOPATHIC SHOOTERS	Charles Whitman	Testicular surgery in 11th grade; fear of sterility
	Robert Poulin	Chest deformity; poor eyesight prevented him from being a pilot like his father; late onset of puberty
	Brenda Spencer	Short: reportedly 5'1", 85 lbs
	Gang Lu	Short: reportedly 5'4", 130 lbs
	Valery Fabrikant	Short: estimated height of 5'4"; fear of sterility[a]
	Wayne Lo	Short: reportedly 5'5"
	Barry Loukaitis	Short / thin: reportedly teased about his body
	Andrew Golden	Very short and thin: reportedly barely 4' tall
	Eric Harris	Chest deformity resulting in two surgeries; birth defect in legs; hated his looks; teased for having a big head on a skinny body
	Tim Kretschmer	Possibly short as a child; nicknamed Mini-Timmi
PSYCHOTIC SHOOTERS	Laurie Dann[b]	Very short; corrective surgery on ears and nose
	Marc Lépine	Cruelly mocked for severe acne
	Kip Kinkel	Reportedly upset that he was short as a child
	Seung Hui Cho	A sickly child; despite working out as adult, autopsy noted an unusual lack of muscle
	Matti Saari	Delayed growth; as adult, below average height
	Pekka-Eric Auvinen	Reportedly suffered because he was so short
	Wellington de Oliveira	Mocked due to a limp
	Adam Lanza	Extraordinarily thin; 6' tall, only 112 lbs
TRAUMATIZED SHOOTERS	Eric Houston	As infant had meningitis, encephalitis, and severe pneumonia; had delayed development
	Jamie Rouse	Reportedly bullied because he was short
	Scott Pennington	Reportedly picked on because he was short
	James Wilson[c]	Reportedly ridiculed for being overweight
	Jason Hoffman	Had a bad skin condition that oozed blood
	Asa Coon	Short and markedly overweight

a Valery Fabrikant, "What Really Happened at Concordia University and How the Media Lied About It," http://fabrikant.webs.com/GZT1.txt

b Also psychopathic.

c Also psychotic.

Spencer—she wanted to be powerful and had to compensate for being small.

Though body issues seem most common among psychopathic shooters, they also occurred among other shooters. As discussed in previous chapters, psychotic shooters often struggled with profound identity issues. Biological deficits presumably were just one more obstacle to developing a healthy sense of themselves. Traumatized shooters may have dealt with body-related issues due to physical, and sometimes sexual, abuse. Sexual abuse in particular can disrupt the relationship with one's body. For males, molestation by a male also raises concerns about one's sense of masculinity. Biological problems simply compounded their difficulties.

Knowing how hard it is for adolescents to feel good about their bodies, the challenges faced by many of the shooters may have resulted in severe self-consciousness, anguish, and the desire to prove their masculinity through violence.

MILITARY FAILURES

John Douglas, the FBI agent who made criminal profiling famous, noticed that many serial killers were either police buffs or had wanted to be police officers. Despite such aspirations, however, Douglas found that "Frequently serial killers had failed in their efforts to join police departments."[11] Similarly, an article titled "The Sexually Sadistic Serial Killer" noted that 35 percent of the subjects in their study were interested in working in security or law enforcement.[12] Dr. Stanton Samenow observed a comparable trend among people with criminal personalities, stating that they "admire policemen and imagine themselves in badge and uniform."[13]

Rather than failing to become police officers, many school shooters had thwarted military aspirations. In fact, approximately 50 percent of those who were old enough to enlist were rejected, discharged prematurely, or denied the opportunity to apply. Here is a brief summary:

- Charles Whitman joined the marines but was miserable there. His parents worked "tirelessly" for his early discharge, lobbying government officials to get him out.[14]
- Robert Poulin applied to an officer-training program but was rejected for being too immature.[15]
- Edward Allaway joined the marines but did not last long; he was dishonorably discharged.[16]

- Patrick Purdy had military aspirations but never applied, perhaps because of his many arrests.[17]
- Marc Lépine applied to the Canadian Army but was rejected as "unsuitable" or "asocial."[18]
- Eric Houston wanted to join the army but failed to graduate high school and thus could not apply.[19]
- Jillian Robbins served in the army reserve but was discharged for failing to complete high school.[20]
- Eric Harris applied to the marines. Though he was rejected, his attack on Columbine High School reportedly occurred before he received the news.[21] Nonetheless, he may have suspected this would happen.
- Jason Hoffman was rejected by the navy and committed his attack less than twenty-four hours later.[22]
- Alvaro Castillo joined the national guard but hated it; after a suicide attempt he was able to obtain a discharge.[23]
- Kimveer Gill enrolled in a military-leadership course but dropped out—or was discharged—after a month.[24]
- Duane Morrison served in the navy for six months but was discharged after he went AWOL.[25]
- Pekka-Eric Auvinen's military service was deferred due to mental health concerns.[26] It is not clear if he had military aspirations or if he was simply called up to serve. Regardless, this rejection may have been a significant blow to his identity.
- Steven Kazmierczak joined the army but was discharged after military personnel discovered he had lied about his history of psychiatric problems.[27]
- Matti Saari joined the military, but a military physician recommended that he be discharged, and Saari wanted to leave. He lasted less than two months.[28]
- Tim Kretschmer apparently did not want to join the military, even though service is essentially mandatory in Germany. Both he and his parents reported his depression to the army.[29] Though he may not have had thwarted military ambition, his inability or unwillingness to serve may have been a blow to his identity.
- Bruco Eastwood had military aspirations but no high school diploma; he studied for his GED for two years, but shortly before his attack he failed the test, preventing his enlisting.[30]
- Adam Lanza wanted to join the marines, but his mother talked him out of applying.[31]

Other shooters were also interested in the military. Robert Flores served and may have had a military rejection; when the army released his paperwork after his attack, his discharge status was blacked out.[32] Jeffrey Weise had military aspirations but committed his attack before he was old enough to serve. Wayne Lo was obsessed with the marines and had "USMC" (United States Marine Corps) shaved in his hair but never enlisted. Sebastian Bosse (a German shooter not covered in this book) was obsessed with the military, frequently wore combat gear, and "dreamt of an army career."[33] Other shooters not included in this book also aspired to serve in the military or law enforcement but went on their rampages when they were too young to have done so. This includes Michael Slobodian, Nathaniel Brazill, Charles "Andy" Williams, Jose Reyes, and Jared Padgett.

Why were so many shooters focused on the military? Perhaps it was their attempt to establish themselves as men. Dr. Katherine Newman noted that school shooters often "failed at the very specific task of 'manhood.'"[34] As discussed above, many perpetrators faced significant biological challenges to their identities. They may have sought to repair their sense of damaged masculinity through becoming soldiers. Their failure may have been devastating. The distress may have been particularly acute for those shooters whose relatives served successfully in the military. Perhaps they felt that they failed not only themselves but their families.

For example, Adam Lanza's uncle had been a marine. Lanza looked up to him and aspired to follow in his footsteps, commenting, "I'm going to be just like Uncle Jim."[35] Later, when he wanted to apply, his mother dissuaded him, saying he would "never be a marine."[36] Lanza reportedly "took the news harder than even his mother expected."[37] Nonetheless, "in the months leading up to the massacre, Lanza would dress himself up head to toe in a camouflage military uniform and target shoot with a pellet gun in his basement."[38] The day of his attack, he dressed in military gear. Maybe for Lanza aspiring to the military equaled aspiring to manhood.

Jillian Robbins, the one female shooter who experienced a military rejection, reportedly idolized her father who was in the army reserves.[39] Perhaps she sought to follow in his footsteps. Though her failure had nothing to do with masculinity, it may have been a profound disappointment to her and her father.

Not only were many shooters drawn to the military, but many had relatives who served. At least sixteen out of the forty-eight shooters (33 percent) presented in this book had relatives in the armed services or law enforcement—another traditionally masculine profession that also involves firearms. Other shooters outside my sample also had family connections to these two professions. Even for those shooters who did not experience thwarted military aspirations, simply having relatives in the armed services may have presented them with role models for masculinity with whom they felt they could not compare. Alternatively, these professions might have represented the government or law and order, which some shooters may have rebelled against.

Table 8.2 presents the shooters with relatives in the military or law enforcement.

Not only did many shooters grow up with relatives who were trained in firearm use, but two interesting patterns exist relating to firearms within their families. At least 92 percent of the psychopathic shooters (not counting those who were also psychotic) came from families where firearms had a prominent place and were used appropriately, whether in the military, law enforcement, hunting, or target shooting. Conversely, at least 58 percent of traumatized shooters had older male relatives who engaged in the *misuse* of firearms (67 percent, if Eric Houston's uncle used a firearm when he killed three men). Misuse included armed robbery, shooting pets, threatening people with guns, and possibly murder. The psychopathic shooters rejected the morality of their parents, defiantly going against their upbringing in the appropriate use of guns. In contrast, the traumatized shooters followed in their family members' footsteps by misusing firearms.

Unlike the psychopathic and traumatized perpetrators, few psychotic shooters grew up in families where firearms had a prominent place. Those who did were college or aberrant adult shooters; no psychotic secondary school shooter grew up with parents in the military, in law enforcement, or otherwise significantly involved with guns.

EDUCATIONAL FAILURES

An oft-repeated misconception is that school shooters commit their crimes in retaliation for bullying. In reality, though approximately 40 percent of shooters were harassed, only one out of forty-eight perpetrators targeted a bully. In contrast, at least sixteen shooters targeted teachers or administrators. In fact, school personnel were targeted more than any other category of victim. This suggests that many shooters were driven by rage regarding failures or conflicts at school. (See chapter 10 for data on bullying and targeted victims.)

In fact, nearly all shooters had bad educational experiences, including academic difficulties (failing classes, repeating grades, not graduating) or disciplinary problems (detention, suspension, expulsion, etc.). Whereas 40 percent of shooters were bullied, at least 92 percent had negative academic or disciplinary experiences. These experiences often

Table 8.2: Relatives in Military or Law Enforcement

SECONDARY SCHOOL SHOOTERS	Robert Poulin	Father: pilot in Canadian Air Force Grandfather: military Relatives on both sides: military
	Brenda Spencer	Father: Navy
	[Brent Fleming][a]	[Father: police officer]
	Andrew Golden	Grandfather: fish and game warden
	Mitchell Johnson	Mother: corrections officer
	Eric Harris	Father: pilot in Air Force Maternal grandfather: military
	Jeffrey Weise	Paternal grandfather: police officer Grandfather's brother: Navy
COLLEGE SHOOTERS	Valery Fabrikant	Father: reportedly physician in Russian Army
	Gang Lu	(Mother: military hospital; family lived in compound)[b]
	Wayne Lo	Father: pilot in Taiwanese Air Force
	Robert Flores	Father: police officer
	One Goh	Brother: United States Army
ABERRANT ADULT SHOOTERS	Patrick Purdy	Father: military
	Marc Lépine	Uncle: Algerian military Father: possibly in Algerian military
	Kimveer Gill	Family served in military in India
	Jiverly Wong	Father: South Vietnamese Army
	Jillian Robbins	Father: Army Reserve
	Adam Lanza	Uncle: Marines and law enforcement
OTHER SHOOTERS	Seth Trickey	Father: U.S. Navy (Mother: Veterans Affairs)[b] Great-uncle #1: U.S. Navy Great-uncle #2: U.S. Navy Great-uncle #3: law enforcement Other more distant relatives: military
	Charles "Andy" Williams	Mother: U.S. Army Grandfather: military Great-grandfather: marines (Father: lab technician in Naval Medical Center)[b]
	John Jason McLaughlin	Father: sergeant in county sheriff's department
	Duane Morrison	Father: military
	Charles Roberts IV	Father: police officer
	Jared Padgett	Brother: Army Reserve
	Robert Butler, Jr.	Father: Navy, police detective

a He supported Spencer's homicidal intentions without participating in the shooting.
b A connection to the military, rather than military service.

appear to have determined whom they targeted. For example, multiple shooters who were disciplined apparently targeted, or contemplated targeting, those in authority:

- Wayne Lo was fined for a disciplinary infraction related to his college residence; he threatened to kill residential staff.
- Michael Carneal had five disciplinary infractions in the three months before his attack; he talked about shooting school administrators.
- Michael Slobodian (a Canadian shooter not included in my sample) intended to kill two teachers who called his mother to complain about his skipping class; one he did not find, but he killed the other.[40]
- Evan Ramsey had seventeen disciplinary infractions in the year and a half before his attack; he killed the principal.
- Jason Hoffman sought revenge against the dean of his school, perhaps due to disciplinary actions, failure to graduate, or other concerns. He found the dean and said, "I've got you"; he fired at him but missed.
- Eric Hainstock had both in-school and out-of-school suspensions shortly before his attack; he killed the principal.
- Robert Butler Jr. (not covered in this book) was suspended following an arrest on school grounds. A few hours after his suspension, he returned to his school and shot the principal and vice principal.
- When Nathaniel Brazill (not covered in this book) was suspended on the last day of school, he intended to shoot the guidance counselor he held responsible; he returned to the school the same day, but before he found the guidance counselor, he shot a teacher who refused to let him into a classroom to talk to a girl he had a crush on.

Similarly, shooters with academic failures targeted those they held responsible:

- Gang Lu did not win the prize for best dissertation; he shot the student who won, as well as others he blamed.
- Robert Flores murdered two professors who failed him and a third with whom he had a conflict.
- Eric Houston killed the teacher who failed him in a class, which had prevented him from graduating.
- Gary Scott Pennington killed a teacher who gave him an unacceptably low grade on a midterm.

- Phu Cuong Ta (not covered in this book) shot "two faculty members because he was angry over his grades."[41]
- Asa Coon shot the teacher whose class he was in danger of failing.
- Robert Steinhäuser was angry with both faculty and administrators; the faculty for repeated academic failures, including twice failing twelfth grade, and administrators for expelling him for forging a physician's note. He killed twelve teachers and a vice principal.

In a different scenario, Marc Lépine had a long history of educational failures, with his last failure apparently determining the location of his attack. He first failed two classes at St. Laurent Junior College and dropped out of the program. He then enrolled in two summer classes but dropped them before they started. He subsequently took computer courses but left the program before completing a degree. He applied to École Polytechnique in 1987 and 1989 and was rejected both times. Later in 1989, he attacked the school.

Not only was there a widespread pattern of educational failure and conflicts among shooters, but many had family members involved in education. At least 38 percent of shooters had relatives who worked or volunteered in schools. Educational failures may have been particularly painful for these shooters. Having parents who were teachers or professors may have exacerbated the students' shame and caused greater conflict with their parents.

In fact, some perpetrators' choices of venue for their attacks may have been related to their parents' vocations. For example, Jillian Robbins's mother and stepfather worked in higher education. Robbins dropped out of high school and argued with her mother, who wanted her to continue her education.[42] Though Robbins never attended Penn State, she attacked the main campus. Why? Perhaps because this was where her mother had studied and worked. It was also where students were doing what her mother wanted her to do—moving ahead with their educations.

Similarly, Kimveer Gill's father had been a college professor. Gill's failure to go beyond one semester of college created conflict in the family, with his parents reportedly pressuring him to continue with his education. It is also interesting that Gill's mother had taken courses at Vanier College, the same college that Gill dropped out of after one semester. Perhaps her success there exacerbated his sense of failure. In fact, Gill had considered Vanier as the site for his rampage.[43] For unknown reasons, he stormed a random college. He gunned down strangers at the same kind of institution where his father had worked, his mother succeeded, and students were doing what his parents wanted him to do—continuing their education.

It would not have occurred to me to include Marc Lépine's mother in this section because she did not work in higher education, but she herself made the connection. She wondered if her son's rage against feminists was at some level really rage against her. "I asked myself if it wasn't directed at me," she said. "Maybe I'd be considered a feminist— I earned a living, I had a paying job."[44] Lépine's mother had been a female university student and he targeted female university students. Even if his hostility toward feminists was not related to his mother, her academic success may have magnified his sense of failure in higher education.

Laurie Dann's educational failures are of particular interest. She aspired to teach elementary school but flunked classes and dropped out of four universities, failing miserably in her pursuit of a teaching career. The fact that her sister-in-law succeeded as a schoolteacher may have made Dann's failure even more damaging. In fact, Dann "admitted on several occasions that she felt badly outclassed by other women in her husband's life."[45] Notably, on the day of her rampage, she not only shot elementary-school students but also tried to burn down two elementary schools—the very type of school where she had aspired to teach. Perhaps she was trying to obliterate symbols of her failure.

One of the most disturbing aspects of rampage attacks is the murder of family members. Such deaths are hard to fathom because, with the exception of Alvaro Castillo's father, none of the relatives killed had been abusive. Is there any pattern among these cases? The only consistency I've found is that of the six shooters who killed family members, five of them (83 percent) killed relatives involved in education. (The sixth shooter who killed relatives—Jeffrey Weise—murdered his grandfather, a police officer.)

Kip Kinkel was the only shooter who killed both his parents. Both parents were schoolteachers, and his father had taught at the school where Kinkel committed his rampage.[46] Kinkel, who was dyslexic and had repeated first grade, had a highly conflicted relationship with his father, reportedly driven at least in part by Kinkel's failure to perform academically to his father's expectations. Is it significant that the only perpetrator who murdered both of his parents had parents who were both teachers? How much did his failure to live up to their academic standards play into Kinkel's rage?

Luke Woodham, like Kinkel, killed his mother. Also like Kinkel, Woodham repeated a grade—ninth. In addition, he had multiple suspensions in sixth and seventh grades. Though Woodham's mother was not teaching at the time of the attack, she had worked as a substitute when Woodham was younger.[47] As a trained teacher, she presumably valued academic success, making Woodham's academic and behavioral issues particularly distressing for him and frustrating for her. Interestingly, Grant Boyette, the boy who commanded Woodham to murder his mother and commit a school shooting, also had a mother who was a teacher.[48]

Charles Whitman's wife was an excellent student who quickly established herself as a teacher.[49] He, meanwhile, floundered academically, lost his military scholarship for failing to keep up his grades, and drifted from one course of study to another without completing a degree. He beat his wife and eventually killed her. Why? Perhaps her success in education highlighted his educational failures, feeding his sense of inadequacy. His biographer commented, Whitman "may have interpreted her success in teaching as a blow to his ego."[50]

Adam Lanza's mother was involved in education in two ways. First, she had volunteered at Sandy Hook Elementary School while he was a student there;[51] it has been hypothesized that Lanza was jealous of the attention she gave to other students.[52] She later homeschooled Lanza during his adolescence. Perhaps supervising his education created friction between them. Was her death related to her roles in education? Furthermore, Lanza's grandmother worked in an elementary school, his father taught at two universities, and his stepmother was a university librarian. Lanza failed to graduate from high school, a college, and a university.[53] Perhaps the prominence of education in his family magnified his sense of failure.

Alvaro Castillo killed his father who was a custodian in a public school.[54] In this case, the father's workplace may not have been a factor. First, there is no evidence that Castillo had major academic failures. Second, though his father worked in a school, he was a custodian, not a teacher, which may have resulted in different dynamics (though he allegedly put great pressure on his children to succeed academically). Furthermore, Castillo reportedly killed his father in response to his violent behavior.

Finally, though Robert Poulin did not kill his parents, he contemplated doing so.[55] His father was a high school teacher, his mother a lunchroom supervisor. The reason for his animosity is unknown. Academic performance was a concern, however, and one diary entry about being depressed began, "Today is April 7, 1975. I think I just flunked my first test."[56] His parents reported that he was very concerned about his grades because he wanted to get into officer training. They commented that he was "very upset that he didn't get 100 percent"[57] in all his courses. Educational failure appears to have been a factor in his attack; whether his parents' involvement in education played a role remains unknown.

We cannot know for sure why the perpetrators killed members of their own families. The impact of academic failures in families where education had a prominent presence, however, may have been one out of many factors.

Beyond those who killed relatives, nearly all shooters had negative academic or disciplinary experiences, and many of them had family members involved in education. Though having a relative who worked in a school may not have been relevant in every case, the pattern seems noteworthy. Table 8.3 lists the shooters with known family connections to education.

OCCUPATIONAL FAILURES

Many shooters had trouble getting or holding jobs. This includes most of the adults in the sample—Charles Whitman, Edward Allaway, Patrick Purdy, Laurie Dann, Marc Lépine, Thomas Hamilton, Biswanath Halder, Kimveer Gill, Steven Kazmierczak, Jiverly Wong, and One Goh. Here are a few examples of major occupational setbacks as well as repeated, smaller failures:

- Gang Lu had a PhD from a prestigious physics program but failed to get hired as a professor despite sending out hundreds of letters.
- Amy Bishop was let go from a position in Boston and failed to get tenure at the University of Alabama.
- Valery Fabrikant failed to get tenure.
- Besides his failed military career, Charles Whitman worked briefly as a bill collector, bank teller, NASA assistant, insurance agent, and real estate broker who never sold a single property.[58]
- By the time Patrick Purdy was twenty-four, he had quit or been fired from at least twenty-one jobs.[59]
- Laurie Dann's "inattentiveness, lack of motivation, and other emerging peculiarities made it impossible for her to keep a steady job."[60] She was fired from Kmart, a hospital, two receptionist positions, and a restaurant. She had also been "fired" as a babysitter by many families.
- Steven Kazmierczak was fired after two months at his first retail job, was fired from Walgreen's after a month, was fired from another job after a month, quit his job at UPS, and was fired from

Table 8.3: Family Involvement in Schools

SECONDARY SCHOOL SHOOTERS	Robert Poulin	Mother: lunchroom supervisor Father: schoolteacher
	Brenda Spencer	Father: university audio-visual technician
	Jamie Rouse	Grandmother: schoolteacher Grandfather: schoolteacher Aunt: schoolteacher Uncle: schoolteacher
	Evan Ramsey	Foster Mother: school superintendant
	Luke Woodham	Mother: teacher (murdered)
	[Grant Boyette][a]	[Mother: schoolteacher]
	Kip Kinkel	Mother: schoolteacher (murdered) Father: schoolteacher (murdered)
	Dylan Klebold	Mother: worked at community college
	Alvaro Castillo	Father: elementary school custodian (murdered)
COLLEGE SHOOTERS	Charles Whitman	Wife: schoolteacher (murdered) Mother-in-law: schoolteacher
	Edward Allaway	Sister: university secretary
	Wayne Lo	Mother: Schoolteacher
	Steven Kazmierczak	Sister: completed graduate degree at university he was attending at time of his attack; maybe employed in special education
	Amy Bishop	Father: college professor Self: college professor
ABERRANT ADULT SHOOTERS	Laurie Dann	Self: studied to be elementary teacher Sister-in-law: schoolteacher
	Marc Lépine	(Mother: university student)[b]
	Jillian Robbins	Mother: college instructor and administrator Stepfather: college professor
	Kimveer Gill	Father: college professor
	Adam Lanza	Mother: home-schooled Lanza; school volunteer (murdered) Father: instructor at two universities Stepmother: university librarian Grandmother: elementary school nurse
OTHER SHOOTERS	Tyrone Mitchell	Fiancée: preschool teacher Sister: teacher's aide
	Seth Trickey	Grandfather: high school teacher Grandmother: elementary school teacher Great-aunt: elementary school teacher Great-uncle #1: high school teacher Great-uncle #2: high school teacher Great-uncle #3: teacher
	Stephen Morgan	Father: college professor

a He was not a school shooter, but commanded Luke Woodham to kill.

b She did not work in education, but her success in academia may have exacerbated Lépine's sense of failure, particularly given his obsession with feminists.

Kmart after a few weeks.[61] In addition, he had five other jobs that did not last long.[62]

These failures may have been blows to both the shooters' identities and financial stability, adding to their depression, desperation, and rage.

ROMANTIC FAILURES

Most shooters either failed to establish any romantic or sexual relationships or else suffered breakups or rejections that contributed to their anguish and anger. These failures were often devastating. Even among the ten shooters who managed to get married, only two appear to have had stable relationships—Valery Fabrikant and Amy Bishop. The others' relationships ended in separation, divorce, or, in the case of Charles Whitman, domestic violence that brought them to the verge of separation.

Many shooters engaged in violence against intimate partners, those they desired relationships with, romantic rivals, or members of the opposite sex in general.

- Charles Whitman beat and eventually murdered his wife.
- Robert Poulin raped and killed a girl he had a crush on who was dating someone else.
- Laurie Dann stabbed her ex-husband.
- Marc Lépine struggled with relationships and targeted women in his attack.
- Barry Loukaitis killed the boy who was dating the girl he had a crush on.
- Luke Woodham killed his ex-girlfriend.
- Andrew Golden shot a girl who broke up with him.
- Mitchell Johnson shot a girl who broke up with him.
- Michael Carneal shot a girl he had a crush on and a girl who rejected him.
- Robert Flores reportedly beat his wife, who then took their two children and left him.
- Peter Odighizuwa assaulted his wife; she left him, taking their four children.
- Tim Kretschmer appeared to target women in his attack; one of the first victims was a woman who had recently rejected him.
- Wellington de Oliveira reportedly targeted girls in his attack.
- T. J. Lane killed the boy who was dating his ex-girlfriend.

- Elliot Rodger's attack (not covered in this book) was motivated by hatred for women. In his last video, he said, "I don't know why you girls aren't attracted to me, but I will punish you all for it. . . . If I can't have you, girls, I will destroy you."[63]

Multiple shooters suffered breakups or rejections shortly before their attacks—Eric Houston, Gary Scott Pennington, Jamie Rouse, Jillian Robbins, Evan Ramsey, and Eric Harris. Other perpetrators, such as Kip Kinkel and Dylan Klebold, were consumed with anguish over their inability to have a girlfriend. For most shooters, intimacy was one more domain in which they failed.

FREQUENT AND SIGNIFICANT RELOCATIONS

Traumatized shooters often experienced frequent relocations. Such disruptions can cause significant stress, creating a sense of instability and anxiety about what the future will bring. These individuals faced repeated challenges to making friends and establishing themselves among their peers. This was true of the following traumatized shooters: Eric Houston, Gary Scott Pennington, Evan Ramsey, Mitchell Johnson, Jeffrey Weise, Eric Hainstock, T. J. Lane, and Patrick Purdy. They, however, were not the only perpetrators to experience relocations. For example:

- Charles Whitman's family moved eight times in his first six years, and he relocated frequently as an adult.
- Eric Harris moved several times due to his father's military career.
- Matti Saari's family moved twelve times, resulting in six changes of schools within nine years.
- Marc Lépine's family moved fifteen times, including stints in Costa Rica and Puerto Rico, where he did not know the language.

Several shooters were immigrants who may not have had frequent relocations but were faced with the significant challenge of adapting to life in a foreign country. This includes Gang Lu, Valery Fabrikant, Wayne Lo, Peter Odighizuwa, Biswanath Halder, Jiverly Wong, Seung Hui Cho, and One Goh. Even after arrival in this country, there were often additional relocations.

The challenges of relocating, whether several smaller moves or the one major move of immigration, may have contributed to the perpetrators' stress.

PSYCHOTIC SHOOTERS: SIBLING RIVALRY

Many psychotic shooters were the youngest children in their families and grew up in the shadows of higher-functioning siblings. In almost every case where there was a family history of severe mental illness, only the shooters were affected. Their brothers or sisters were untouched by psychological disturbances. This caused significant sibling rivalry.

- Luke Woodham resented his older brother, who was higher functioning and "Mr. Popular."
- Andrew Wurst's older brothers were typical kids; Wurst was the misfit in his family.
- Michael Carneal's older sister, Kelly, was talented, academically successful, and socially popular; she was everything Carneal wasn't.
- Kip Kinkel's older sister was a pretty, popular, successful young woman, while Kinkel was immature and psychologically troubled.
- Dylan Klebold complained that his older brother was popular and athletic and always "ripped" on him.
- Seung Hui Cho's older sister was highly successful; she graduated from Princeton and was hired by the State Department. Cho went to a less-prestigious university and was incapable of functioning socially.
- Laurie Dann's older brother was athletic, academically capable, and successful in his career: "Laurie always envied and admired her brother."[64]
- Adam Lanza left no record of envy toward his older brother, Ryan, but "unlike Adam, Ryan was socially well adjusted, one of the popular kids at Newtown High."[65] Two years before Lanza's rampage, he broke off contact with his brother, suggesting some level of hostility.
- Marc Lépine was plagued by his younger sister, who emotionally terrorized him. He was so full of rage toward her that he made a mock grave and tombstone with her name on it.[66]
- Steven Kazmierczak's older sister was psychologically stable and an outstanding student. She completed her graduate degree at the

University of Illinois—the same university Kazmierczak was attending when he went on his rampage. Their relationship was so conflicted that after his attack, his sister was surprised he had not murdered her instead of students he didn't know. When Kazmierczak was in eighth grade, he was once so angry with her that he chased her out of the house with a knife.[67]

- Amy Bishop killed her brother. If this was deliberate, then it constitutes the most extreme case of sibling rivalry among school shooters.

All of the shooters just listed were psychotic. Sibling envy was not an issue for the psychopathic or traumatized shooters. Many psychotic shooters, however, were not only social misfits but misfits in their own families as well. Not measuring up to their siblings, not fitting in at home or school, and disappointing their parents contributed to their insecurity, identity issues, and rage.

OTHER POSSIBLE FACTORS

Three other factors deserve a brief mention. First, at least half of the perpetrators engaged in substance abuse (illegal drugs, prescription drugs, or alcohol). What role, if any, this played in their attacks is unknown. No shooters in the sample were drunk or high during their attacks. Their substance use, however, may have impaired their judgment, added to their distress, contributed to their academic, occupational, or relationship difficulties, or exacerbated their psychotic symptoms.

A second factor is that at least 42 percent of the shooters had a history of legal troubles, including arrests, contempt of court, and loss of a driver's license. The psychological impact of being arrested, taken to the police station, and being brought before a judge should not be underestimated. These events may have been humiliating, resulted in feeling like a failure, or spurred resentment and outrage toward the police or society in general. How the shooters responded depended on who they were.

- In the marines, Charles Whitman was court martialed, reduced from corporal to private, and sentenced to thirty days' confinement and ninety days' hard labor. This not only caused him to hate the marines but affected his relationship with his wife. Whitman wrote, she "seems pretty disgusted with me."[68]

- Jiverly Wong's multiple arrests apparently led to paranoid delusions about police. He wrote bizarre allegations in his suicide note about how police harassed and mistreated him. Because Wong wore body armor in his attack, the chief of police in Binghamton concluded that Wong "was going to take the police on";[69] Wong apparently changed his mind and killed himself.
- Jamie Rouse lost his driver's license due to multiple traffic violations. Three days before his attack he had a fender bender, panicked about losing his license again, and felt like killing the woman who confronted him about the incident. His parents "remember Jamie saying there was no use living if he could not drive."[70]
- Eric Harris identified his arrest as the most embarrassing experience of his life and said "cops" were the "one person" he hated the most.[71] He fantasized about killing cops and tried to do so during his attack.

Interestingly, two attacks may have been triggered by impending court appearances. Valery Fabrikant committed his attack the day before his hearing for contempt of court. Similarly, Sebastian Bosse (not covered in this book) went on his rampage the day before appearing in court for illegal possession of a firearm. Both perpetrators had contemplated violence for a long time, but the prospect of being in court may have pushed them to action.

The third possible factor motivating a shooter to attack is the loss of loved ones. Many traumatized shooters, for example, lost one or both parents to prison, death, disability, or abandonment. Others shooters lost their spouses, and sometimes children, to separation or divorce. Beyond this, several shooters experienced one or more significant deaths:

- Several classmates of Alvaro Castillo had been killed in a car accident a couple of months before his attack.
- Matti Saari's brother died of a congenital disease; several friends of his had been killed in a car accident a few months before his attack.
- Steven Kazmierczak's mother had died less than a year and a half before his attack.
- Within three years of his attack, Wellington de Oliveira had lost both his adoptive parents.
- One Goh's mother had died and his brother had been killed in a car accident within approximately a year of his attack.

Such losses, particularly for those who were psychotic (as were all the shooters listed above), may have been overwhelming. For instance, Wellington de Oliveira barely functioned throughout his life and reportedly became more reclusive and strange following his adoptive mother's death, going on his rampage eight months later. The psychologist who conducted a posthumous evaluation of Steven Kazmierczak concluded that his mother's death precipitated "an unstoppable, downward slide that would carry him to even greater depths of despair than he had experienced in his worst times as an adolescent."[72]

EXTERNAL INFLUENCES

Many shooters found support for committing their attacks in a variety of external sources. These included their peers, violent media, and real-life role models or ideologies. Though it is not possible to quantify or prove the significance of these factors, the evidence suggests that in many cases external influences contributed to the shooters' decisions to commit their attacks.

Peer Support

When people talk about peer influence on school shootings, they generally mean bullying. There has been little focus on the supportive role played by the shooters' friends. In many cases, however, peers supported the violent intentions of shooters. Without such support, it seems likely that some attacks would not have occurred. Interestingly, peer support appears to have been most relevant among secondary school shooters, while few college and aberrant adult shooters shared their plans with friends. Perhaps the older shooters did not require encouragement, or perhaps they were more careful not to leak their intentions.

The most direct type of peer influence occurred when one person convinced another to join him in an attack—as with Golden and Johnson and again with Harris and Klebold. Grant Boyette exercised another kind of direct influence by bombarding Luke Woodham with commands to kill his mother and his ex-girlfriend. Similarly, two friends talked Evan Ramsey into committing his attack.

Many other shooters received indirect support for their rampages. They often shared their plans with friends and may have interpreted their friends' silence or lack of protest as tacit approval. As noted by Dr. Marisa Reddy, "some people, if they've threatened and there's no response, they may take that as permission to move forward with a plan."[73]

Ideologies and Role Models

Many shooters were attracted to ideologies of power and role models for violence. Ideologies such as Nazism, Satanism, or black magic (casting spells with an intent to hurt people) confer a sense of power that is highly appealing to people who feel weak and helpless. Luke Woodham said of his involvement in black magic, "One second I was some kind of heart-broken idiot, and the next second I had power over many things."[74] Those drawn to Nazi ideology included Marc Lépine, Luke Woodham, Andrew Wurst, Eric Harris, Jeffrey Weise, Kimveer Gill, and Steven Kazmierczak. Several shooters were drawn to the philosophy of Friedrich Nietzsche, including Luke Woodham, Eric Harris, Pekka-Eric Auvinen, and Steven Kazmierczak. (For a discussion of Nietzsche's appeal to Eric Harris, and potentially other shooters, see my article "Influences on the Ideology of Eric Harris," 2008, http://www.schoolshooters.info.)

In addition to latching onto ideologies that provided a framework to support their fragile identities, many shooters also had specific role models for violence, including serial killers, mass murderers, and other school shooters. It is noteworthy that most of the shooters with role models or ideologies were psychotic (82 percent). In general, the psychopathic and traumatized shooters carried out their attacks as independent acts, not in imitation of other killers.

Similarly, the shooters who viewed their attacks as global rather than local events were usually psychotic. Seung Hui Cho wrote about his attack triggering a massive social revolution, and Pekka-Eric Auvinen envisioned that his rampage would lead to the toppling of totalitarian regimes. Biswanath Halder believed his attack had "saved mankind." Eric Harris was the only nonpsychotic shooter who conceived of his rampage as having global significance.

In general, psychopathic shooters felt no need to attach themselves to a source of power; they *were* the source of power. They did not give their attacks any global significance—theirs were local acts done for personal reasons. Psychotic shooters, in contrast, often sought out ideologies and role models, looking for sources of power they could connect with to bolster their unstable identities—sometimes entertaining a delusion that shooting people at school would cause a positive transformation of the world.

Media Violence

Though there is no evidence that media violence—by itself—causes school shootings, there is anecdotal evidence suggesting that some school shooters were influenced by violent video games, films, or books. This doesn't mean that media violence caused their rampage attacks, but it may have been one of many factors that shaped the behavior of the shooters. Here are several examples:

- Jamie Rouse cited the film *Natural Born Killers* as an influence, commenting, "It made killing look easy and fun . . . it fascinated me."[75]
- Eric Houston was fascinated by the movie *The Terminator*, watching it twenty-three times, including the night before his attack.[76]
- One of Jeffrey Weise's favorite films was *Elephant*, which is about a school shooting. He liked to fast-forward to scenes of the attack, and he watched the movie with friends shortly before his own rampage.
- Kimveer Gill apparently identified with "Postal Dude" and wanted the game *Postal* to become "so realistic that it looks and feels like it's actually happening." Perhaps he sought to make the game real by going on a rampage.
- Gang Lu's letter to the world cited multiple movies that portrayed individuals who used violence to obtain justice, including *Die Hard* and "Clint Eastwood's movies."[77]
- Steven Kazmierczak played violent video games and once wrote to a friend that "practicing with virtual weapons translates into ?"[78]—not finishing the thought but apparently suggesting a connection between practicing violence and committing violence. Kazmierczak was also fascinated by violent films, including *Saw*, *Saw IV*, *Mr. Brooks*, and *Fight Club*. The official report on his attack cited these films as probable influences.
- After watching the movie *The Basketball Diaries* (which includes a dream sequence of a boy shooting his classmates), Michael Carneal "said that it would be neat to go in the school and shoot people that you don't like."[79] Dr. Dewey Cornell noted another media influence on Carneal: "In one of his favorite games, Nintendo's *Doom*, he often pretended that he was shooting the bullies at school."[80] Dr. Katherine Newman's team of researchers concluded that "Michael's exposure to media violence can be regarded as a factor which contributed to the attitudes, perceptions, and judgment which led to his violent behavior."[81]

- Eric Harris and Dylan Klebold's code name for their attack was "NBK" after the film *Natural Born Killers*. In addition, Harris was obsessed with the video game *Doom*. He wrote, "I wished I lived in *Doom*"[82] and "What I can't do in real life, I try to do in *Doom*."[83] He even made a direct connection between *Doom* and his upcoming attack: "I have a goal to destroy as much as possible, so I must not be sidetracked by my feelings of sympathy, mercy, or any of that, so I will force myself to believe that everyone is just another monster from *Doom* . . . so it's either me or them."[84]

The issue of media influence is of particular interest with Barry Loukaitis, warranting a more in-depth review. First, like other shooters, he was fascinated with *Natural Born Killers*[85] and liked to quote it to his peers. He was also reportedly influenced by the song "Jeremy" by Pearl Jam, the video of which depicted a school shooting.[86] The primary influence on his attack, however, may have been the novel *Rage*, written by Stephen King under the name Richard Bachman. Loukaitis had multiple books by King, but "none was as worn as his copy of *Rage*."[87] In the novel, a boy named Charlie Decker shoots his algebra teacher and holds the class hostage. Loukaitis also shot his algebra teacher and held the class hostage. Decker makes a comment that his attack "sure beats panty raids."[88] Loukaitis commented, "it sure beats algebra."[89] Also, like the book's protagonist, Loukaitis targeted his attack against a boy who was both a popular athlete and romantic rival.

Two other aspects of the novel may be relevant. Decker says that the attack was really "misplaced aggression" and that he wished he had killed his father instead of his teacher. Loukaitis had written poems wishing his father were dead.[90] Finally, on the page in *Rage* after Decker kills his teacher, there is a reference to "a little kid in a Halloween cowboy suit."[91] The day of the attack, Loukaitis was "dressed from head to toe in a Western-style black hat, boots, and duster."[92] Though *Rage* did not cause Loukaitis to commit murder, he apparently related to the story and modeled his behavior after it.

* * *

Did external influences cause rampage attacks? No, but in many cases they appear to have been contributing factors. Making up one's mind to commit mass murder presumably is not done lightly. Having friends, ideologies, or role models (fictional and nonfictional) that supported violent action apparently made it easier for the shooters to proceed with their attacks.

It is interesting that all three types of external influences—peer support, role models and ideologies, and media violence—were most relevant among younger shooters. This includes secondary school shooters and college or aberrant adult shooters in their teens or twenties. External influences do not appear to have been relevant for shooters in their thirties through sixties. Perhaps as adults they were able to act on their own, whereas younger shooters were more likely to seek out the influence of, or be influenced by, external factors.

SUMMARY

The patterns identified in this chapter appear to be relevant to understanding school shooters. This doesn't mean, however, that the factors were equally relevant for all shooters. For example, having a parent involved in education may have been significant for Jillian Robbins but not for Dylan Klebold. Nonetheless, the high percentages of shooters with biological problems, military failures, relatives in the military, and so on suggests that these factors played a role in the shooters' lives.

As I have noted, the vast majority of people who are psychopathic, psychotic, or traumatized do not commit school shootings. This means that other factors contribute to rampage attacks. Hopefully, this chapter has shed light on at least some of these additional influences.

9

PREVENTING SCHOOL SHOOTINGS

Threat Assessment and Warning Signs

There is no one way to prevent school shootings. Most public discussion has focused on what can be done to stop an assailant once he or she has arrived at school: lockdown procedures, armed guards, and so on. These practices can minimize the damage a shooter inflicts, but they are emergency-response procedures, not prevention. For example, Virginia Tech had armed campus police, Columbine High School had an armed security guard, and Red Lake High School had an armed guard and metal detector. Clearly, physical security measures cannot be counted on to stop rampage attacks.

Many schools attempt to restrict access to their buildings in order to keep out strangers. It should never be assumed, however, that an attacker can be kept out. At Sandy Hook Elementary School, for instance, Adam Lanza simply shot out a window and entered the school. It is important to note that keeping strangers out of the school does not guarantee safety. Some shooters gunned down children as they arrived at school, while they played at recess, or upon dismissal. A school shooting does not always happen inside the building.

Of course, shooters usually attack schools they are attending, so unless they are visibly armed, there is no reason to keep them out of the building. A more proactive approach to prevention is to keep people from reaching the point where taking a gun to school seems like a good idea. Within schools, this can take the form of promoting a positive environment, minimizing peer harassment, and creating a physically and emotionally safe space. At the broader societal level, it means improving child-protective services to minimize child abuse and its damaging effects, as well as expanding mental health services to treat people long before they reach the point of violence.

Then, of course, there is the issue of access to firearms. The key here, at least as it applies to youths, is to limit access to guns within their own homes or those of friends and relatives. All too often secondary school shooters obtained firearms at home. In addition, family members can keep impaired adults from using firearms. For example, despite his mental health problems, Adam Lanza's mother trained him to use firearms and kept weapons accessible in the home.[1] Failure to secure the guns cost not only her own life but those of twenty-six others. This is not about gun control, but about people doing a better job of securing their firearms.

The best method of preventing school shootings, however, is through threat assessment. This means identifying potential shooters before they show up at schools armed and with an urge to kill. Threat assessment involves knowing the warning signs of potential violence, having teams of school personnel who are trained to evaluate threats of violence, and taking whatever action is necessary to maintain safety. Before discussing threat assessment and warning signs, a few preliminary comments are in order.

THE MANY FACES OF SCHOOL SHOOTERS

Recognizing the diversity of school shooters is important for prevention. If we are confined by the belief that shooters are white males, we may miss the warning signs of those who don't fit this stereotype. We need to know that rampage shooters can come from any racial or ethnic background. And though the vast majority of school shooters are male, female students who exhibit warning signs of violence need to be taken just as seriously as male students.

School shooters are often thought to be odd kids on the periphery of their peer groups who are depressed, unathletic, harassed, uninvolved at school, and disconnected from their communities. This is a dangerous assumption. For example, Mitchell Johnson had friends, dated several girls, played on the school's football, baseball, and basketball teams, and sang in a church choir that performed for the elderly. Similarly, Andrew Golden had friends, dated at least one girl, played trumpet in the school band, raced go-karts, played baseball, and was a mischievous class clown.

Though Eric Harris has been portrayed as an ostracized loner, he had many friends, dated girls, played sports, and was a successful student. On his report card three teachers indicated he exhibited a "positive attitude and good cooperation," and one added that he showed "strong interest and participation."[2] On a progress report, one teacher wrote, "Eric is doing awesome!"[3] What did Harris's teachers see when they looked at him? A bright, eager student who was a pleasure to have in class. If we think all shooters look like Adam Lanza, we will miss the warning signs in an Eric Harris.

Contrary to expectations, the smallest, least intimidating kids may be the most dangerous. Some shooters were large and scary, such as surly Jason Hoffman. Very often, however, students who seemed least likely to be violent have gone on rampages. Students who are unusually small or physically undeveloped may be the most likely to use guns to establish a sense of power.

It is essential that we resist stereotyping school shooters. As long as we believe that students do not pose a risk because they have friends, play sports, are too small to hurt anyone, or are not white males, we will put ourselves and our communities at risk.

THREAT ASSESSMENT

The best way for schools to prevent rampage attacks is to have threat assessment teams to evaluate and respond to potential threats of violence. Threat assessment is for preventing not just rampage attacks but also any school-related violence. The details of setting up such teams are beyond the scope of this book, but a few comments will be made.

Many students make threats with no intention to hurt anyone. For instance, a student who feels insulted may threaten, "If you say that again, I'm going to kill you." Maybe he means this literally, but in most cases, he doesn't. The job of a threat assessment team is to conduct an investigation to distinguish real threats from false alarms. What does this involve? As stated by Dr. Brian Van Brunt in his book *Ending Campus Violence: New Approaches to Prevention*, threat assessment "involves viewing the student from multiple perspectives, collecting information about their past academic, social, and legal history, understanding their family of origin, how they interact with others, their access to lethal means and their interactions with other students, faculty, and staff."[4]

Who serves on threat assessment teams? Drs. Dewey Cornell and Peter Sheras address this issue in their book, *Guidelines for Responding to Student Threats of Violence*. They advise that secondary school threat assessment teams should include the principal or assistant principal, a school resource officer, a school psychologist or social worker, and a school counselor.[5] Not every school has all these professionals, so the team membership will vary.

In higher education the membership primarily includes the dean of students or vice-president of student affairs, campus law enforcement, and the counseling center director. Additional members can represent residential life, academic affairs, health services, or legal counsel.[6]

All school personnel need to be trained to recognize warning signs of potential violence so they know when to alert the threat assessment team. Teachers, administrators, and guidance counselors, office workers, cafeteria staff, and maintenance workers—all are on the front line of violence prevention.

Most importantly, *students* must be trained to recognize and report warning signs of potential violence. As emphasized in an FBI report by Dr. Mary Ellen O'Toole, "The School Shooter: A Threat Assessment Perspective," "students are often in the best position to see and hear signs or cues of potential violence, and training should stress that ignoring those cues or remaining silent can be dangerous for themselves as well as others. Training should also confront the common teenage 'code of silence' and students' reluctance to be branded as a 'snitch' or to violate a friend's confidence."[7] All too often, students have observed warning signs without reporting them. On the positive side, most foiled attacks have been due to students communicating their concerns.

WHAT ARE THE WARNING SIGNS?

Most school shooters leave a trail of warning signs that are either not noticed or not responded to. As noted by Dr. James Alan Fox and Harvey Burstein in their book *Violence and Security on Campus: From Preschool through College*, "in the aftermath of virtually any high-profile episode of school violence, much of the focus (and finger-pointing) surrounds the warning signs that were reportedly missed or ignored by parents, teachers, peers, and law enforcement officials."[8]

What constitutes a potential warning sign of violence? Warning signs do not relate to students' clothing, video games, musical preferences, or other aspects of their lifestyles. Warning signs are actions that constitute *attack-related behaviors*. These are behaviors related to preparing a rampage: stockpiling weapons, diagramming the school, recording plans, making a hit list, and so on.

A key aspect of attack-related behavior is *leakage*—leaking plans to other people. Leakage is important because it is how people are most likely to learn about a perpetrator's intentions. Leakage takes many forms and can be direct or indirect. Ironically, even the clearest leakage may fail to generate an intervention.

Forms of Leakage

Students often miss obvious warning signs because they do not take them seriously. For instance, Michael Carneal told students "he was gonna come to school and start shooting people."[9] Standing on a cafeteria table, Andrew Golden announced, "You're all going to die."[10] Mitchell Johnson told peers, "Tomorrow you will find out if you live or die."[11]

Why, despite clear threats, did nobody intervene? First, people may have believed the students were too young to commit murder. Second, sometimes the students making the threats were considered weird and were known for saying strange things. Third, sometimes shooters made direct threats but, when questioned by friends, denied actual intent. Finally, people may assume that anyone intending to commit mass murder won't announce it publicly. This is where school shooters differ from other killers, often leaving a long trail of leakage.

Students sometimes attempt to recruit peers to join the attack. Andrew Golden convinced Mitchell Johnson to be his partner. That same year, Andrew Wurst tried to recruit a friend but was turned down. Unfortunately, the friend did not notify adults about Wurst's plans. A better outcome occurred in 2008 when Dillon Cossey asked a friend to join his attack. The friend told authorities, who arrested Cossey and foiled a potential rampage.

Occasionally, shooters asked friends to provide supplies for their attacks. Barry Loukaitis wanted ammunition; Eric Harris asked for guns. Though, as in these cases, peers may not know why they wanted weapons, attempts to illegally obtain weapons should raise red flags.

Some shooters wanted their friends to be safe, warning them to avoid school on a particular day. Michael Carneal, for example, told friends to stay away from school on the Monday after Thanksgiving. If someone had spoken up, his rampage that day might have been prevented.

Sometimes students communicate their plans less directly, leaking their intentions by praising other school shootings. They may refer to a rampage as "cool" or say, "Somebody should do that here." Andrew Wurst made such comments about Golden and Johnson's shooting. A month later, Wurst carried out his own attack. Kip Kinkel was similarly fascinated by the Jonesboro shooting, saying somebody should do that at his school. Two months later, he went on his rampage.

Making a pilgrimage to the site of a school shooting shows intense admiration. Matti Saari was fascinated by Pekka-Eric Auvinen's attack; he traveled to Jokela, took photographs of Auvinen's school, and ordered guns from the shop where Auvinen had bought his weapons. Similarly, Alvaro Castillo was so obsessed with Columbine that he convinced his mother to take him from their North Carolina home to see the Colorado school, Harris's home, and the pizzeria where Harris had worked. Pilgrimages like these are warning signs.

School Assignments

Shooters sometimes foreshadowed their attacks through school assignments. This is another form of leakage. For example, Kip Kinkel, who told peers he wanted to be the next Unabomber, gave an oral report on how to make bombs. Though his attack did not involve bombs, he left numerous explosives in his home. Furthermore, when asked to write about love at first sight, Kinkel wrote an ominous essay that included the following sentences: "That is why you go to a pawn shop and buy an AR-15 because you are going to execute every last mother fucking one of you" and "My firearms will be the only things to fight my isolation."[12] The entire essay is strange and disturbing, especially considering it was supposed to be about love.

At least five shooters wrote essays about school shootings, including how to prevent them—Eric Harris, Seung Hui Cho, Pekka-Eric Auvinen, Steven Kazmierczak, and Tim Kretschmer. Of course, students may write about rampage attacks without being at risk for violence. If a student who writes on this topic, however, shows other warning signs, the interest in school shootings may not be innocent and should be investigated.

Apart from nonfiction essays on school shootings, other assignments foreshadowed future violence. Eric Harris and Dylan Klebold made a film for their video-production class called *The Trench Coat Mafia: Hitmen for Hire*. The film portrays Harris and Klebold as hit men who are hired by a student who is picked on. They come to school and gun down the bullies. Later, Klebold wrote a story about a man killing students. Likewise, Michael Carneal wrote about a boy who goes on a rampage against "preps." There is no way of knowing how many students write stories like Carneal's and Klebold's without committing school shootings. Nonetheless, any story in which students murder other students should raise concern.

Though there is no sure way to predict violence based on fictional writings, several aspects of Klebold's and Carneal's stories are disturbing. First, both writers identified with the killer. Klebold described the killer as left-handed, 6'4", and wearing a black trench coat. Klebold was left-handed, approximately 6'4", and wore a black trench coat. In Carneal's story, the killer is named Michael, just like Carneal himself. In addition, the names of murdered students in the story were the names of actual students in his school, giving the story a sense of imminent danger.

Beyond identifying with him, Klebold wrote about the killer with admiration—almost worship. "If I could face an emotion of god," he wrote, "it would have looked like the man. I not only saw in his face, but also felt emanating from him power, complacence, closure, and godliness. The man smiled, and in that instant, thru no endeavor of my own, I understood his actions."[13] Furthermore, both boys' stories revel in brutal violence. Carneal's is particularly graphic and sadistic. In a passage about killing five students, he wrote, "The first one he crucified on a metal cross that had been heated up to a glowing red temperature. . . . The third one he heated up a drill bit and drilled it into one of his eyes."[14] The sadistic nature of the violence may help to distinguish this paper from typical student writings.

Finally, Carneal's paper contains bizarre elements that suggest disorganized thinking. For example, he wrote, "Michael's Mom's birthday was the next day so he decided to get a present from the 'Your Mom Has a Birthday Only When There's a Riot' store."[15] Other elements of the story are illogical or bizarre, suggesting cognitive disorganization, a symptom of schizophrenia. When evidence of psychosis occurs alongside warning signs of violence, a risk assessment and a mental health evaluation are important.

Warning Signs at Home

Some parents of school shooters were aware of their children's disturbing behavior but did not follow through effectively. For example, Kip Kinkel's parents knew he was obsessed with guns and knives, was building bombs, and was explosively angry and severely depressed. If they had searched his room after finding his bomb-making materials, they might have found his journal documenting his suicidal anguish and homicidal rage.

Alvaro Castillo's parents knew he was obsessed with Harris's attack (his mother drove him on his "pilgrimage"). They knew he had planned to kill himself on the seventh anniversary of Columbine. They knew he had significant mental health issues and was obsessed with his firearms. Taken together, this was a dangerous combination.

Parents need to respond to warning signs that their children may become violent. Sadly, Kinkel's parents and Castillo's father were among the murdered. Their failure to act cost them their lives.

Warning Signs Online

Several perpetrators posted text, photographs, or videos online that foreshadowed their upcoming attacks. As previously noted, one might doubt that someone would publicize an upcoming killing spree, yet shooters have done just that. Eric Harris posted explicit homicidal rants, including, "God I can't wait till I can kill you people. . . . I don't care if I live or die in the shootout, all I want to do is kill and injure as many of you pricks as I can."[16] He even named a student he wanted to kill.

Finnish shooters Pekka-Eric Auvinen and Matti Saari each posted online videos. Auvinen showed himself shooting a gun and praised Harris and Klebold, Timothy McVeigh, and the Unabomber. His manifesto echoed and quoted Harris. Notably, Auvinen even announced his intention to carry out a rampage, naming his school and the date of the attack. Unfortunately, these details were posted the morning of his rampage. Because explicit online messages may be posted with little time to spare, an immediate response is imperative.

Like Auvinen, Saari posted online clips of himself shooting a gun and publicized that his favorite videos were about Columbine. In one video he said, "You will die next" and fired a series of shots.[17] These videos came to the attention of police, who interviewed him. Saari denied violent intent and was allowed to keep his gun. The next day he went on his rampage.

Sudden Purchase of Firearms

Leakage is just one type of attack-related behavior. Other actions often indicate a risk of violence. For example, several shooters who had conflicts with their universities bought firearms and began practicing with them months before their rampages. This is notable because these shooters had no prior histories of hunting or target shooting. Firearm purchases in the midst of significant conflict with schools, particularly if other warning signs are present, could indicate impending danger. In hindsight, this behavior occurred in the following cases:

- Never a hunter or shooter for sport, Gang Lu bought a gun and began target practice six months before his attack. This was around the time he learned he did not win the prize for the best dissertation.

- Peter Odighizuwa had no history of firearm use but bought a gun and began training six months before his attack.
- Two months before his rampage, Seung Hui Cho became a first-time gun owner and went to a target range.
- Valery Fabrikant told university colleagues he had applied for a permit to carry a concealed weapon. Two months later he attacked.

How should friends, colleagues, or relatives respond when people who are unstable and bitterly angry toward their schools become first-time gun owners? They should report their concerns to school administrators or law enforcement officials.

* * *

Preventing violence is difficult. Students may make threats or display warning signs without any intention to commit violence. Any one behavior does not prove that an attack is imminent. The behaviors cited here do not necessarily predict impending violence. They are signals, however, that there may be a risk and that investigation is necessary.

SCHOOL EMPLOYEES

Three of the shooters in my sample were school employees, including two professors—Valery Fabrikant and Amy Bishop. Despite their disturbing behavior and threats, no preventive actions were taken. Why? Perhaps what John Cowan referred to as the "tolerance for eccentricity" in academia inhibited people from taking action.[18] For example, when an administrator voiced reservations about Fabrikant's recommended promotion due to his problematic behavior, the chair of the department commented, "I was always under the impression that we took decisions on promotions, reappointments, and salary . . . increases purely on the basis of scholarly achievements and academic excellence rather than on the individual's behavior. . . . I hope my understanding is still valid."[19]

Cowan's report about Fabrikant noted that the concept of academic freedom may be mistakenly interpreted to mean the total absence of restraints on faculty behavior. He commented, however, "One extension of the concept I have yet to come to terms with," which "is the 'academic freedom' to be brutish and miserable to colleagues and students. . . . There is no academic freedom to harass. There is no academic freedom to be disruptive. There is no academic freedom to intimidate."[20]

Cowan also commented on the inhibitory effect of university hierarchies, administrators' lack of clarity about their authority, and hesitation in using it. "When faced with the challenge of a 'bad' colleague, whose behavior is disruptive, threatening, or merely unethical," he writes, "they do not in general know what their powers are, and are massively risk-averse when it comes to exercising those powers, even when they are aware of them."[21]

Cowan wrote this in 1994. Since then, multiple campus shootings, particularly the massacre at Virginia Tech, have made campus safety a much greater priority. Institutions of higher education are presumably more responsive to threats of violence than they were twenty years ago. Nonetheless, Amy Bishop's attack in 2010 shows that even in the face of disturbing and threatening behavior a university can still fail to respond effectively.

In addition, Edward Allaway was a university employee who went on a rampage. Though he did not exhibit the same warning signs as Fabrikant and Bishop, his case further highlights the need for colleges and universities to respond to concerns about potentially dangerous employees by referring them to their threat assessment or behavioral intervention teams. Unfortunately, as noted by Gregory Eells, "Many campuses have teams that focus only on student behavior and do not include a more comprehensive approach to campus safety that includes a review of troubling behavior from faculty and staff."[22]

ABERRANT ATTACKS

Preventing aberrant attacks is particularly difficult because schools are unaware that the perpetrators exist. In these cases, the burden of prevention falls more heavily on the potential shooters' family and friends. These are the cases in which physical security measures take on the greatest importance. Even if the attacks cannot be foreseen and prevented, solid safety procedures and prompt emergency response may minimize casualties.

Schools are not completely helpless to prevent violence from outsiders. Alert systems that notify school officials whenever the name of their school appears online may catch leakage on the Internet, particularly when accompanied by other content that indicates potential danger. Dr. Brian Van Brunt notes that "One new trend being used in threat assessment is the process of data mining, or knowledge discovery, on social media sites and the Internet. They search for key words or phrases that indicate a communicated threat to an individual or location."[23]

Also, some aberrant adult shooters spent time at or around the schools they eventually attacked. For example, less than two weeks before his rampage at Cleveland Elementary School, Patrick Purdy was seen sitting in his car behind the school. A few days later, he talked with a janitor inside a middle school and was seen walking back and forth between the middle school and high school. Two days later, he was again spotted.[24]

Purdy was not the only aberrant adult shooter to scope out the venue for his attack:

- Marc Lépine was captured on video at the École Polytechnique at least seven times in the two months before his attack.[25]
- Kimveer Gill was captured on video near Dawson College a month prior to his rampage.[26]
- Bruco Eastwood entered Deer Creek Middle School, chatted with teachers, left the building, and began shooting students as they exited the school.[27]

These examples show that it is crucial for school personnel to watch for people who have no business at the school. This is particularly relevant for primary and secondary schools. The openness and size of colleges and universities may make it difficult to identify someone who does not belong on campus. Nonetheless, anyone who causes suspicion should be reported to the administration, security, or the police.

THE UNPREDICTABILITY OF VICTIM SELECTION

Threat assessment procedures dictate that specific people who are threatened should be notified and kept safe from the potential perpetrator. School shooters, however, sometimes fantasized about killing—or threatened to kill—one person but ended up choosing other victims instead.

For instance, Charles Whitman made a comment about killing his father, whom he reportedly hated. He did not, however, kill his father but instead murdered his wife and mother, both of whom he allegedly loved. He then went on a rampage, shooting random people. Robert Poulin and Andrew Wurst both thought about killing their parents.

Neither one did so; they killed other people. Kip Kinkel fantasized about killing a boy who starred on the football team and dated the girl he had a crush on. Kinkel made no effort to kill him but instead shot his parents and random students.

The night before his attack, Jamie Rouse told a friend "he was going to kill a girl at school, the principal, a coach, and a state trooper who had given him two speeding tickets."[28] Rouse, however, targeted none of these people. Instead, he shot teachers he had no reason to dislike. Eric Harris wrote about killing and torturing specific people but then tried to blow up the school and kill as many people as possible.

Simply keeping the apparent intended victim safe does not mean that danger has been averted; people with enough rage to kill may lash out in unexpected directions.

IMMEDIATE AFTERMATH

When prevention efforts failed and attacks occurred, how did they end? What situations confronted school personnel and first responders? The scenarios have been remarkably varied.

Most commonly, the shooter committed suicide at the school. This was not always straightforward, however. Though many shooters turned their guns on themselves, about 30 percent of those who killed themselves at the school first exchanged gunfire with security or police. Though several shooters may have wanted to be killed by police—"suicide by cop"—only Charles Whitman died in this manner. Jason Hoffman reportedly sought suicide by cop; he was hit by gunfire but survived. He later took his life in jail.

Many shooters, however, had no desire to die. In fact, several took hostages. Eric Houston, Barry Loukaitis, and Gary Scott Pennington appeared to plan this in advance. Whereas Houston and Pennington surrendered, Loukaitis's gun was ripped from his grasp and he was apprehended. Valery Fabrikant also took hostages, but it is unknown whether this was part of his original plan. He, too, was overpowered and apprehended.

Two shooters called the police to turn themselves in. Wayne Lo did this while still on campus; Edward Allaway fled campus and called the police from a nearby hotel. Both shooters surrendered peacefully to the police. Other shooters, such as Amy Bishop and T. J. Lane, fled the scene and were arrested nearby, offering no resistance. Andrew Golden and Mitchell Johnson attempted to flee but were intercepted and apprehended by police. Luke Woodham also attempted to escape, but his car got stuck in mud and he was apprehended at gunpoint by the assistant principal.

Two shooters escaped from the schools they attacked and eluded the police long enough to do further damage. Laurie Dann drove off, eventually leaving her car and fleeing on foot. She entered a house, held the residents hostage, and shot and wounded one of them. When officers surrounded the house, Dann killed herself. Tim Kretschmer was on the run for three hours; he hijacked a vehicle, forcing a man to drive as he continued to shoot people. Kretschmer was wounded twice by police before he ended his life.

Not only do first responders need to be prepared for any course of action on the part of the perpetrators, they also need to be prepared for the challenges presented by different shooters and their chosen weapons. Although the term *school shooters* may conjure up images of teenagers, one cannot assume the perpetrator is a student. At Dunblane Primary School, Sandy Hook Elementary School, and the Amish schoolhouse in West Nickel Mines, Pennsylvania, the victims were young children, but the perpetrators were adults. In fact, some shooters have been ex-military marksmen. First responders might encounter well-trained gunmen with high-powered weapons.

School shooters were sometimes armed with more than guns. A dangerous situation occurred when Kip Kinkel was at the police station after his arrest. Kinkel's guns had been confiscated, but he had a knife hidden on his person. When the detective left the room briefly and then returned, Kinkel lunged at him with his knife. Though in this instance the detective subdued Kinkel with mace, the failure to fully search and disarm a perpetrator could have deadly consequences.

Some shooters were also arsonists—Laurie Dann, Pekka-Eric Auvinen, and Matti Saari—so first responders need to be prepared to encounter fires. Though not an arsonist, Sebastian Bosse—a German shooter not covered in this book—set off smoke grenades in the school; sixteen police officers were treated for smoke inhalation.

Bosse also had three bombs strapped to his body, five in his backpack, and four in his car. Similarly, Eric Harris and Dylan Klebold used bombs in the school and set explosives in their cars to go off after their attacks. Kip Kinkel left behind a house full of explosives. The neighborhood had to be evacuated while a bomb squad cleared the home. Police have to proceed with caution in handling the body of the perpetrator, as well as the perpetrator's vehicle and other possessions, due to the possibility of explosives.

First responders need to be prepared for all potential outcomes. They might be faced with a hostage situation, a military-trained sniper, raging fires, or explosives. Perpetrators might surrender peacefully or shoot at the police. They may fight to the death or attempt to escape. Once on the run, some might turn themselves in, and others may continue their rampage. School shooters exhibit remarkable diversity; their behavior when confronted by law enforcement cannot be predicted.

10

KEY FINDINGS

After reviewing forty-eight school shooters, what conclusions can we draw? How accurate are commonly held beliefs about the perpetrators and their attacks? Are school shooters really white, male, middle-class loners who are bullied into retaliation? Do they really seek out and kill the kids who picked on them? Moving beyond the stereotype to other issues, which categories of shooters were the most deadly? The most suicidal? The answers to these questions are sometimes surprising.

FINDINGS VERSUS CONVENTIONAL WISDOM

Most school shooters were not victims of bullying.

Despite the widespread belief that school shooters are virtually always victims of bullying, this does not appear to be true. The connection between bullying and school shootings, however, is difficult to untangle. It is even hard to define *bullying*, as people use widely different definitions. For my purposes, bullying refers to a pattern of behavior that includes insults, taunts, harassment (including sexual harassment), stalking, threats, intimidation, or physical assault. Because the available information is often incomplete and contradictory, the findings in table 10.1 are tentative. Nonetheless, there are interesting patterns.

Psychopathic shooters were frequently bullies and infrequently victims of bullying. The opposite was true of traumatized shooters, who rarely picked on others but were often picked on. Thus, those shooters who were most mistreated at home were also most mistreated at school.

Table 10.1: **Peer Harassment by Type and Population**

	Sample	Harassed	Harassing
SECONDARY SCHOOL:			
Psychopathic	7	29%	86%
Psychotic	7	57%	57%
Traumatized	10	70%	20%
Total	24	54%	50%
COLLEGE:			
Psychopathic	8	13%	100%
Psychotic	8	38%	71%
Total	13[a]	23%	83%
ABERRANT ADULT:			
Psychopathic	2	0%	100%
Psychotic	10	36%	36%
Traumatized	2	100%	0%
Total	11[a]	45%	36%
Total Psychopathic	17	18%	94%
Total Psychotic	25	44%	48%
Total Traumatized	12	75%	17%
Overall Total	48[a]	40%	54%

a Because some shooters fall into two categories, the total does not represent the sum of the categories but the actual number of shooters.

The rates of bullying and victimization among the psychotic shooters were approximately equal, except among college shooters, who were more often perpetrators than victims.

Across the three populations of shooters—secondary school, college, aberrant adult—victimization by bullying was least prevalent among college shooters, more common among the aberrant adults, and most common among secondary school shooters. Among the aberrant adult shooters, the harassment occurred years before their attacks. In these cases, it was not an immediate trigger for violence, but it may have left deep psychological scars.

Overall, at least 40 percent of shooters experienced peer harassment at some point in their lives. How this compares to students in general depends on which survey you read, how the survey defines bullying, and what questions are asked. A recent study by the US Department of Education reported that 27.8 percent of students ages twelve to eighteen reported being bullied in the last six months.[1] A survey of seventh graders in California found that 42 percent reported being bullied in the last year.[2] A report by the American Psychological Association noted that "70 percent of middle and high school students have experienced bullying at some point."[3] Based on these results, it is not clear that school shooters were harassed more than other students.

On a different note, at least 54 percent of the shooters teased, harassed, stalked, threatened, or intimidated others. Thus, it appears that school shooters bullied others more than they were victims of bullying. In some cases, shooters were both perpetrators and victims of harassment.

The fact that some shooters were harassed does not account for their attacks. After all, the vast majority of students who are harassed never commit murder. This does not mean that bullying was never a factor in school shootings. For some shooters, it was one more problem on top of many others. It was never, however, the only problem. There were always other issues.

Only one out of forty-eight shooters targeted a student who had bullied him.

Although many people believe that rampage attacks are revenge for bullying, only Evan Ramsey sought out and killed a boy who had harassed him. Notably, homicide was not even his idea; his friends convinced him to kill. Out of 631 people killed or wounded by the forty-eight shooters discussed in this book, only one was targeted because he had harassed the perpetrator. This is a remarkable statistic.

More shooters targeted school personnel than any other category of victim.

At least sixteen shooters (33 percent) shot or tried to shoot specific faculty members or administrators. In contrast, nine shooters (19 percent) targeted girls or women, six shooters (13 percent) targeted family members, three (6 percent) targeted rivals, and, as just noted, only one (2 percent) targeted a bully. Overall, 69 percent of the shooters had one or more specific targets or category of targets (e.g., either a specific girl or women in general, young children, etc.).

The data presented in table 10.2 is an attempt to tally the different types of targeted victims across the populations of shooters. These conclusions are tentative because it was not always clear if victims were targeted or random. Even when they were targeted, decisions had to be made regarding how to categorize them. For example, female teachers could have been targeted as females or as teachers. I placed them in the category that seemed most relevant according to the shooters' apparent motives. I counted Charles Whitman's wife and mother as both "family" and "females."

Secondary school and college shooters targeted school personnel most, whereas aberrant adult shooters never did, even when they were attacking schools they had previously attended. The high number of females targeted by aberrant adult shooters was the result of only two shooters (Lépine and de Oliveira), whereas six secondary school shooters targeted females. In contrast, no college shooters targeted females at their schools, though Whitman killed his wife and mother. Among secondary school shooters, none of the psychotic perpetrators targeted teachers or administrators, whereas more than half of the psychopathic and traumatized shooters did.

One other category of victim should be noted—children. Seven of the eleven aberrant adult shooters gunned down children in elementary or middle schools. Though no specific children were killed, the perpetrators deliberately sought out victims much younger than themselves. Whereas most school shootings involved kids killing kids (and sometimes adults) or adults killing adults, these seven perpetrators were adults killing children. These shooters killed or wounded 137 children—more than all the other categories of victims combined. In addition, though Brenda Spencer was not an adult, she was a sixteen-year-old gunning down children aged approximately seven to ten.

Table 10.2: Targeted Victims by Populations of Shooters

	Bullies	Rivals	Family	Females	Staff	Children
Secondary School	1	2	6	14	28	8
College	0	1	2[a]	2[a]	21	0
Aberrant Adult	0	0	1	32	0	129[b]
Total	1	3	9	48	49	137

a   Charles Whitman's wife and mother are counted both as family and female victims.

b   This includes ten girls who were also counted as female victims of Wellington de Oliveira.

In two out of three populations of school shooters, white males were not a majority.

One of the most common stereotypes of school shooters is that they are virtually always white males. This is a misconception. Among the shooters covered in this book, only 58 percent were white males. The percentage differed significantly, however, among secondary school perpetrators (79 percent), college shooters (39 percent), and aberrant adult shooters (36 percent). Though white males were a majority among secondary school shooters, they were a minority in the other two populations.

Why might this be? Perhaps a key factor was immigration. No secondary school shooters were immigrants, and only one (4 percent) was the child of immigrants. In contrast, at least 54 percent of college shooters were immigrants, and 36 percent of aberrant adult shooters were either immigrants (9 percent) or the children of immigrants (27 percent). Though within my sample being nonwhite does not correlate exactly with being an immigrant, for many of the older shooters these categories overlapped. Dr. James Alan Fox noted that international students may "come from cultures where failure is seen as shame on the entire family," exacerbating the stresses of academia and acculturation.[4]

Also, three of the four female shooters were college or aberrant adult shooters (and Latina Williams, an African American female who is not covered in this book, was a college shooter). Whether or not this is significant or an artifact of the small sample size is unknown.

In addition to the shooters included in this book, several others were not white males. Among secondary school shooters this includes Phu Cuong Ta (Asian), Jose Reyes (Latino), Nathaniel Brazill (African American), Seth Trickey (Native American), and Robert Butler Jr. (African American father). Among college shooters, as just noted, Latina Williams was an African American female. Nonwhite aberrant adult shooters include Tyrone Mitchell (African American) and Elliot Rodger (Asian mother).

Most school shooters were not socially isolated loners.

After Adam Lanza's attack at Sandy Hook, there were comments online such as "Of course he was a loner—school shooters are always loners." This is wrong. Though they often didn't have the social success they desired, school shooters were usually *not* loners. Even among those who appear to have been loners during the last few months before their attacks, most had social connections through most of their lives. Those shooters who were loners most commonly were psychotic shooters who either never had close relationships or withdrew from others as they sank into their psychosis. Most shooters, however, had friends, dated, and interacted with classmates or colleagues; ten even got married. The extreme isolation of Adam Lanza was not typical of school shooters but an anomaly.

School shooters are not always middle class.

School shooters are sometimes said to come exclusively from middle-class families. Their relative economic privilege has been highlighted in contrast to the perpetrators of violence among the urban poor. To say school shooters are middle class may be largely true, but it is misleading. Multiple shooters, primarily traumatized ones, came from low-income families who struggled to get by. In addition, several college and aberrant adult shooters struggled financially. Thus, economic issues affected both the younger shooters, several of whom grew up in poverty, as well as older shooters, who faced financial crises that were factors in their violence.

Most school shootings did not occur in urban settings.

School shootings have been said to occur primarily in small towns, rural areas, or suburbs, rather than in major metropolitan centers. This is largely true. There are, however, exceptions. For example, Tyrone Mitchell committed a shooting in Los Angeles in 1984 (not covered in this book). There have been two school shootings in San Diego (Brenda Spencer and also Frederick Davidson, who was not covered in this book), two in Cleveland (Biswanath Halder and Asa Coon), three in Montreal (Marc Lépine, Valery Fabrikant, and Kimveer Gill), one in Toronto (Phu Cuong Ta, not covered in this book), one in Oakland (One Goh), and one in Rio de Janeiro (Wellington de Oliveira). College or aberrant adult shooters committed most of the urban attacks.

   Why might smaller communities be more vulnerable to rampage attacks? Dr. Katherine Newman argued that it may be harder for people to raise concerns about someone's child when the families all know each other, do business together, and so on. Newman argued that fear of disrupting communal relationships inhibits the flow of information: "The same multiplex ties that promote the spread of gossip throughout a community can also prevent it from reaching the people who might need to hear it."[5]

   As I wrote in *Why Kids Kill*, another possible factor is that cities offer greater diversity of peer groups, making it easier for kids to find their niche: "A misfit in West Paducah would be expected to have a harder time than a misfit in New York City."[6]

Most shooters were not on psychiatric medications at the time of their attacks.

Many websites blame school shootings on psychiatric medications. These sites are commonly full of errors. Among the perpetrators in my sample, only four (8 percent) were on medications at the time of their attacks. Two or three others had taken medications within a month of their attacks (6 percent). Most shooters had never been on psychiatric medication. For those who did take medications, there is no evidence that they caused mania, psychosis, or violence. (For a detailed discussion of this issue, see my article "Psychiatric Medications and School Shooters" at http://www.schoolshooters.info.)

THE MAGNITUDE OF THEIR ATTACKS

Though all the perpetrators included in my sample intended to shoot multiple people, the number of casualties they caused varied dramatically by psychological type, attack type, population of shooters, and perpetrator age.

Regardless of psychological type or population of shooter, young adults had the highest victim rate.

The age of the perpetrators appears to have been a significant factor in the victim rate. The fourteen shooters with twenty or more victims had an average age of twenty-three. Figure 10.1 shows the relationship between perpetrator age and number of victims, with those between the ages of eighteen and twenty-seven being the most dangerous.

Among secondary school perpetrators, psychopathic shooters had the highest victim rate.

Psychopathic shooters had an average of 14.4 victims. Psychotic shooters came close to this, with an average of 12.7 victims. In contrast, traumatized shooters averaged 5.9 victims, less than half the rate of the psychopathic and psychotic shooters.

Another way of looking at this is that only 20 percent of the traumatized shooters had ten or more victims, whereas 57 percent of the

Figure 10.1: **Number of Victims by Age of Perpetrator**

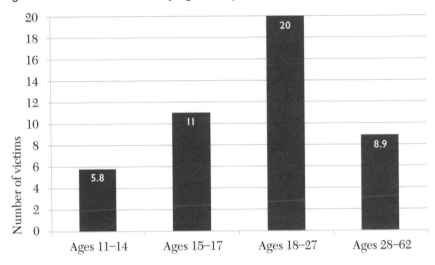

psychotic shooters and 71 percent of the psychopathic shooters had ten or more victims. This cannot be accounted for by the assailants' ages, as all three groups of attackers had an average age of sixteen to sixteen and a half. Psychopathic shooters were the most bloodthirsty or the most skilled in planning and executing their attacks.

Among college shooters, random attackers had five times the victim rate of targeted attackers.

College shooters who committed targeted attacks had a few intended victims, and after shooting them, the attacks were done. The perpetrators of random attacks, however, had no defined end point for their attacks. As a result they had more than five times as many victims as targeted college shooters (average of 27.2 victims versus 5 victims).

Among the three populations, aberrant adult shooters had the highest victim rate.

The average number of victims increases from secondary school shooters (10.4 victims) to college shooters (14.2 victims) to aberrant adult shooters (18.9 victims). Two factors may account for this. First, all of the aberrant adult attacks were random—insofar as no specific individuals were targeted, though females or children in general were sometimes targeted—and, as just mentioned, random attacks averaged far more victims than targeted attacks.

The second possible factor is age. As we saw in figure 10.1, young adults had the highest numbers of casualties, and the average age of aberrant adult shooters was 27.4, at the top of the age range of young adults. In comparison, secondary school shooters averaged 16.2 years of age, and college shooters averaged 35.8.

Figure 10.2 compares the victim rates across the different groups of shooters. The chart follows the groupings of the shooters as presented in the book, with the secondary school shooters organized by psychological type, the college shooters by attack type, and the entire sample by the three populations of shooters.

Figure 10.2: **Average Number of Victims (Killed and Wounded)**

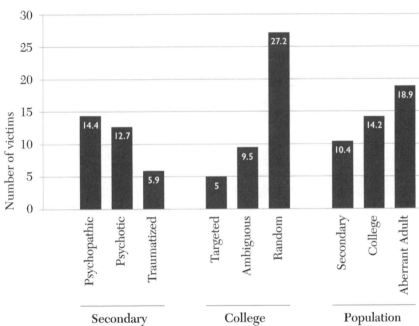

SUICIDE AMONG SCHOOL SHOOTERS

Though many shooters were suicidal, many others were not. It is impossible, however, to say for sure who was suicidal at the time of their attacks. Some shooters intended to die in their attacks but didn't, either because others apprehended them or because they changed their minds. Conversely, some shooters apparently expected to survive but ended up taking their own lives when escape became impossible. The results presented here include those who killed themselves (including one suicide by cop), regardless of their intention going into the attack. Of the forty-eight shooters, twenty-two died by suicide (46 percent). There were notable differences, however, across the types and populations.

Among secondary school perpetrators, psychopathic shooters had the highest suicide rate.

The rate of suicide among psychopathic secondary school shooters was 57 percent. In contrast, psychotic shooters had a suicide rate of 29 percent and traumatized shooters only 20 percent. This seems surprising because the psychotic and traumatized shooters generally appeared to be in far greater distress than the psychopathic shooters.

It is not surprising that some psychotic shooters killed themselves. After all, the suicide rate for schizophrenics is a thousand times higher than for the general population. Why some psychotic shooters killed themselves and others did not remains unknown.

Despite the traumatized shooters' anguish, they were the least suicidal of the three types. Why were some suicidal and not others? One factor may have been their mothers' levels of functioning. All fathers of traumatized shooters were dysfunctional, violent, or absent. Several mothers were also violent, alcoholic, or otherwise problematic. This might explain the suicidal urges of Evan Ramsey, Asa Coon, Jeffrey Weise, and Patrick Purdy. Four of the five suicidal traumatized shooters not only had dysfunctional fathers but dysfunctional mothers, too.

Why would psychopathic shooters take their own lives? Though psychopaths are sometimes said to be free of psychological distress, this is not always the case. They can become discouraged, depressed, and hopeless.[7] Yochelson and Samenow discuss the *zero state* that psychopaths are prone to experiencing: "[He] fears being reduced to a 'nothing' more than he fears almost anything else. He is said to be in a 'zero state' when his self-esteem is at rock bottom."[8] Yochelson and Samenow cite one criminal's state of mind as an example: "He had no faith in things now, no faith in people, and no faith in the future. He seriously questioned whether he could go through life this way—gloomy, pessimistic, with faith in nothing."[9]

This describes Eric Harris. The first thing he wrote in his journal was, "I hate the fucking world," then going on to call it "Hell on earth."[10] He referred to the world as "this worthless place"[11] and commented, "it's all doomed."[12] He had no belief in anything, rejected morals and values, and seemed incapable of, or uninterested in, love. With no belief in anything, what was the point of living? As stated by Yochelson and Samenow, the criminal "is chronically dissatisfied with the world."[13]

Why are psychopaths so dissatisfied with the world? Because it fails to meet their expectations. They believe that they are entitled to whatever they want and should be treated like exalted beings. The world, however, does not respond accordingly. Thus, they are chronically disappointed and enraged. Yochelson and Samenow mention a case that sheds light on the suicide of Eric Harris and possibly other psychopathic shooters. This person "believed that it was better 'to be under the sod than not to be God.'"[14] Harris could not achieve the godlike status he desired, so he felt there was no point to living.

Why did some psychopathic secondary school shooters kill themselves while others did not? One possibility is age. The three oldest—eighteen, eighteen, and nineteen—were suicidal, and the three youngest—eleven, fourteen, and sixteen—were not. Interestingly, Tim Kretschmer at seventeen was right in the middle; like the younger shooters in this group, he did not intend to kill himself, but like the older shooters, he did (after being twice wounded by police gunfire).

Among college shooters, random attackers had more than twice the suicide rate of targeted attackers.

Based on their psychological dynamics and the triggers for their attacks, it makes sense that random attackers were more suicidal (80 percent to 33 percent). The targeted shooters believed they had legitimate grievances; in their minds, the problem wasn't in them but in the universities. The random shooters generally had a greater level of despair about themselves.

Among the three populations, aberrant adults had the highest suicide rate.

Secondary school shooters had the lowest suicide rate (33 percent), with college shooters somewhat higher (46 percent) and aberrant adult shooters much higher (73 percent). The frequency of suicide among aberrant adult shooters could be due to their high rate of psychosis (the suicide rate among schizophrenics is extraordinarily high).

Aberrant adult shooters seem to have been the most disturbed of the three populations, having the highest victim rate and the highest suicide rate. They were the most destructive and the most self-destructive.

Figure 10.3 shows variations in suicide rate by age. This figure is strikingly similar to the figure on the rate of victims by perpetrator age (figure 10.2). There is the same rise and fall according to age, with young adults being the most homicidal and the most suicidal.

Figure 10.4 presents the suicide rates across various groupings of shooters.

THE TYPOLOGY ACROSS THE POPULATIONS OF SHOOTERS

The three psychological types—psychopathic, psychotic, and traumatized—are not evenly distributed among the sample as a whole, nor within the three populations of shooters—secondary school, college, and aberrant adult. In fact, there are remarkable differences across the populations.

Traumatized perpetrators were the most common type among secondary school shooters but absent among college shooters and nearly absent among aberrant adult shooters.

Among secondary school shooters, 42 percent were traumatized, with psychotic and psychopathic perpetrators accounting for 29 percent

Figure 10.3: **Suicide Rate by Age**

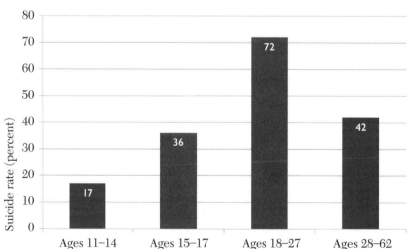

Figure 10.4: **Comparitive Suicide Rates**

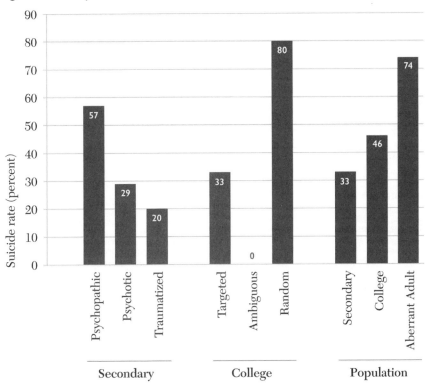

each. Traumatized shooters, however, were absent from the college population. Perhaps due to the poverty and chaos of their families, such youths are not likely to attend college. Alternatively, perhaps traumatized shooters reach their breaking point sooner than other shooters. Even among the aberrant adult shooters, the two traumatized individuals—James Wilson and Patrick Purdy—committed their attacks at nineteen and twenty-four. In contrast, there were shooters with psychopathic and/or psychotic traits who went on rampages in their thirties, forties, fifties, and sixties.

Over half of the shooters in the entire sample had psychotic features.

Figure 10.5 shows the percentages of the three types of shooters. In my sample, 52 percent had psychotic features, 35 percent had psychopathic features, and 25 percent were traumatized (these numbers total more than 100 percent because six shooters had features of two types). The frequency of mental illness among school shooters is often overlooked or minimized, yet over half had symptoms of schizophrenia or schizotypal personality disorder. This highlights the importance of early detection and intervention for people suffering from psychosis.

The rate of psychosis was higher in the two populations of older shooters. This makes sense because schizophrenia typically has an adult onset. In fact, 91 percent of aberrant adult shooters, and 62 percent of college shooters, had psychotic features. In contrast, only 29 percent of secondary school shooters were psychotic.

I categorized six shooters as belonging to two types—three each among college and aberrant adult shooters. Five of the six combined

Figure 10.5: **Percentage of Shooters by Type**

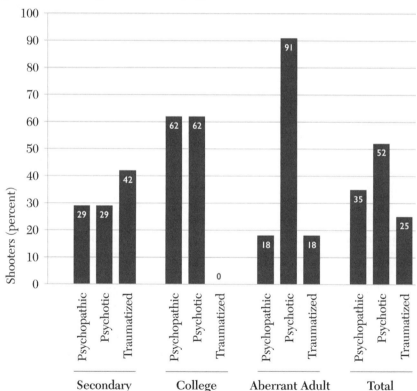

Note: the percentages for college, aberrant adult, and total shooters add up to more than 100% because of shooters who fit in more than one type.

features of psychotic and psychopathic shooters; one was both psychotic and traumatized.

Some shooters, rather than fully belonging to two types, may warrant a primary as well as a secondary classification. For example, Alvaro Castillo, Charles Whitman, Marc Lépine, and Wayne Lo all grew up with domestic violence, physical abuse, or harsh discipline. I did not categorize them as traumatized because it is not clear how much violence they witnessed or endured and what impact this had on them. Furthermore, their families did not have the extreme dysfunction that characterized the families of traumatized shooters. Finally, their psychopathic or psychotic features appeared to best illuminate the dynamics that drove them to violence. Nonetheless, in addition to their primary categorizations as psychotic or psychopathic, they might warrant a secondary identification as traumatized.

OTHER OBSERVATIONS

There were dramatic differences between random vs. targeted college attackers across multiple domains.

As noted above, random college shooters caused five times the casualties of targeted attackers. Another significant difference is that the average age of random college shooters was twenty-three, whereas the average age of targeted shooters was forty-five. Not only were targeted shooters older, but most of them had children and were financially responsible for themselves or their families. Thus, educational and occupational failures loomed larger for them than for the random shooters. Furthermore, two targeted attackers had spouses who had left them and taken their children. Between their familial, occupational, and educational failures, their lives were falling apart in multiple domains, increasing their rage and desperation.

Their desperation manifested in their preattack behavior. All six were belligerent, abrasive, and entitled with administrators and faculty. All six waged extensive grievance campaigns within their universities, often going outside appropriate channels to seek attention and support for their causes. Three of the six sued their universities, and one threatened to sue. Three took their causes outside the university to the media or government agencies. Five of the six threatened violence, causing faculty or administrators to fear for their safety.

In contrast, random shooters did not have comparable financial responsibilities, and none had children. They also kept a lower profile on campus. The warning signs among random shooters varied, but none had long-term grievances, sued their schools, contacted the media, or stirred up fear to the extent the targeted attackers did. Unfortunately, though the random shooters exhibited fewer warning signs, they were far more deadly than targeted attackers.

Table 10.3 illustrates the differences in preattack circumstances and behavior between random and targeted attackers.

Table 10.3: **College Shooters: Random vs Targeted Attackers**

	Had children	Faced financial crisis	Abrasive behavior w/ staff	Grievance campaign	Sued (or threatened to sue)	Sought external publicity	Violent threats	Students/ staff afraid
RANDOM:								
Whitman								
Lo							X	X
Cho								X
Kazmierczak								
Saari								
TARGETED:								
Lu		X	X	X	(X)	X		
Fabrikant	X	X	X	X	X	X	X	X
Odighizuwa	X	X	X	X	X[a]		X	X
Flores	X	X	X	X			X	X
Halder		X	X	X	X[b]	X	X	X
Bishop	X	X	X	X	X		X	X

a Odighizuwa had sued a previous employer (not Appalachian Law School).

b Besides a lawsuit at Case Western reserve University, Halder had also sued past employers or potential employers.

Psychopathic shooters blamed their victims more than psychotic and traumatized shooters did.

Psychopaths often justify their behavior by blaming their victims. For example, during his attack Eric Harris claimed he was getting revenge, blaming students for their own deaths as he gleefully and sadistically killed people who had never done him any harm. Similarly, Gang Lu believed he made the world a better place by killing people who denied him a prize. Valery Fabrikant was proud that he killed four "scoundrels" in his department, and Robert Flores justified murdering his professors because they had given him poor grades. In the eyes of these killers, their victims were to blame for their own deaths.

The appalling nature of this attitude is particularly notable when compared to the attitudes of other shooters. For example, Jamie Rouse had a long history of physical and emotional abuse. He grew up with violence and chronic instability. Despite this, he did not rationalize his behavior or consider his attack justified. In fact, he suffered horribly after his rampage. He repeatedly tried to kill himself, and when his mother tried to comfort him, he said, "Mama, people are dead because of me."

Similarly, Mitchell Johnson, who had a violent, abusive father and had been raped again and again for years, did not try to excuse his actions by pointing to his history of abuse. He said, "I don't look at myself as a victim. I look at myself as, you know, having done a crime. . . . Am I a victim? No."[15]

Despite being psychotic, Michael Carneal was sufficiently in touch with reality to be devastated by his attack. He repeatedly tried to kill himself, commenting, "I thought if I killed myself I would make the world a better place."[16] Similarly, after murdering his parents, Kip Kinkel was full of anguish and wrote, "I'm so sorry. I am a horrible son. I wish I had been aborted."[17] Luke Woodham said, "If they could give the death penalty in this, I deserve it. I'm guilty."[18]

What these cases illustrate is that shooters who were victimized by abuse or devastated by mental illness accepted responsibility for their actions. They did not blame their schizophrenia, their abusers, their victims, or anybody else. In contrast, the psychopathic shooters justified murdering innocent people. The psychopaths believed they made the world a better place by killing people; other shooters thought the world would be better off if they were dead.

Psychopathic shooters were most likely to shoot at police.

Among the three psychological types, 35 percent of psychopathic perpetrators fired on the police, compared to 17 percent of psychotic and 17 percent of traumatized shooters (one shooter was psychotic and psychopathic and was counted in both categories). Because psychopathic shooters tend to be both fearless and hostile toward authorities, it is not surprising that they most often attacked law enforcement officers.

Female school shooters resembled male shooters on multiple dimensions but had fewer external influences.

Because female school shooters are rare, it is interesting to compare them to male shooters. The four females in this sample fit within the psychological typology previously established among male shooters. The females were either psychopathic (Brenda Spencer), psychotic (Jillian Robbins), or both (Laurie Dann and Amy Bishop). Female shooters appeared in each of the three populations (secondary school, college, aberrant adult) and engaged in both random and targeted attacks.

The female perpetrators shared characteristics with male shooters. They had relatives in the military (Spencer and Robbins) and in education (Spencer, Dann, Robbins, and Bishop). They had military failure (Robbins), educational or occupational failure (Spencer, Dann, Robbins, and Bishop), marital failure (Dann and Robbins), and biological challenges (Spencer and Dann).

They differed from males in the relative lack of external influences. Whereas male shooters often were attracted to Nazism, Nietzsche's philosophy, Satanism, mass murderers, serial killers, or other school shooters, none of the females had role models or ideologies. Similarly, apart from Spencer's pleasure in seeing police get killed in television shows, there was apparently no interest in violent media. Also, Spencer was the only female shooter with peer encouragement to kill. Finally, based on available information, none of the female shooters was traumatized, and none appears to have endured significant peer harassment.

School shooters in other countries resemble those in the United States.

The ten international perpetrators included in this sample shared many characteristics with American shooters. They fit the typology as either psychotic, psychopathic, or both. Interestingly, no foreign shooters were traumatized. Many had features that were common among

American shooters: romantic rejections, relatives in the military, military failures, relatives in education, educational failures, biological challenges, peer harassment, and external influences—such as peer encouragement, role models, and ideologies.

Nonschool shooters, such as Jared Loughner and James Holmes, share numerous features with school shooters.

Though Jared Loughner and James Holmes were not school shooters, they were students shortly before their attacks. In fact, both had grudges against their schools and could well have attacked them. Instead, Loughner shot Gabrielle Giffords and eighteen others in Tucson, Arizona, in 2011, and Holmes attacked a movie theater in Aurora, Colorado, in 2012.

These two killers share many features with school shooters. For example, Jared Loughner had two grandfathers who had served in the military. In addition, he applied to the army but was rejected.[19] He also had major academic failures; he dropped out of high school and was asked to leave Pima Community College due to his bizarre and frightening behavior. He had run-ins with police regarding drugs and vandalism,[20] as well as five encounters with campus police.[21] He also was fired from at least five jobs and a volunteer position.[22]

James Holmes had relatives in both education and the military. A grandfather served in the armed forces and later became a schoolteacher, and a grandmother was a school librarian. In addition, Holmes's father conducted research for the navy and the marines. Though Holmes's father did not work in education, he had achieved a high level of academic success, earning three degrees from prestigious universities. His successes contrasted sharply with Holmes's failure when he dropped out of his PhD program at the University of Colorado.[23]

Both Loughner and Holmes appear to have functioned well through most of their lives, experiencing psychological deterioration as young adults. This suggests that, like Kimveer Gill, they had adult-onset schizophrenia. Loughner became socially bizarre and Holmes socially withdrawn. Loughner and Holmes also had external influences. Loughner was drawn to Hitler and had a bizarre political ideology. Holmes appeared to have been influenced by Batman movies. They both abused substances, and both suffered romantic failures.

The attacks by Loughner and Holmes are particularly hard to fathom. They both were hostile toward the schools they had recently attended but conducted attacks elsewhere. Why they did not commit rampages at their schools remains a mystery.

CONCLUSION

At first glance, school shooters may all look alike—angry, alienated youths who go to school with guns and kill people. A closer look at the perpetrators, however, reveals both their diversity and the complexity of their circumstances. Although school shootings might appear incomprehensible, in-depth analysis brings to light a web of factors and motives that propelled the shooters into violence. Dividing the perpetrators into meaningful groups allows patterns to emerge that would otherwise remain hidden. It is my hope that the information provided in this book will help us as a society to keep our schools and communities safe, because every life lost to violence is one life too many.

NOTES

2. PSYCHOPATHIC SECONDARY
SCHOOL SHOOTERS

1. Robert Hare, *Without Conscience: The Disturbing World of the Psychopaths Among Us* (New York: Guilford, 1999).

2. Theodore Millon and Roger Davis, "Ten Subtypes of Psychopathy," in *Psychopathy: Antisocial, Criminal, and Violent Behavior*, ed. Theodore Millon et al., 161–70 (New York: Guilford, 1998).

3. Samuel Yochelson and Stanton Samenow, *The Criminal Personality, Volume I: A Profile for Change* (New York: Jason Aronson, 1976), 261.

4. Chris Cobb and Bob Avery, *The Rape of a Normal Mind* (Markham, Ontario: PaperJacks, 1977), 160–61. Unless otherwise noted, information on Poulin is from Cobb and Avery.

5. Cobb and Avery, *The Rape*, 39.

6. Cobb and Avery, *The Rape*, 63.

7. Cobb and Avery, *The Rape*, 30–31.

8. Cobb and Avery, *The Rape*, 60–61.

9. Cobb and Avery, *The Rape*, 39.

10. Cobb and Avery, *The Rape*, 156.

11. Cobb and Avery, *The Rape*, 60.

12. Cobb and Avery, *The Rape*, 62.

13. Cobb and Avery, *The Rape*, 62.

14. Cobb and Avery, *The Rape*, 61.

15. Cobb and Avery, *The Rape*, 61.

16. Cobb and Avery, *The Rape*, 66.

17. "Coroners Try to Unravel Details of Shootings," *Leader-Post* (Regina, Saskatchewan), October 30, 1975, 27.

18. Cobb and Avery, *The Rape*, 54.

19. Theodore Millon, *Disorders of Personality: DSM-IV and Beyond*, 2nd ed. (New York: John Wiley & Sons, 1996), 453.

20. J. Reid Meloy, *The Psychopathic Mind: Origins, Dynamics, and Treatment* (Northvale, NJ: Jason Aronson, 1992), 65.

21. Eric Hart, *Does Anyone Like Mondays? The Brenda Spencer Murder Case* (N.p.: Hart Publishing, LLC, 2012).

22. Jonathan Fast, *Ceremonial Violence: A Psychological Explanation of School Shootings* (New York: Overlook, 2008), 69.

23. Fast, *Ceremonial Violence*, 71.

24. Fast, *Ceremonial Violence*, 72.

25. Fast, *Ceremonial Violence*, 72.

26. Hart, *Does Anyone Like Mondays?* 34–35.

27. Hart, *Does Anyone Like Mondays?* 22.

28. Hart, *Does Anyone Like Mondays?* 26–27.

29. Hart, *Does Anyone Like Mondays?* 34.

30. Hart, *Does Anyone Like Mondays?* 34.

31. Hart, *Does Anyone Like Mondays?* 36.

32. Hart, *Does Anyone Like Mondays?* 82.

33. Hart, *Does Anyone Like Mondays?* 70.

34. Hart, *Does Anyone Like Mondays?* 77.

35. Hart, *Does Anyone Like Mondays?* 24.

36. Hart, *Does Anyone Like Mondays?* 82.

37. Hart, *Does Anyone Like Mondays?* 47.

38. Hart, *Does Anyone Like Mondays?* 78.

39. Fast, *Ceremonial Violence*, 81.

40. Fast, *Ceremonial Violence*, 81–82.

41. Hart, *Does Anyone Like Mondays?* 151.

42. Fast, *Ceremonial Violence*, 82.

43. Hart, *Does Anyone Like Mondays?* 79.

44. Martha Stout, *The Sociopath Next Door* (New York: Three Rivers Press, 2005), 107.

45. Millon and Davis, "Ten Subtypes," 164.

46. Peggy Andersen, "Loukaitis' Mother Testifies She Told Him about Suicide Plans," *Moscow-Pullman Daily News* (Moscow, Idaho, and Pullman, Washington), September 8, 1997, 3.

47. "Loukaitis' Parents Testify about Pre-shootings Days," *Ellensburg Daily Record*, September 9, 1997, 3.

48. "Loukaitis' Parents Testify."

49. William Miller, "'Cold Fury' in Loukaitis Scared Dad, Father Says He Was Horrified by Change after Shootings," *Spokesman-Review* (Spokane, Washington), September 27, 1996.

50. "How Barry 'Pulled Away': Loukaitises Describe What Prompted Changes in Boy's Behavior," *Wenatchee World* (Washington), September 27, 1996, 2.

51. Peggy Andersen, "His Classmates Say Barry Loukaitis Knew He Was a Killer," *Spokesman-Review* (Spokane, Washington), September 16, 1997, 25.

52. Lynda V. Mapes, "Bloody Movie, Random Violence Thrilled Loukaitis, Classmates Say," *Spokesman-Review* (Spokane, Washington), August 28, 1997, A1.

53. Bonnie Harris, "Witnesses Say Loukaitis Vowed to Kill, Prosecution Tries to Show Premeditation in Rampage," *Spokesman-Review* (Spokane, Washington), April 17, 1996, A1.

54. Harris, "Witnesses Say Loukaitis Vowed to Kill."

55. Harris, "Witnesses Say Loukaitis Vowed to Kill."

56. "School Shootings: Classmate Says Loukaitis Expected to Kill," *Kitsap Sun* (Washington), September 16, 1997, http://www.kitsapsun.com/news/1997/sep/16/school-shootings-classmate-says-loukaitis-to/?print=1.

57. "On Tape, Moses Lake Boy Talks about School Rampage," *Seattle Times*, April 18, 1996, http://community.seattletimes.nwsource.com/archive/?date=19960418&slug=2324775.

58. *State of Washington v. Barry D. Loukaitis*, No. 17007-1-III, (1999), 2, available online at http://www.schoolshooters.info.

59. Bonnie Harris, "Detective Says He Saw No Remorse in Loukaitis," *Spokesman-Review* (Spokane, Washington), April 16, 1996, A1, http://www.spokesman.com/stories/1996/apr/16/detective-says-he-saw-no-remorse-in-loukaitis/.

60. Lynda V. Mapes, "Loukaitis' Dark Moods Recalled," *Spokesman-Review* (Spokane, Washington), September 4, 1997, B1.

61. Mapes, "Loukaitis' Dark Moods."

62. *State of Washington v. Barry D. Loukaitis*, 3.

63. Lynda V. Mapes, "Loukaitis' Mom Tells Court about Suicidal Moods Defense Portrays Teen as Disturbed by Parents' Broken Marriage," *Spokesman-Review* (Spokane, Washington), September 9, 1997, http://www.spokesman.com/stories/1997/sep/09/loukaitis-mom-tells-court-about-suicidal-moods/.

64. William Miller, "Psychiatrist Says Loukaitis Snapped before Rampage," *Spokesman-Review* (Spokane, Washington), September 25, 1996, A1, http://www.spokesman.com/stories/1996/sep/25/psychiatrist-says-loukaitis-snapped-before/.

65. Millon and Davis, "Ten Subtypes," 164.

66. Millon and Davis, "Ten Subtypes," 168.

67. Sandy Davis and Jeff Porter, "Illness Faked, the Weapons Were Gathered," *Arkansas Democrat-Gazette*, March 26, 1998, http://www.arkansasonline.com/news/1998/mar/26/illness-faked-weapons-were-gathered/?print; Katherine Newman, *Rampage: The Social Roots of School Shootings* (New York: Basic Books, 2004), 39.

68. John Kifner, "From Wild Talk and Friendship to Five Deaths in a Schoolyard," *New York Times*, March 29, 1998, 1, http://www.nytimes.com/1998/03/29/us/from-wild-talk-and-friendship-to-five-deaths-in-a-schoolyard.html.

69. David Usborne, "Jonesboro Massacre: Two Macho Boys with 'a Lot of Killing to Do,'" *Independent* (London), March 27, 1998, http://www.

independent.co.uk/news/jonesboro-massacre-two-macho-boys-with-a-lot-of-killing-to-do-1152649.html.

70. Newman, *Rampage*, 40.

71. Sandy Davis and Linda Satter, "Differing Views Depict Character of Suspect, 11," *Arkansas Democrat-Gazette*, March 29, 1998, http://www.arkansasonline.com/news/1998/mar/29/differing-views-depict-character-suspect-11/.

72. Newman, *Rampage*, 40.

73. Newman, *Rampage*, 40.

74. Cybelle Fox, Wendy D. Roth, and Katherine Newman, "A Deadly Partnership: Lethal Violence in an Arkansas Middle School," in *Deadly Lessons: Understanding Lethal School Violence*, ed. National Research Council, 113 (Washington, DC: National Academies Press, 2003).

75. Fox, Roth, and Newman, "A Deadly Partnership," 112.

76. Newman, *Rampage*, 40.

77. Peter Langman, *Why Kids Kill: Inside the Minds of School Shooters* (New York: Palgrave Macmillan, 2009), 23.

78. Andy Lines and Emily Compston, "In Dock with a Smile on His Face: Boys Charged with Jonesboro Killings Make First Court Appearance," *Mirror* (Britain), March 26, 1998.

79. Millon and Davis, "Ten Subtypes," 162.

80. Peter Langman, "Themes in the Writings of Eric Harris," http://www.schoolshooters.info. Please note that the Jefferson County Sheriff's Office (JCSO) has released over twenty thousand pages of documents relating to the attack at Columbine High School. In some cases, I cite the specific pages in these original documents. In other cases, for ease of finding the information, I cite other documents that are based on the original material, such as "Eric Harris's Journal, April 10, 1998–April 3, 1999" and "Themes in the Writing of Eric Harris." These documents cite the page numbers from the original JCSO documents for those who want to see the source material. Both the original material and the edited documents are available at http://www.schoolshooters.info.

81. Langman, "Themes in the Writings of Eric Harris," 4.

82. Eric Harris, "Eric Harris's Journal, April 10, 1998–April 3, 1999," transcr. and annot. Peter Langman, available online at http://www.schoolshooters.info.

83. Harris, "Eric Harris's Journal," 8.

84. Harris, "Eric Harris's Journal," 11.

85. Langman, "Themes in the Writings of Eric Harris," 4.

86. Janet Warren, Robert R. Hazelwood, and Park Dietz, "The Sexually Sadistic Serial Killer," in *Serial and Mass Murder: Theory, Research, and Practice*, ed. Thomas O'Reilly-Fleming, 88 (Toronto: Canadian Scholars' Press, 1996).

87. Harris, "Eric Harris's Journal," 9.

88. Harris, "Eric Harris's Journal," 8–9.

89. Harris, "Eric Harris's Journal," 9.

90. Harris, "Eric Harris's Journal," 9.

91. Jefferson County Sheriff's Office, "Columbine Documents: JC-001-025923 through JC-001-026859" (Jefferson County, CO: Jefferson County Sheriff's Office, n.d.), 26,343, available online at http://www.schoolshooters.info.

92. Nancy Gibbs and Timothy Roche, "The Columbine Tapes," *Time Magazine*, December 20, 1999, http://content.time.com/time/magazine/article/0,9171,992873,00.html.

93. Dave Cullen, *Columbine* (New York: Twelve, 2009), 227.

94. Erich Fromm, *The Anatomy of Human Destructiveness* (New York: Holt, Rinehart and Winston, 1973), 292.

95. Jefferson County Sheriff's Office (JCSO), "Columbine Documents: Columbine High School, 99-7625; Library Injured, A-1" (Jefferson County, CO: Jefferson County Sheriff's Office, n.d.), 445 and 556, available online at http://www.schoolshooters.info.

96. Jefferson County Sheriff's Office, "Columbine Documents: JC-001-025923 through JC-001-026859," 26,859.

97. Hare, *Without Conscience*, 28.

98. Harris, "Eric Harris's Journal," 5.

99. Langman, "Themes in the Writings of Eric Harris," 6.

100. Harris, "Eric Harris's Journal," 3.

101. Harris, "Eric Harris's Journal," 1–2.

102. Millon and Davis, "Ten Subtypes," 166.

103. Millon and Davis, "Ten Subtypes," 166.

104. Brooks Brown and Rob Merritt, *No Easy Answers: The Truth behind Death at Columbine* (New York: Lantern, 2002), 72, 93.

105. Millon and Davis, "Ten Subtypes," 166.

106. Millon and Davis, "Ten Subtypes," 169.

107. Charles Wallace, "Massacre in Erfurt," *Time Europe* 159, no. 18 (2002): 24.

108. Wallace, "Massacre in Erfurt," 24.

109. Dietmar Henning, "Germany: Two Years Since the Erfurt School Shooting," *World Socialist Web Site*, May 11, 2004, http://www.wsws.org/en/articles/2004/05/erfu-m11.html.

110. Thomas Schadt and Knut Beulich, *Amok in der Schule—Die Tat des Robert Steinhäuser* (film), 2004, part 1 available online at https://www.youtube.com/watch?v=dCNtVUII6sc, part 2 at https://www.youtube.com/watch?v=7tapQBivtO8, part 3 at https://www.youtube.com/watch?v=9scsLtoH-IU, part 4 at https://www.youtube.com/watch?v=FNCkP8cpKWE, part 5 at https://www.youtube.com/watch?v=Yc5QMaZKbGI, and part 6 at https://www.youtube.com/watch?v=dwkpAXOEWvU.

111. Allan Hall, "A Bright but Troubled Boy Who Wanted to Exact a Terrible Revenge," *Scotland on Sunday* (Edinburgh), April 28, 2002, http://www.scotsman.com/news/world/a-bright-but-troubled-boy-who-wanted-to-exact-a-terrible-revenge-1-1372744.

112. Matthew Beard, "Unsuspecting Parents Wished Gunman 'Good Luck' before School Killings," *Independent* (London), April 29, 2002.

113. Heinz Gasser, Malte Creutzfeldt, Markus Näher, Rulolph Rainer, and Peter Wickler, *Bericht der Kommission Gutenberg-Gymnasium* (Erfurt, Ger.: Freistaat Thüringen, 2004), 297.

114. Yochelson and Samenow, *The Criminal Personality*, 145.

115. Yochelson and Samenow, *The Criminal Personality*, 262.

116. Gasser et al., *Bericht der Kommission*, 298.

117. Schadt and Beulich, *Amok in der Schule*.

118. Gasser et al., *Bericht der Kommission*, 16–17, 299–303.

119. John Hooper, "Killer's Secret behind Revenge Attack," *Guardian*, April 29, 2002.

120. Gasser et al., *Bericht der Kommission*, 304.

121. Gasser et al., *Bericht der Kommission*, 12.

122. Gasser et al., *Bericht der Kommission*, 118, 334.

123. Wallace, "Massacre in Erfurt."

124. Millon and Davis, "Ten Subtypes," 162.

125. Tomislav Mamic, "Waffen waren in der Familie nichts Ungewöhnliches," *WAZ*, March 13, 2009, http://www.derwesten.de/ nachrichten/waffen-waren-in-der-familie-nichts-ungewoehnliches-id525374. html.

126. Julia Jüttner, "Sie haben Tim alles dekauft, was er wollte," *Spiegel Online*, March 12, 2009, http://ml.spiegel.de/article.do?id=613025.

127. Mamic, "Waffen waren."

128. Bojan Pancevskiin, "Mass Killer 'Rejected' by Girl at Party," *Sunday Times* (Britain), March 15, 2009.

129. Pancevskiin, "Mass Killer 'Rejected.'"

130. State Court of Stuttgart, Criminal Division 18, "Criminal Case against Jorg Wilhelm Kretschmer, born January 12, 1959, in Stuttgart," Case Number 18 KLs 112 Js 21916/09 (Stuttgart, Ger.: State Court of Stuttgart), 102.

131. Petra Von Bornhöft, Klaus Brinkbäumer, Ulrike Demmer, Wiebke Hollersen, Simone Kaiser, Sebastian Knauer, Ansbert Kneip, Sven Röbel, Samiha Shafy, Holger Stark, and Katja Thimm, "113 Kugeln Kalte Wut," *Der Spiegel*, March 16, 2009, http://www.spiegel.de/spiegel/print/d-64628264.html.

132. Mamic, "Waffen waren."

133. Von Bornhöft et al., "113 Kugeln Kalte Wut."

134. Udo Andriof, "Prävention, Intervention, Opferhilfe, Medien: Konsequenzen Aus Dem Amoklauf in Winnenden Und Wendlingen Am 11. Marz 2009," Baden-Württemberg.de, 2009.

135. Andriof, "Prävention."

136. Hendrik Vöhringer, "Amoklauf in Winnenden," *Spiegel TV Reportage*, September 19, 2009.

137. Von Bornhöft et al., "113 Kugeln Kalte Wut."

138. State Court of Stuttgart, "Criminal Case against Jorg Wilhelm Kretschmer," 63.

139. "16 Die in Rampage in German School, Towns," *Associated Press*, March 11, 2009, available online at http://www.nbcnews.com/id/29630925/ns/world_news-europe/t/german-school-rampage-happened-seconds/#.U8b8h6jPbhM.

140. Andriof, "Prävention."

141. Vöhringer, "Amoklauf in Winnenden."

142. Von Bornhöft et al., "113 Kugeln Kalte Wut."

143. State Court of Stuttgart, "Criminal Case against Jorg Wilhelm Kretsch-mer," 47.

144. State Court of Stuttgart, "Criminal Case against Jorg Wilhelm Kretsch-mer," 45.

145. State Court of Stuttgart, "Criminal Case against Jorg Wilhelm Kretsch-mer," 65.

146. Andriof, "Prävention."

147. Pancevskiin, "Mass Killer 'Rejected.'"

148. Carter Dougherty, "Portrait of German Gunman Emerges," *New York Times*, March 14, 2009, http://www.nytimes.com/2009/03/14/world/europe/14germany.html.

149. "School Shooting Hostage Speaks Out: 'Tim Kretschmer Told Me Was Killing People for Fun,'" *Bild.com*, April 2009, http://www.bild.de/news/bild-english/news/tim-kretschmer-told-me-he-was-killing-for-fun-7725950.bild.html.

3. PSYCHOTIC SECONDARY SCHOOL SHOOTERS

1. E. Fuller Torrey, *Surviving Schizophrenia: A Manual for Families, Patients, and Providers* (New York: HarperCollins, 2006), 2.

2. Torrey, *Surviving Schizophrenia*, 1.

3. Torrey, *Surviving Schizophrenia*, 10.

4. Nancy McWilliams, *Psychoanalytic Diagnosis: Understanding Personality Structure in the Clinical Process*, 2nd ed. (New York: Guilford, 2011), 60.

5. American Psychiatric Association, *Diagnostic and Statistical Manual of Mental Disorders, Fourth Edition, Text Revision* (Arlington: American Psychiatric Association, 2000), 304.

6. American Foundation for Suicide Prevention, "Facts and Figures: Suicide Deaths," http://www.afsp.org/understanding-suicide/facts-and-figures.

7. Jon Bellini, *Child's Prey* (New York: Kensington, 2001), 127.

8. "A Community and Its Shooter," *Courier-Journal* (Louisville), December 8, 1998.

9. Lisa Popyk, "'I Knew It Wouldn't Be Right,'" *Cincinnati Post*, November 9, 1998.

10. Bellini, *Child's Prey*, 36.

11. Bellini, *Child's Prey*, 87.

12. "A Community and Its Shooter."

13. "Teen Killer Sobs as Confession Played in Court," CNN.com, June 11, 1998, http://www.cnn.com/US/9806/11/school.shooting/.

14. "Teen Killer Sobs."

15. Popyk, "'I Knew It Wouldn't Be Right.'"

16. "Teen-Ager Accused of Killing Says He Got Demons' Orders," *New York Times*, June 5, 1998, http://www.nytimes.com/1998/06/05/us/teen-ager-accused-of-killing-says-he-got-demons-orders.html.

17. Bellini, *Child's Prey*, 64, 68.

18. *Luke T. Woodham v. State of Mississippi*, NO. 1998-KA-01479-SCT (1998), 4, available online at http://www.schoolshooters.info.

19. Popyk, "'I Knew It Wouldn't Be Right.'"

20. "Conspiracy Charges are Dropped in Mississippi School Shootings," *New York Times*, July 23, 1998, http://www.nytimes.com/1998/07/23/us/conspiracy-charges-are-dropped-in-mississippi-school-shootings.html.

21. "Teen Apologizes for School Killings," *Associated Press*, November 11, 1997.

22. Bellini, *Child's Prey*, 205, 76.

23. Bellini, *Child's Prey*, 109.

24. American Psychiatric Association, *Diagnostic and Statistical Manual of Mental Disorders*, 697–98.

25. Bellini, *Child's Prey*, 154.

26. Bellini, *Child's Prey*, 45.

27. "A Community and Its Shooter."

28. Katherine Newman, *Rampage: The Social Roots of School Shootings* (New York: Basic Books, 2004), 24.

29. Dewey Cornell, *School Violence: Fears Versus Facts* (Mahwah, NJ: Lawrence Erlbaum, 2006), 46.

30. Cornell, *School Violence*, 46.

31. Newman, *Rampage*, 26.

32. Cornell, *School Violence*, 41.

33. Cornell, *School Violence*, 41.

34. Newman, *Rampage*, 134.

35. Newman, *Rampage*, 64.

36. Newman, *Rampage*, 98.

37. David Harding, Jal Mehta, and Katherine Newman, "No Exit: Mental Illness, Marginality, and School Violence in West Paducah, Kentucky," in *Deadly Lessons: Understanding Lethal School Violence*, ed. National Research Council (Washington, DC: National Academies Press, 2003), 146.

38. Cornell, *School Violence*, 42.

39. Harding, Mehta, and Newman, "No Exit," 150.

40. "Boy Says He Was 'Mad at the World' When He Shot Classmates," *Oak Ridger Online* (Tennessee), April 6, 2000.

41. Newman, *Rampage*, 31.

42. Jim Adams and James Malone, "Outsider's Destructive Behavior Spiraled into Violence," *Courier-Journal* (Louisville), March 18, 1999, 17A.

43. Adams and Malone, "Outsider's Destructive Behavior."

44. Cornell, *School Violence*, 42.

45. *Commonwealth of Kentucky v. Michael Carneal*, Nos. 2006-SC-000653-DG, 2007-SC-000203-DG (2008), available online at http://www.schoolshooters.info.

46. William DeJong, Joel Epstein, and Thomas Hart, "Bad Things Happen in Good Communities: The Rampage Shooting in Edinboro, Pennsylvania, and Its Aftermath," in *Deadly Lessons: Understanding Lethal School Violence*, ed. National Research Council (Washington, DC: National Academies Press, 2003), 77.

47. DeJong, Epstein, and Hart, "Bad Things Happen," 80.

48. DeJong, Epstein, and Hart, "Bad Things Happen," 77.

49. DeJong, Epstein, and Hart, "Bad Things Happen," 73.

50. "A Portrait of Conflict," *Erie Times-News*, March 7, 1999.

51. DeJong, Epstein, and Hart, "Bad Things Happen," 86.

52. DeJong, Epstein, and Hart, "Bad Things Happen," 86.

53. DeJong, Epstein, and Hart, "Bad Things Happen," 85.

54. DeJong, Epstein, and Hart, "Bad Things Happen," 87.

55. DeJong, Epstein, and Hart, "Bad Things Happen," 82.

56. DeJong, Epstein, and Hart, "Bad Things Happen," 78.

57. Joseph Lieberman, *School Shootings: What Every Parent and Educator Needs to Know to Protect Our Children* (Kensington: New York, 2008), 67.

58. Lieberman, *School Shootings*, 167–69.

59. Elisa Swanson, "Comment: 'Killers Start Sad and Crazy'; Mental Illness and the Betrayal of Kipland Kinkel," *Oregon Law Review* 79, no. 4 (2000): 1094, available online at http://law.uoregon.edu/org/olrold/archives/79/79olr1081.pdf.

60. Lieberman, *School Shootings*, 119–20.

61. Frontline, "Dr. Orin Bolstad's Testimony," *Frontline: The Killer at Thurston High*, http://www.pbs.org/wgbh/pages/frontline/shows/kinkel/trial/bolstad.html.

62. Frontline, "Dr. Orin Bolstad's Testimony."

63. Frontline, "Dr. Orin Bolstad's Testimony."

64. Swanson, "Comment: 'Killers Start Sad and Crazy,'" 1083.

65. Frontline, "Transcript," *Frontline: The Killer at Thurston High*, January 18, 2000, http://www.pbs.org/wgbh/pages/frontline/shows/kinkel/etc/script.html.

66. Lieberman, *School Shootings*, 165.

67. Lieberman, *School Shootings*, 26.

68. Lieberman, *School Shootings*, 27.

69. Lieberman, *School Shootings*, 26.

70. Mike Anton and Lisa Ryckman, "In Hindsight, Signs to Killings Obvious," *Denver Rocky Mountain News*, May 2, 1999.

71. American Psychiatric Association, *Diagnostic and Statistical Manual of Mental Disorders*, 718.

72. Theodore Millon, *Disorders of Personality: DSM-IV and Beyond*, 2nd ed. (New York: John Wiley & Sons, 1996), 626.

73. Peter Langman, ed., "Jefferson County Sheriff's Office Columbine Documents Organized by Theme," 1, 3, 10, 23, available online at http://www.schoolshooters.info. Please note that the Jefferson County Sheriff's Office (JCSO) has released over twenty thousand pages of documents relating to the attack at Columbine High School. In some cases, I cite the specific pages in these original documents. In other cases, for ease of finding the information, I cite other documents that are based on the original material, such as "Dylan Klebold's Journal" or "The Search for Truth at Columbine." These documents cite the page numbers from the original JCSO documents for those who want to see the source material. Both the original material and the edited documents are available online at http://www.schoolshooters.info.

74. Dylan Klebold, "Dylan Klebold's Journal and Other Writings," transcr. and annot. Peter Langman (n.d.), 2, available online at http://www.schoolshooters.info.

75. Klebold, "Dylan Klebold's Journal," 2.

76. Klebold, "Dylan Klebold's Journal," 6.

77. Klebold, "Dylan Klebold's Journal," 6.

78. Klebold, "Dylan Klebold's Journal," 8.

79. Klebold, "Dylan Klebold's Journal," 11.

80. Peter Langman, *Why Kids Kill: Inside the Minds of School Shooters* (New York: Palgrave Macmillan, 2009), 66–69.

81. Peter Langman, "The Search for Truth at Columbine," 2008, http://www.schoolshooters.info.

82. Klebold, "Dylan Klebold's Journal," 2.

83. Klebold, "Dylan Klebold's Journal," 9.

84. A Columbine Site, "Basement Tapes," n.d., http://www.acolumbinesite.com/quotes1.html.

85. Klebold, "Dylan Klebold's Journal," 3.

86. Klebold, "Dylan Klebold's Journal," 3.

87. Klebold, "Dylan Klebold's Journal," 2.

88. *State of North Carolina v. Alvaro Rafael Castillo*, No. COA10-814 (2010), available online at http://www.schoolshooters.info.

89. *State of North Carolina v. Alvaro Rafael Castillo*, 4.

90. *State of North Carolina v. Alvaro Rafael Castillo*, 5.

91. Anne Blythe, "Castillo's Family Says Father Was Violent," *NewsObserver* (North Carolina), August 11, 2009, http://www.newsobserver.com/2009/08/11/75904/castillos-family-says-father-was.html.

92. Beth Karas, "Insanity Defense Takes Center Stage," CNN.com, August 12, 2009, http://insession.blogs.cnn.com/2009/08/12/insanity-defense-takes-center-stage/.

93. *State of North Carolina v. Alvaro Rafael Castillo*, 5.

94. Matthew Burns, "Accused School Shooter's Mother, Sister Testify," WRAL.com, August 11, 2009, http://www.wral.com/news/local/story/5770869/.

95. *State of North Carolina v. Alvaro Rafael Castillo*, 5.

96. *State of North Carolina v. Alvaro Rafael Castillo*, 6.

97. Kelly Hinchcliffe, "Accused Shooter's Journal: 'Planning Your Suicide Is So Fun,'" WRAL.com, August 19, 2009, http://www.wral.com/news/local/story/5815701/.

98. *State of North Carolina v. Alvaro Rafael Castillo*, 11.

99. *State of North Carolina v. Alvaro Rafael Castillo*, 6–7.

100. *State of North Carolina v. Alvaro Rafael Castillo*, 12.

101. *State of North Carolina v. Alvaro Rafael Castillo*, 15.

102. Beth Karas, "Defendant's Eerie Words Heard at Murder Trial," CNN.com, August 3, 2009, http://insession.blogs.cnn.com/2009/08/03/defendants-eerie-words-heard-at-murder-trial/.

103. *State of North Carolina v. Alvaro Rafael Castillo*, 16.

104. *State of North Carolina v. Alvaro Rafael Castillo*, 20.

105. *State of North Carolina v. Alvaro Rafael Castillo*, 20.

106. *State of North Carolina v. Alvaro Rafael Castillo*, 21.

107. Pekka-Eric Auvinen, "Pekka-Eric Auvinen Online," n.d., available online at http://www.schoolshooters.info.

108. Finland Ministry of Justice, "Jokela School Shooting on 7 November 2007: Report of the Investigation Commission," translation of the original Finish report (Helsinki: Ministry of Justice, Finland, 2009), available online at http://www.schoolshooters.info, 50.

109. Finland Ministry of Justice, "Jokela School Shooting," 46.

110. Tomi Kiilakoski and Atte Oksanen, "Soundtrack of the School Shootings: Cultural Script, Music and Male Rage," *Young* 19, no. 3 (2011): 261–62.

111. Finland Ministry of Justice, "Jokela School Shooting," 50.

112. Atte Oksanen, Johanna Nurmi, Miika Vuori, and Pekka Räsänen, "Jokela: The Social Roots of a School Shooting Tragedy in Finland," in *School Shootings: International Research, Case Studies, and Concepts for Prevention*, ed. Nils Böckler, Thorsten Seeger, Peter Sitzer, and Wilhelm Heitmeyer, 198 (New York: Springer, 2013), 189–216

113. Oksanen et al., "Jokela," 198.

114. Brendan O'Neill, "Rating Humanity: Finland's School Shooting Highlights a Link Between Environmentalism and the Rise of a New Form of Antihumanist Nihilism," *Guardian* (Britain), November 14, 2007, http://www.theguardian.com/commentisfree/2007/nov/14/ratinghumanity.

115. Finland Ministry of Justice, "Jokela School Shooting," 51.

116. Finland Ministry of Justice, "Jokela School Shooting," 115.

117. Finland Ministry of Justice, "Jokela School Shooting," 17.

118. Finland Ministry of Justice, "Jokela School Shooting," 48.

119. Kiilakoski and Oksanen, "Soundtrack of the School Shootings," 262.

120. "Police: Finland Shooter Left Suicide Note," *Associated Press*, November 8, 2007, available online at http://www.nbcnews.com/id/21686096/ns/world_news-europe/t/police-finland-teen-shooter-left-suicide-note/ -. U8d6KKjPbhM.

121. Finland Ministry of Justice, "Jokela School Shooting," 18.

122. Finland Ministry of Justice, "Jokela School Shooting," 49.

123. Tomi Kiilakoski and Atte Oksanen, "Cultural and Peer Influences on Homicidal Violence: A Finnish Perspective," *New Directions for Youth Development* 33, no. 129 (2011): 35, available online at http://www.academia.edu/1130441/Cultural_and_peer_influences_on_homicidal_violence_A_Finnish_perspective.

124. Kiilakoski and Oksanen, "Soundtrack of the School Shootings," 263.

125. Kiilakoski and Oksanen, "Soundtrack of the School Shootings," 264.

126. Kiilakoski and Oksanen, "Cultural and Peer Influences," 37.

127. Kiilakoski and Oksanen, "Soundtrack of the School Shootings," 257.

128. Langman, ed., "Pekka-Eric Auvinen Online."

129. Finland Ministry of Justice, "Jokela School Shooting," 48.

130. "Police: Finland Shooter."

131. Millon, *Disorders of Personality*, 624.

132. Langman, ed., "Pekka-Eric Auvinen Online."

133. Langman, ed., "Pekka-Eric Auvinen Online."

134. Millon, *Disorders of Personality*, 628.

135. Millon, *Disorders of Personality*, 627.

136. Harding, Mehta, and Newman, "No Exit," 147.

137. Lisa Popyk, "Teen Lives Out Murderous Dream," *Cincinnati Post*, November 10, 1998, 1A.

138. "A Portrait of Conflict."

139. Klebold, "Dylan Klebold's Journal," 3.

140. David Shapiro, *Autonomy and Rigid Character* (New York: Basic, 1981), 113.

141. Shapiro, *Autonomy*, 109.

4. TRAUMATIZED SECONDARY SCHOOL SHOOTERS

1. *People of the State of California v. Eric Christopher Houston*, S035190, Napa County Superior Court No. 14311 (2008), available online at http://www.schoolshooters.info. Unless otherwise noted, the information on Houston is from the court case cited here.

2. *People of the State of California v. Eric Christopher Houston*, 112.

3. *People of the State of California v. Eric Christopher Houston*, 113.

4. Jonathan Fast, *Ceremonial Violence: A Psychological Explanation of School Shootings* (New York: Overlook, 2008), 26.

5. *People of the State of California v. Eric Christopher Houston*, 100.

6. *People of the State of California v. Eric Christopher Houston*, 91.

7. *People of the State of California v. Eric Christopher Houston*, 84.

8. *People of the State of California v. Eric Christopher Houston*, 89.

9. *People of the State of California v. Eric Christopher Houston*, 79.

10. Jerry Buckley, "The Tragedy in Room 108: An Angry Teen Killed His Teacher and Forever Changed a Kentucky Town," *US News & World Report*,

October 31, 1993, http://www.usnews.com/news/articles/1993/10/31/the-tragedy-in-room-108.

11. Fast, *Ceremonial Violence*, 28.

12. Fast, *Ceremonial Violence*, 28.

13. Susan Reed, "Reading, Writing, and Murder," *People* 39, no. 23, June 14, 1993, http://www.people.com/people/archive/article/0,,20110610,00.html.

14. Fast, *Ceremonial Violence*, 28.

15. Buckley, "The Tragedy in Room 108."

16. Buckley, "The Tragedy in Room 108."

17. Fast, *Ceremonial Violence*, 28.

18. Lee Mueller, "Jurors Hear Tape of Pennington Confession," *Lexington Herald-Leader*, February 17, 1995, B1.

19. Mueller, "Jurors Hear Tape."

20. Mueller, "Jurors Hear Tape."

21. Chris Poore and Lee Mueller, "Move to Carter School Was Difficult for Teen," *Lexington Herald-Leader*, January 21, 1993, A1.

22. Fast, *Ceremonial Violence*, 28.

23. Lee Mueller, "Pennington's Teacher Was Told to Contact Police, Social Workers," *Lexington Herald-Leader*, February 18, 1995, B1.

24. Mueller, "Pennington's Teacher."

25. Fast, *Ceremonial Violence*, 29.

26. Buckley, "The Tragedy in Room 108."

27. Mueller, "Pennington's Teacher."

28. Buckley, "The Tragedy in Room 108."

29. Buckley, "The Tragedy in Room 108."

30. Richard Meyer, "When the Shooting Stops," *Los Angeles Times*, April 22, 2000, http://articles.latimes.com/2000/apr/22/news/ss-24169.

31. Meyer, "When the Shooting Stops."

32. Meyer, "When the Shooting Stops."

33. 48 Hours, "The Mind of a School Shooter," *CBS News*, April 14, 2004, http://www.cbsnews.com/news/the-mind-of-a-school-shooter/.

34. Meyer, "When the Shooting Stops."

35. Meyer, "When the Shooting Stops."

36. Meyer, "When the Shooting Stops."

37. Meyer, "When the Shooting Stops."

38. Meyer, "When the Shooting Stops."

39. Meyer, "When the Shooting Stops."

40. "The Mind of a School Shooter."

41. "The Mind of a School Shooter."

42. Meyer, "When the Shooting Stops."

43. *Donald Lee Ramsey v. State of Alaska*, 834 P.2d 811 (1992), available online at http://www.schoolshooters.info.

44. 60 Minutes, "Rage: A Look at a Teen Killer," *CBS News*, March 7, 2001, http://www.cbsnews.com/news/rage-a-look-at-a-teen-killer/.

45. Steve Fainaru, "Many Struggle to Put Their World Together," *Boston Globe*, October 20, 1998.

46. Sheila Toomey, "Brothers Testify to Hard Life, Then Ramsey Defense Rests," *Anchorage Daily News*, February 3, 1998, A1.

47. Peter Langman, "Court Cases in the Ramsey Family," n.d., http://www.schoolshooters.info.

48. Steve Fainaru, "Alaska School Murders: A Window on Teen Rage," *Boston Globe*, October 18, 1998.

49. Steve Fainaru, "A Tragedy Was Preceded by Many Overlooked Signals," *Boston Globe*, October 19, 1998.

50. Fainaru, "Alaska School Murders."

51. Fainaru, "Alaska School Murders."

52. Fainaru, "Alaska School Murders."

53. Toomey, "Brothers Testify."

54. Langman, "Court Cases in the Ramsey Family."

55. Fainaru, "Alaska School Murders."

56. Fainaru, "Alaska School Murders."

57. Fainaru, "A Tragedy Was Preceded."

58. Carol Marin, "Portrait of a High School Killer," *60 Minutes* (*CBS News* transcripts), March 6, 2001, http://www.cbsnews.com/news/portrait-of-a-high-school-killer/.

59. Toomey, "Brothers Testify."

60. Fainaru, "Alaska School Murders."

61. Fainaru, "A Tragedy Was Preceded."

62. Jim Clarke, "Teen Gunman Opens Fire in School, Killing Principal, Student," *Associated Press*, February 20, 1997, http://www.apnewsarchive.com/1997/Teen-gunman-opens-fire-in-school-killing-principal-student/id-0aea0da200b450d6d553e36668b5c97b.

63. Fainaru, "A Tragedy Was Preceded."

64. Fainaru, "Alaska School Murders."

65. "Mitchell Johnson Deposition," Craighead County, Arkansas, April 2, 2007, available online at http://www.schoolshooters.info.

66. Katherine Newman, *Rampage: The Social Roots of School Shootings* (New York: Basic, 2004), 12.

67. Newman, *Rampage*, 158.

68. Rick Bragg, "Judge Punishes Arkansas Boys Who Killed 5," *New York Times*, August 12, 1998, http://www.nytimes.com/1998/08/12/us/judge-punishes-arkansas-boys-who-killed-5.html.

69. "Mitchell Johnson Deposition," 104.

70. Newman, *Rampage*, 35.

71. Cybelle Fox, Wendy Roth, and Katherine Newman, "A Deadly Partnership: Lethal Violence in an Arkansas Middle School," in *Deadly Lessons: Understanding Lethal School Violence*, ed. National Research Council, 103 (Washington, DC: National Academies Press, 2003).

72. "Mitchell Johnson Deposition," 78.

73. Fox, Roth, and Newman, "A Deadly Partnership," 103.

74. "Mitchell Johnson Deposition," 78.

75. Fox, Roth, and Newman, "A Deadly Partnership," 104.

76. Fox, Roth, and Newman, "A Deadly Partnership," 105.

77. Fox, Roth, and Newman, "A Deadly Partnership," 105.

78. Newman, *Rampage*, 36.

79. Fox, Roth, and Newman, "A Deadly Partnership," 105.

80. Fox, Roth, and Newman, "A Deadly Partnership," 105.

81. "Mitchell Johnson Deposition," 32.

82. Tony Perry, "Armed Youth Was Hoping for 'Suicide by Cop,'" *Los Angeles Times*, October 31, 2001, http://articles.latimes.com/2001/oct/31/local/me-63853.

83. Greg Krikorian, "Violence Marks Life of School Gunfire Suspect," *Los Angeles Times*, April 20, 2001, http://articles.latimes.com/2001/apr/20/local/me-53339.

84. Krikorian, "Violence Marks Life."

85. Krikorian, "Violence Marks Life."

86. Krikorian, "Violence Marks Life."

87. Alex Roth, "Psychiatrist Says Pills Hoffman Took Are Safe," *San Diego Union-Tribune*, April 19, 2001.

88. Alex Roth, "Schoolmates Feared Hulking Teen before Shooting," *San Diego Union-Tribune*, March 23, 2001, http://legacy.utsandiego.com/news/metro/granitehills/20010323-9999_1n23jason.html.

89. Roth, "Schoolmates Feared."

90. Roth, "Schoolmates Feared."

91. Karen Kucher and Alex Roth, "Teen's Motive Emerges: Suspect Blamed Dean for Rejection from Navy," *San Diego Union-Tribune*, March 24, 2001, A-1.

92. Rich Gibson, "Lonely Privilege in Despair: Aiming for Unfeigned Hope," in *The Evolution of Alienation: Trauma, Promise, and the Millennium*, ed. Lauren Langman and Devorah Kalekin-Fishman, 163 (New York: Rowman & Littlefield, 2006).

93. Perry, "Armed Youth."

94. Kucher and Roth, "Teen's Motive."

95. Alex Roth, "Shooting at Granite Hills High School," *San Diego Union-Tribune*, May 11, 2001, B-1.

96. Alex Roth, "'Suicide by Cop' Had Been Goal of Gunman," *San Diego Union-Tribune*, October 31, 2001, B-1, http://legacy.utsandiego.com/news/metro/granitehills/20011031-9999_7m31jason.html.

97. Alex Roth, "Dean Recalls Chaos of School Shooting," *San Diego Union-Tribune*, May 11, 2001, B-1, http://legacy.utsandiego.com/news/metro/granitehills/20010511-9999_1m11jason.html.

98. Peter Langman, "Jeffrey Weise: Timeline," n.d., available online at http://www.schoolshooters.info. Unless otherwise noted, the information on Weise's life is derived from this source.

99. Kimberly Sevcik, "Reservation for Death," *Salon*, August 8, 2005, http://www.salon.com/2005/08/08/red_lake/.

100. Heron Marquez Estrada, Ron Nixon, and John Stefany, "An Internet Trail of a Boy's Death Wish," *Star Tribune* (Minneapolis), March 23, 2005, http://www.startribune.com/local/11574966.html.

101. Frank J. Zenere, "Tragedy at Red Lake: Epilogue," *Communiqué* 34, no. 1 (2005), www.nasponline.org/publications/cq/cq341redlake.aspx.

102. David Hanners, "Web Postings Show Many Sides to Weise," *Duluth News-Tribune*, March 26, 2005, 1A.

103. Peter Langman, *Why Kids Kill: Inside the Minds of School Shooters* (New York: Palgrave Macmillan, 2009), 118.

104. Chuck Haga, Howie Padilla, and Richard Meryhew, "Jeff Weise: Teen Was a Mystery in a Life Full of Hardship," *Star Tribune*, March 23, 2005, 1A.

105. Peter Langman, ed., "Jeffrey Weise Online," available online at http://www.schoolshooters.info.

106. Langman, ed., "Jeffrey Weise Online."

107. Sevcik, "Reservation for Death."

108. Sevcik, "Reservation for Death."

109. Estrada, Nixon, and Stefany, "An Internet Trail."

110. Jodi Rave, "Family Still Struggling to Understand Teenager's Rampage in Minnesota," *Missoulian*, July 10, 2005, available online at http://missoulian.com/jodirave/teen-suicides-series-part-family-still-struggling-to-understand-teenager/article_cad5494b-ffaf-55e4-b62b-388c05f40b90.html.

111. Chuck Haga and Terry Collins, "Did Friendship Spiral into Conspiracy?" *Star Tribune* (Minneapolis), November 19, 2005, http://www.startribune.com/local/11577741.html.

112. Haga, Padilla, and Meryhew, "Jeff Weise: Teen was a Mystery."

113. Rave, "Family Still Struggling."

114. Ted Gregory, "Friend Says Shooter Had Threatened Violence at School Before," *Chicago Tribune*, March 23, 2005.

115. Jodi Rave, "Portrait Emerges of Youth Who Did Not Seem Violent," *Journal Star* (Lincoln), August 5, 2005, http://journalstar.com/special-section/news/portrait-emerges-of-youth-who-did-not-seem-violent/article_b9ec2b08-5c12-5b48-a1cc-1c991460db2f.html.

116. Langman, "Jeffrey Weise: Timeline."

117. Jeffrey Weise, "Thoughts of a Dreamer," available online at http://www.schoolshooters.info.

118. Weise, "Thoughts of a Dreamer."

119. Weise, "Thoughts of a Dreamer."

120. Haga, Padilla, and Meryhew, "Jeffrey Weise: Teen was a Mystery."

121. Pam Louwagie and Chuck Haga, "Jourdain Plea Deal Avoids Trial," *Star Tribune* (Minneapolis), November 29, 2005, http://www.startribune.com/local/11575931.html.

122. Monica Davey, "Behind the Why of a Rampage, Loner with a Taste for Nazism," *New York Times*, March 23, 2005, http://www.nytimes.com/2005/03/23/national/23shoot.html?_r=0.

123. Zenere, "Tragedy at Red Lake."

124. Estrada, Nixon, and Stefany, "An Internet Trail."

125. Hanners, "Web Postings Show."

126. Langman, ed., "Jeffrey Weise Online."

127. Todd Richmond, "Jury Convicts Teen in School Shooting," *Washington Post*, August 3, 2007, http://www.washingtonpost.com/wp-dyn/content/article/2007/08/02/AR2007080201748_pf.html.

128. Bill Lueders, "Eric Hainstock: Free at Last," *Isthmus*, July 31, 2008, http://www.isthmus.com/isthmus/article.php?article=23349.

129. Associated Press, "Wis. Teen Who Complained About Being Teased Fatally Shoots Principal," *Fox News*, September 30, 2006, http://www.foxnews.com/story/2006/09/30/wis-teen-who-complained-about-being-teased-fatally-shoots-principal/.

130. Richmond, "Jury Convicts Teen."

131. Tom Held, "Accusations Shake Teen's Family," *Milwaukee Journal-Sentinel*, October 6, 2006, http://www.jsonline.com/news/wisconsin/29184069.html.

132. Mike Nichols, "Home Life, Not School, Hardened Hainstock," *Milwaukee Journal-Sentinel*, October 7, 2006, http://www.jsonline.com/news/milwaukee/29199204.html.

133. Bill Lueders, "The Life of Eric Hainstock: A Timeline," *Isthmus/Daily Page*, July 31, 2008, http://www.isthmus.com/daily/article.php?article=23364.

134. Lueders, "The Life of Eric Hainstock."

135. Lueders, "Free at Last."

136. Lueders, "The Life of Eric Hainstock."

137. Lueders, "Free at Last."

138. Lueders, "The Life of Eric Hainstock."

139. Held, "Accusations Shake Teen's Family."

140. Lueders, "Free at Last."

141. Lueders, "Free at Last."

142. Eric Hainstock, "Eric Hainstock: Letters," available online at http://www.schoolshooters.info.

143. Lueders, "Free at Last."

144. Lueders, "Free at Last."

145. "Teen 'Enjoyed Playing Victim,' Counselor Says," *Milwaukee Journal-Sentinel*, July 31, 2007, http://www.jsonline.com/news/wisconsin/29494304.html.

146. Lueders, "The Life of Eric Hainstock."

147. "Hainstock Accused of Fatally Shooting Principal," *WISC-TV* (online trial blog from July 26 through August 3, 2007).

148. Richmond, "Jury Convicts Teen."

149. *State of Wisconsin v. Eric J. Hainstock*, Appeal No. 2009AP2905-CR (2011), 5, available online at http://www.schoolshooters.info.

150. "Hainstock Accused."

151. Christopher Maag, "Short but Troubled Life Ended in Shooting and Suicide," *New York Times*, October 12, 2007, http://www.nytimes.com/2007/10/12/us/12cleveland.html?pagewanted=print.

152. Emily Bazar and Marisol Bello, "Lesson of Shootings: Schools Act Too Late," *USA Today*, October 11, 2007, http://usatoday30.usatoday.com/news/nation/2007-10-11-school-shooting_N.htm; Joe Milicia, "Cleveland Gunman Ridiculed by Others," *Associated Press/Star Beacon* (Ashtabula, OH), October 11, 2007, http://www.starbeacon.com/local/x343668779/Cleveland-gunman-ridiculed-by-others.

153. "SuccessTech's Shooter's Father Says Teen Snapped," *LiveLeak*, December 18, 2007, http://www.liveleak.com/view?i=bf8_1198051894.

154. Joe Milicia, "Gunman's Uncle: Teen Upset with Teachers," *USA Today*, October 12, 2007, http://usatoday30.usatoday.com/news/nation/2007-10-12-cleveland-uncle_N.htm.

155. Karl Turner, "Asa Coon's Brother Speaks about Day of Shooting," *Cleveland Plain Dealer*, December 18, 2007, http://blog.cleveland.com/metro/2007/12/asa_coons_brother_speaks_about.html.

156. Joe Milicia, "School Gunman Had Access Despite Threats," *Associated Press*, October 11, 2007, available online at http://usatoday30.usatoday.com/news/nation/2007-10-10-953360477_x.htm.

157. Karl Turner, "Who Was Asa Coon?" *Cleveland Plain Dealer*, October 10, 2007, http://blog.cleveland.com/metro/2007/10/who_was_asa_coon.html.

158. Rachel Dissell, "Social Workers Delt with Asa Coon," *Cleveland Plain Dealer*, October 11, 2007, http://blog.cleveland.com/metro/2007/10/social_workers_dealt_with_asa.html.

159. Turner, "Who Was Asa Coon?"

160. Gil Kaufman, "Cleveland School Shooter Fit Sadly Predictable Profile: Bullied Loner from Troubled Home," *MTV*, October 11, 2007, http://www.mtv.com/news/1571704/cleveland-school-shooter-fit-sadly-predictable-profile-bullied-loner-from-troubled-home/.

161. Maag, "Short but Troubled Life."

162. Milicia, "School Gunman Had Access."

163. Joe Milicia, "Youth Who Shot 4, Killed Self Was Upset with Teachers, Relative Says," *Associated Press*, October 13, 2007.

164. Turner, "Who Was Asa Coon?"

165. Milicia, "School Gunman Had Access."

166. Milicia, "School Gunman Had Access."

167. "Ohio School Shooter Gave Many Warnings," *CNN.com*, October 11, 2007.

168. Turner, "Asa Coon's Brother."

169. Maag, "Short but Troubled Life."

170. Maag, "Short but Troubled Life."

171. Chris Maag and Ian Urbina, "Student, 14, Shoots 4 and Kill Himself in Cleveland School," *New York Times*, October 11, 2007, http://www.nytimes.com/2007/10/11/us/11cleveland.html.

172. "Ohio School Shooter."

173. Joe Milicia, "Boy Opens Fire at Cleveland School, Then Kills Himself," *Morning Call* (Allentown, PA), October 11, 2007.

174. Associated Press, "Teacher: Cleveland School Shooter Upset about Failing History," *Fox News*, October 15, 2007, http://www.foxnews.com/story/2007/10/15/teacher-cleveland-school-shooter-upset-about-failing-history/.

175. Rachel Dissell, "Accused Chardon High School Gunman T. J. Lane's Early Life Was Full of Turmoil, Documents Show," *Cleveland Plain Dealer*, March 14, 2012, http://www.cleveland.com/chardon-shooting/index.ssf/2012/03/court_files_from_1995_adds_mor.html.

176. Dissell, "Accused Chardon High School Gunman."

177. Ron Regan, "Alleged Chardon High School Gunman Grew Up in Troubled Family Hit by Divorce, Violence," *Newsnet5.com*, February 27, 2012, http://www.newsnet5.com/news/local-news/investigations/alleged-chardon-high-school-gunman-grew-up-in-troubled-family-hit-by-divorce-violence.

178. Melanie Jones, "Ohio School Shooting 2012: T. J. Lane's Father Guilty of Horrific Domestic Violence," *International Business News*, February 28, 2012, http://www.ibtimes.com/ohio-school-shooting-2012-tj-lanes-father-guilty-horrific-domestic-violence-417756.

179. David S. Glasier, "T. J. Lane's History in Focus: Records Indicate Chardon Shooting Suspect Has Troubled Past," *News-Herald* (Northern Ohio), March 11, 2012, http://www.news-herald.com/general-news/20120311/tj-lanes-history-in-focus-records-indicate-chardon-shooting-suspect-has-troubled-past.

180. Rachel Dissell, "Parents of Teen Accused of Shootings Faced Charges," *Cleveland Plain Dealer*, February 28, 2012, http://www.cleveland.com/chardon-shooting/index.ssf/2012/02/parents_of_teen_accused_of_sho.html.

181. Brandon C. Baker, "Neighbors, Friends Describe the T. J. Lane They Knew," *News-Herald* (Northern Ohio), February 28, 2012, http://www.news-herald.com/general-news/20120228/neighbors-friends-describe-the-tj-lane-they-knew; "Ohio School Shooting: Frequently Asked Questions about What Happened and Why," *Cleveland Plain Dealer*, February 29, 2012, http://www.cleveland.com/chardon-shooting/index.ssf/2012/02/ohio_school_shooting_frequentl.html.

182. Kevin Dolak, Christina Ng, and Barbara Lowe, "Ohio High School Shooting: Student Suspect to Be Tried as Adult," *ABC News*, February 29, 2012, http://abcnews.go.com/US/ohio-high-school-shooting-prosecutors-tj-lane-adult/story?id=15814303.

183. "Alleged Ohio Gunman Rarely Spoke about 'Trouble' at Home," *CNN.com*, February 28, 2012, http://www.cnn.com/2012/02/27/justice/ohio-shooting-suspect/.

184. "Ohio School Shooting."

185. Melanie Jones, "Who Is T. J. Lane? 5 Things to Know about Chardon High School Shooting Suspect," *International Business News*, February 28, 2012, http://www.ibtimes.com/who-tj-lane-5-things-know-about-chardon-high-school-shooting-suspect-417514.

186. Paula Mooney, "Thomas TJ Lane's Facebook Page Rants about God, Lucifer and Death," *Examiner.com*, February 27, 2012, http://www.examiner.com/article/thomas-tj-lane-s-facebook-page-rants-about-god-lucifer-and-death.

187. Mooney, "Thomas TJ Lane's Facebook Page."

188. James Garbarino, *Lost Boys: Why Our Sons Turn Violent and How We Can Save Them* (New York: The Free Press, 1999), 44–45.

189. Garbarino, *Lost Boys*, 45, italics in the original.

190. Garbarino, *Lost Boys*, 47.

5. COLLEGE SHOOTERS

1. Edwin Chen, *Deadly Scholarship: The True Story of Lu Gang and Mass Murder in America's Heartland* (New York: Birch Lane Press, 1995). Note that Chen puts the family name of Lu first, which is the Chinese usage; I follow the Western usage of the family name as the last name. Also note that all the information on Lu in this chapter is from this source.

2. Chen, *Deadly Scholarship*, 43.

3. Chen, *Deadly Scholarship*, 67.

4. Chen, *Deadly Scholarship*, 52.

5. Chen, *Deadly Scholarship*, 129, italics mine.

6. Chen, *Deadly Scholarship*, 136, italics mine.

7. Chen, *Deadly Scholarship*, 151.

8. Chen, *Deadly Scholarship*, 152.

9. Theodore Millon and Roger Davis, "Ten Subtypes of Psychopathy," in *Psychopathy: Antisocial, Criminal, and Violent Behavior*, ed. Theodore Millon et al., 167 (New York: Guilford Press, 1998).

10. Millon and Davis, "Ten Subtypes," 168.

11. John Scott Cowan, "Lessons from the Fabrikant File: A Report to the Board of Governors of Concordia University," Montreal, Can., January 6, 1994, 15, available online at http://archives.concordia.ca/sites/default/files/uploaded-documents/pages/2011/07/26/Cowan_report.pdf.

12. Cowan, "Lessons from the Fabrikant File," 15.

13. Cowan, "Lessons from the Fabrikant File," 15.

14. Cowan, "Lessons from the Fabrikant File," 16.

15. Morris Wolfe, "Dr. Fabrikant's Solution," *Essays: New and Selected*, n.d., http://www.grubstreetbooks.ca/essays/fabrikant.html.

16. Cowan, "Lessons from the Fabrikant File," 18.

17. Wolfe, "Dr. Fabrikant's Solution."

18. Wolfe, "Dr. Fabrikant's Solution."

19. Wolfe, "Dr. Fabrikant's Solution."

20. Cowan, "Lessons from the Fabrikant File," 14.

21. Wolfe, "Dr. Fabrikant's Solution."

22. Wolfe, "Dr. Fabrikant's Solution."

23. Wolfe, "Dr. Fabrikant's Solution."

24. Wolfe, "Dr. Fabrikant's Solution."

25. H. W. Arthurs, Roger A. Blais, and Jon Thompson, "Integrity in Scholarship: A Report to Concordia University," The Independent Committee of

Inquiry into Academic and Scientific Integrity, April 1994, 5, available online at http://www.schoolshooters.info.

26. Valery Fabrikant, personal website, n.d., http://web.archive.org/web/20091026234951/http://geocities.com/benny_patrick/.

27. Helen Hickey De Haven, "The Elephant in the Ivory Tower: Rampages in Higher Education and the Case for Institutional Liability," *Journal of College and University Law* 35, no. 3 (2009): 543.

28. Mitch Tobin, "Killer Sends 22-Page Letter to Publisher," *Arizona Daily Star*, October 30, 2002.

29. John Broder, "Arizona Gunman Chose Victims in Advance," *New York Times*, October 30, 2002, http://www.nytimes.com/2002/10/30/us/arizona-gunman-chose-victims-in-advance.html.

30. Tobin, "Killer Sends."

31. Tobin, "Killer Sends."

32. Scott Smallwood, "The Deadly Risk of Giving an F," *Chronicle of Higher Education*, November 15, 2002.

33. De Haven, "The Elephant," 542.

34. De Haven, "The Elephant," 542, note 186.

35. De Haven, "The Elephant," 543.

36. Smallwood, "The Deadly Risk."

37. Nate Buchik, "2 Slain Profs Feared Flores," *Arizona Daily Wildcat*, October 30, 2002, http://wc.arizona.edu/papers/96/47/01_1.html.

38. De Haven, "The Elephant," 544.

39. De Haven, "The Elephant," 545.

40. Millon and Davis, "Ten Subtypes," 169.

41. Millon and Davis, "Ten Subtypes," 168.

42. De Haven, "The Elephant," 528.

43. Chris Kahn, "Appalachian School of Law Killer Still Haunted by Paranoia, Delusions," *Associated Press*, June 11, 2004.

44. De Haven, "The Elephant," 530.

45. De Haven, "The Elephant," 532, text and note 129.

46. De Haven, "The Elephant," 532.

47. De Haven, "The Elephant," 531, text and note 123.

48. Nara Schoenberg, "Appalachian Tragedy," *Chicago Tribune*, March 5, 2002, http://articles.chicagotribune.com/2002-03-05/features/0203050001_1_dean-l-anthony-sutin-coal-miners-tight-knit-campus.

49. De Haven, "The Elephant," 532.

50. Quoted in De Haven, "The Elephant," 531, note 121.

51. Jeffrey Gettleman and Stephanie Simon, "Dean, Professor and Student Killed at Law School in Va.," *Los Angeles Times*, January 17, 2002, http://articles.latimes.com/2002/jan/17/news/mn-23244.

52. Gettleman and Simon, "Dean, Professor and Student."

53. Schoenberg, "Appalachian Tragedy."

54. De Haven, "The Elephant," 532, note 130.

55. De Haven, "The Elephant," 533.

56. Schoenberg, "Appalachian Tragedy."

57. De Haven, "The Elephant," 534.

58. Kahn, "Appalachian School."

59. Kahn, "Appalachian School."

60. Kahn, "Appalachian School."

61. Schoenberg, "Appalachian Tragedy."

62. Chris Kahn, "Ex-Law Student Admits to Slayings," *Washington Post*, February 27, 2004, http://www.washingtonpost.com/wp-dyn/articles/A12363-2004Feb27.html.

63. Millon and Davis, "Ten Subtypes," 166–67.

64. De Haven, "The Elephant," 547–78.

65. *State of Ohio v. Biswanath Halder*, 2007-Ohio-5940, No. 87974, Case No. CR-437717 (2007), 4, available online at http://www.schoolshooters.info.

66. De Haven, "The Elephant," 547.

67. De Haven, "The Elephant," 548.

68. De Haven, "The Elephant," 549.

69. De Haven, "The Elephant," 550, note 245.

70. De Haven, "The Elephant," 548.

71. De Haven, "The Elephant," 550.

72. Arthur J. Pais, "Halder Case: Into the Mind of a Killer," *Rediff.com*, last updated January 19, 2006, http://www.rediff.com/news/2006/jan/19halder.htm.

73. *Brian Wallace, Administrator of the Estate of Norman E. Wallace, v. Biswanath Halder et al.*, Supreme Court of Ohio, Case No. 2009-1817, No. 92046, Case No. CV-591169, 7, available online at http://www.schoolshooters.info.

74. De Haven, "The Elephant," 550.

75. De Haven, "The Elephant," 551.

76. De Haven, "The Elephant," 551.

77. Pais, "Halder Case."

78. *State of Ohio v. Biswanath Halder*, 5.

79. *State of Ohio v. Biswanath Halder*, 6.

80. *Brian Wallace v. Biswanath Halder*, 3.

81. De Haven, "The Elephant," 553.

82. Pais, "Halder Case."

83. Pais, "Halder Case."

84. *State of Ohio v. Biswanath Halder*, 39, note 40.

85. *State of Ohio v. Biswanath Halder*, 16.

86. Amy Wallace, "What Made This University Scientist Snap?" *Wired*, February 28, 2011, http://www.wired.com/2011/02/ff_bishop/all/.

87. Wallace, "What Made This University Scientist Snap?"

88. Patricia C. McCarter, "Prosecutor: Amy Bishop Should Have Been Charged in Brother's 1986 Death," *Everything Alabama*, February 17, 2010.

89. Wallace, "What Made This University Scientist Snap?"

90. Wallace, "What Made This University Scientist Snap?"

91. Shelley Murphy and Eric Moskowitz, "US Orders Review of Attempted Bombing," *Boston Globe*, February 25, 2010, http://www.boston.com/news/

local/massachusetts/articles/2010/02/25/us_orders_review_of_attempted_
bombing/.

92. Shaila Dewan, Stephanie Saul, and Katie Zezima, "For Professor, Fury
Just Beneath the Surface," *New York Times*, February 20, 2010, http://www.
nytimes.com/2010/02/21/us/21bishop.html?pagewanted=all&_r=0.

93. Laurel J. Sweet, Jessica Van Sack, Jessica Fargen, and Ira Kantor,
"'Oddball' Portrait of Amy Bishop Emerges," *Boston Herald*, February 15,
2010.

94. Wallace, "What Made This University Scientist Snap?"

95. Wallace, "What Made This University Scientist Snap?"

96. Wallace, "What Made This University Scientist Snap?"

97. Wallace, "What Made This University Scientist Snap?"

98. Wallace, "What Made This University Scientist Snap?"

99. "Ala. Students Complained about Amy Bishop," *CBS News*, February
17, 2010, http://www.cbsnews.com/news/ala-students-complained-about-amy-
bishop/.

100. *Dr. Jaqueline U. Johnson v. Dr. Vistasp M. Karbhari, Dr. Amy Bishop,
a.k.a. Amy Bishop Anderson, and James Anderson*, Case No. CV-2011-
900038.00 (2011), 4, available online at http://www.schoolshooters.info.

101. *Johnson v. Karbhari, Bishop, Anderson*, 4.

102. Dewan, Saul, and Zezima, "For Professor."

103. Wallace, "What Made This University Scientist Snap?"

104. Tom Bartlett, "Slain Department Head Supported Accused Killer's
Tenure Bid," *Chronicle for Higher Education*, February 13, 2010, http://
chronicle.com/blogs/ticker/slain-department-head-supported-accused-killers-
tenure-bid/21250.

105. *Johnson v. Karbhari, Bishop, Anderson*, 10.

106. *Johnson v. Karbhari, Bishop, Anderson*, 9–10.

107. Wallace, "What Made This University Scientist Snap?"

108. *Johnson v. Karbhari, Bishop, Anderson*, 10.

109. *Johnson v. Karbhari, Bishop, Anderson*, 11.

110. *Johnson v. Karbhari, Bishop, Anderson*, 5.

111. *Johnson v. Karbhari, Bishop, Anderson*, 5.

112. Wallace, "What Made This University Scientist Snap?"

113. Wallace, "What Made This University Scientist Snap?"

114. Susan Donaldson James, "Shooter Amy Bishop Likely Schizophrenic,
Says Lawyer," *ABC News*, February 19, 2010, http://abcnews.go.com/Health/
MindMoodNews/amy-bishop-lawyer-plead-insanity-alleged-university-
alabama-shooter-schizophrenic/story?id=9880257.

115. Jay Reeves, "Former Professor Pleads Not Guilty in Ala Shooting," *Seattle Times*, September 22, 2011, http://seattletimes.com/html/nationworld/
2016284360_apusalaunivershooting.html.

116. Millon and Davis, "Ten Subtypes," 166.

117. Stanton Samenow, *Inside the Criminal Mind*, revised and updated (New
York: Crown, 2004), 89.

6. COLLEGE SHOOTERS

1. Gary M. Lavergne, *A Sniper in the Tower: The Charles Whitman Murders* (Denton: University of North Texas Press, 1997), 5. All the information on Whitman in this chapter is from his biography.

2. Lavergne, *A Sniper*, 2.

3. Lavergne, *A Sniper*, 3.

4. Lavergne, *A Sniper*, 68.

5. Lavergne, *A Sniper*, 71.

6. Lavergne, *A Sniper*, 53.

7. Lavergne, *A Sniper*, 256–67.

8. Lavergne, *A Sniper*, 109.

9. Lavergne, *A Sniper*, 24–25.

10. Lavergne, *A Sniper*, 70–71.

11. Lavergne, *A Sniper*, 91.

12. Lavergne, *A Sniper*, 21.

13. Lavergne, *A Sniper*, 81.

14. Lavergne, *A Sniper*, 48.

15. Lavergne, *A Sniper*, 269.

16. Lavergne, *A Sniper*, 268.

17. Theodore Millon and Roger Davis, "Ten Subtypes of Psychopathy," in *Psychopathy; Antisocial, Criminal, and Violent Behavior*, ed. Theodore Millon et al., 166 (New York: Guilford Press, 1998).

18. Millon and Davis, "Ten Subtypes," 167.

19. Millon and Davis, "Ten Subtypes," 167.

20. Jonathan Fast, *Ceremonial Violence: A Psychological Explanation of School Shootings* (New York: Overlook, 2008), 84.

21. Gregory Gibson, *Gone Boy: A Walkabout* (New York: Anchor Books, 2000), 257.

22. Brian Melley, "Lo Described by Psychiatrist as Suffering from Delusions," *Union-News* (Springfield, MA), January 27, 1994, 12.

23. Fast, *Ceremonial Violence*, 84.

24. Fast, *Ceremonial Violence*, 87.

25. Fast, *Ceremonial Violence*, 90.

26. Fast, *Ceremonial Violence*, 90.

27. Gibson, *Gone Boy*, 159.

28. Fast, *Ceremonial Violence*, 91.

29. Fast, *Ceremonial Violence*, 91.

30. Fast, *Ceremonial Violence*, 97.

31. Fast, *Ceremonial Violence*, 100.

32. Fast, *Ceremonial Violence*, 100.

33. Fast, *Ceremonial Violence*, 92.

34. *Commonwealth v. Wayne Lo*, 428 Mass. 45 (1998), 2, available online at http://www.schoolshooters.info.

35. William Glaberson, "Man and His Son's Slayer Unite to Ask Why," *New York Times*, April 12, 2000, http://www.nytimes.com/2000/04/12/us/man-and-his-son-s-slayer-unite-to-ask-why.html.

36. Gibson, *Gone Boy*, 226.

37. Gibson, *Gone Boy*, 226.

38. Gibson, *Gone Boy*, 227.

39. Fast, *Ceremonial Violence*, 92.

40. Fast, *Ceremonial Violence*, 92.

41. Theodore Millon, *Disorders of Personality: DSM-IV and Beyond*, 2nd ed. (New York: John Wiley & Sons, 1996), 452.

42. Millon, *Disorders of Personality*, 452.

43. TriData Division, System Planning Corporation, "Mass Shootings at Virginia Tech: Addendum to the Report of the Review Panel" (Arlington, VA: TriData Division, 2009), 23–24, available online at http://www.schoolshooters.info.

44. TriData Division, "Mass Shootings," 23.

45. TriData Division, "Mass Shootings," 25.

46. Seung Hui Cho, "Seung Hui Cho's Letter to the English Department of Virginia Tech," mailed on April 16, 2007, author's personal collection.

47. Seung Hui Cho, "Seung Hui Cho's 'Manifesto,'" n.d., 4, available online at http://www.schoolshooters.info.

48. Sari Horwitz, "Va. Tech Shooter Seen as 'Collector of Injustice," *Washington Post*, June 19, 2007, http://www.washingtonpost.com/wp-dyn/content/article/2007/06/18/AR2007061801732.html.

49. TriData Division, "Mass Shootings," 46.

50. TriData Division, "Mass Shootings," 46.

51. Matt Apuzzo, "Gunman's Writings Were Disturbing," *Huffington Post*, April 17, 2007, http://www.huffingtonpost.com/huff-wires/20070417/virginia-tech-shooting/.

52. Amy Gardner and David Cho, "Isolation Defined Cho's Senior Year," *Washington Post*, May 6, 2007, http://www.washingtonpost.com/wp-dyn/content/article/2007/05/05/AR2007050501221.html.

53. N. R. Kleinfield, "Before Deadly Rage, a Lifetime Consumed by a Troubling Silence," *New York Times*, April 22, 2007, http://www.nytimes.com/2007/04/22/us/22vatech.html?pagewanted=all&_r=0.

54. TriData Division, "Mass Shootings," 42.

55. Kleinfield, "Before Deadly Rage."

56. Seung Hui Cho et al., "Cho's English Department E-mails," fall 2005–spring 2007, available online at http://www.schoolshooters.info.

57. Cho, "Seung Hui Cho's 'Manifesto,'" 1.

58. Cho, "Seung Hui Cho's 'Manifesto,'" 1.

59. Cho, "Seung Hui Cho's 'Manifesto,'" 3.

60. Cho, "Seung Hui Cho's 'Manifesto,'" 1.

61. Cho, "Seung Hui Cho's 'Manifesto,'" 1.

62. "Report: Cho Hired an Escort Before Rampage," *ABC News*, April 24, 2007, http://abcnews.go.com/US/VATech/story?id=3071730.

63. TriData Division, "Mass Shootings," 50.

64. Cho et al., "Cho's English Department E-mails."

65. Sari Horwitz, "Paper by Cho Exhibits Disturbing Parallels to Shootings, Sources Say," *Washington Post*, August 29, 2007, A01, http://www.washingtonpost.com/wp-dyn/content/article/2007/08/28/AR2007082801948.html.

66. TriData Division, "Mass shootings," 50.

67. Cho, "Seung Hui Cho's Letter."

68. Northern Illinois University, "Report of the February 14, 2008, Shootings at Northern Illinois University," (DeKalb: Northern Illinois University, 2008), available online at http://www.schoolshooters.info. Unless otherwise noted, the information on Kazmierczak in this chapter is from this source.

69. Northern Illinois University, "Report of the February 14, 2008, Shootings," 24.

70. Northern Illinois University, "Report of the February 14, 2008, Shootings," 34.

71. Northern Illinois University, "Report of the February 14, 2008, Shootings," 21.

72. Northern Illinois University, "Report of the February 14, 2008, Shootings," 39.

73. Finland Ministry of Justice, "Kauhajoki School Shooting on 23 September 2008: Report of the Investigation Commission," translation of the original Finish report (Vantaa: Ministry of Justice, Finland, 2010), 54, available online at http://www.schoolshooters.info. Unless otherwise noted, the information on Saari in this chapter is from this source.

74. Finland Ministry of Justice, "Kauhajoki School Shooting," 56.

75. Finland Ministry of Justice, "Kauhajoki School Shooting," 54.

76. Finland Ministry of Justice, "Kauhajoki School Shooting," 55.

77. Finland Ministry of Justice, "Kauhajoki School Shooting," 56.

78. Tomi Kiilakoski and Atte Oksanen, "Cultural and Peer Influences on Homicidal Violence: A Finnish Perspective," *New Directions for Youth Development* 33, no. 129 (2011): 37, available online at http://www.academia.edu/1130441/Cultural_and_peer_influences_on_homicidal_violence_A_Finnish_perspective.

79. Nick Allen, "Finland School Shooting: Gunman Matti Saari Made Phone Call during Slaughter," *Telegraph* (UK), September 26, 2008, http://www.telegraph.co.uk/news/worldnews/europe/finland/3083996/Finland-school-shooting-Gunman-Matti-Saari-made-phone-call-during-slaughter.html.

80. Finland Ministry of Justice, "Kauhajoki School Shooting," 55, 61.

81. Finland Ministry of Justice, "Kauhajoki School Shooting," 55.

82. Finland Ministry of Justice, "Kauhajoki School Shooting," 57.

83. Finland Ministry of Justice, "Kauhajoki School Shooting," 57.

84. Finland Ministry of Justice, "Kauhajoki School Shooting," 57.

85. Finland Ministry of Justice, "Kauhajoki School Shooting," 52.

86. Finland Ministry of Justice, "Kauhajoki School Shooting," 56.

87. Finland Ministry of Justice, "Kauhajoki School Shooting," 149.

88. Finland Ministry of Justice, "Kauhajoki School Shooting," 57.

89. Nick Allen, "Finland School Shooting: Gunman had Contact with 2007 School Killer," *Telegraph* (UK), September 24, 2008, http://www.telegraph.co.uk/news/worldnews/europe/finland/3075246/Finland-school-shooting-Gunman-had-contact-with-2007-school-killer.html.

90. Jane Applegate, "10 Years after Murderous Rampage, Campus Killer Says He Is Now Sane," *Los Angeles Times*, July 6, 1986, http://articles.latimes.com/1986-07-06/local/me-23088_1_murderous-rampage.

91. Nicole Smith, "History of a Cal State Fullerton Killer," *Daily Titan* (California State University, Fullerton), December 29, 2008, http://www.dailytitan.com/2006/05/history-of-a-cal-state-fullerton-killer/.

92. Smith, "History of a Cal State."

93. Smith, "History of a Cal State."

94. Nicole Smith, "The Quiet Custodian," *Tusk Magazine*, May 15, 2006, available online at http://www.hearstfdn.org/hearst_journalism/competitions.php?type=Writing&year=2007&id=1.

95. Applegate, "10 Years after."

96. Applegate, "10 Years after."

97. Applegate, "10 Years after."

98. Smith, "The Quiet Custodian."

99. Smith, "The Quiet Custodian."

100. Smith, "The Quiet Custodian."

101. Smith, "The Quiet Custodian."

102. Smith, "The Quiet Custodian."

103. Smith, "The Quiet Custodian."

104. Smith, "The Quiet Custodian."

105. Smith, "The Quiet Custodian."

106. Jeffrey Perlman, "Doctor Says 'Other Force' May Have Guided Allaway," *Los Angeles Times*, August 25, 1977, OC1, 7.

107. Smith, "The Quiet Custodian."

108. Nicole M. Smith, "Blood Spills in Library Hallways," *Daily Titan* (California State University, Fullerton), May 16, 2006, http://www.dailytitan.com/2006/05/bloodspillsinlibraryhallways/.

109. Smith, "History of a Cal State."

110. Matthias Gafni, Thomas Peele, Joshua Melvin, and Matt Krupnick, "Oakland University Shooting: Accused Oikos University Shooter One Goh Was 'Troubled,' 'Angry,' Said Those Who Knew Him," *Oakland Tribune*, April 3, 2012, available online at http://www.insidebayarea.com/top-stories/ci_20314383/oakland-school-rampage-suspect-sought-revenge-against-administrator.

111. Elizabeth Flock, "Who Is One Goh, Oakland School Shooting Suspect?" *Washington Post*, April 3, 2012, http://www.washingtonpost.com/blogs/worldviews/post/who-is-one-goh-oakland-school-shooting-suspect/2012/04/03/gIQACiZysS_blog.html.

112. Terry Collins, "One L. Goh, Oikos University Shooting Suspect, Was Upset about Being Teased over Poor English Skills: Police," *Huffington Post*,

April 3, 2012, http://www.huffingtonpost.com/2012/04/03/one-l-goh-oikos-university-shooting-suspect_n_1399256.html.

113. Gafni et al., "Oakland University Shooting."

114. Gafni et al., "Oakland University Shooting."

115. Jaxon Van Derbeken and Henry K. Lee, "Oikos Shooting: Shooter's Apparent Target Revealed," *SFGate*, April 6, 2012, available online at http://www.sfgate.com/crime/article/Oikos-shooting-Shooter-s-apparent-target-revealed-3461501.php.

116. Gafni et al., "Oakland University Shooting."

117. Collins, "One L. Goh."

118. Norimitsu Onishi and Malia Wollan, "Troubled History Emerges for Suspect in Fatal Oakland Attack," *New York Times*, April 3, 2012, http://www.nytimes.com/2012/04/04/us/oikos-university-gunman-lined-up-victims.html?pagewanted=all.

119. Matt Krupnick, Kristin J. Bender, and Paul Thissen, "Oikos University Reopens Three Weeks after Gunman Killed Seven," *San Jose Mercury News*, April 23, 2012, http://www.mercurynews.com/breaking-news/ci_20460160/oakland-oikos-university-reopens-today-three-weeks-after.

120. Candice Choi, Terry Collins, and Garance Burke, "One Goh, Oakland Shooting Suspect, Didn't Show Violent Signs: Official," *Huffington Post*, April 7, 2012, http://www.huffingtonpost.com/2012/04/07/one-goh-oakland-shooting_n_1410210.html.

121. Van Derbeken and Lee, "Oikos Shooting."

122. Onishi and Wollan, "Troubled History."

123. Van Derbeken and Lee, "Oikos Shooting."

124. Terry Collins, "One Goh, Oikos University Shooting Suspect, Deemed Unfit for Trial," *Huffington Post*, January 7, 2013, http://www.huffingtonpost.com/2013/01/07/one-goh-oikos_n_2428444.html.

125. Demian Bulwa, "One Goh Incompetentin Oakland Masscare," *San Francisco Chronicle*, January 7, 2012, http://www.sfgate.com/crime/article/One-Goh-incompetent-in-Oakland-massacre-4173068.php.

126. Collins, "One Goh, Oikos University."

127. Van Derbeken and Lee, "Oikos Shooting."

7. ABERRANT ADULT SHOOTERS

1. Monique Lépine and Harold Gagné, *Aftermath: The Mother of Marc Lépine Tells the Story of Her Life before and after the Montreal Massacre*, trans. Diana Halfpenny (Toronto: Viking, 2008), 156.

2. Lépine and Gagné, *Aftermath*, 54.

3. Lépine and Gagné, *Aftermath*, 62–63, 135, 154, 193.

4. Lépine and Gagné, *Aftermath*, 151–52.

5. Kate Fillion, "Maclean's Interview: Monique Lépine; Monique Lépine Talks with Kate Fillion about Shame, Guilt, and Living with the Fact that Her

Son Killed 14 Women," *Maclean's*, November 3, 2008, http://www.macleans.ca/general/monique-lepine/.

6. Lépine and Gagné, *Aftermath*, 31.

7. Fillion, "Maclean's Interview."

8. Lépine and Gagné, *Aftermath*, 32.

9. Greg Weston and Jack Aubry, "The Montreal Massacre," *Ottawa Citizen*, February 8, 1990, available online at http://www.canada.com/ottawacitizen/features/rapidfire/story.html?id=bd7367a7-1f49-4c5d-949d-7e5a85941b40.

10. Marc Lépine, "Marc Lépine's Suicide Note," presumed December 6, 1989, available online at http://www.schoolshooters.info.

11. "The Montreal Massacre," *Guardian* (UK), September 15, 2006, http://www.theguardian.com/g2/story/0,,1872900,00.html.

12. Lépine and Gagné, *Aftermath*, 158–59.

13. Vicki Cheng, "Robbins' Mother Struggles to Comprehend HUB Shooting," *Centre Daily Times* (central Pennsylvania), August 24, 1997.

14. Vicki Cheng, "Who Is Jillian Robbins?" *Centre Daily Times* (central Pennsylvania), October 13, 1996.

15. Cheng, "Who Is Jillian Robbins?"

16. Cheng, "Who Is Jillian Robbins?"

17. Cheng, "Robbins' Mother Struggles."

18. Cheng, "Who Is Jillian Robbins?"

19. Cheng, "Robbins' Mother Struggles."

20. Jim MacKinnon, "Friends, Co-workers Recall Friendly, Artistic Robbins," *Centre Daily Times* (central Pennsylvania), September 19, 1996.

21. Jim MacKinnon, "Police Detail New Findings," *Centre Daily Times* (central Pennsylvania), September, 24, 1996.

22. Cheng, "Who Is Jillian Robbins?"

23. Tom Gibb, "Shooter in 1996 Penn State Killing Recounts Her Past," *Pittsburgh Post-Gazette*, February 25, 2003, http://old.post-gazette.com/localnews/20030225sniper0225p3.asp.

24. MacKinnon, "Friends, Co-workers."

25. Cheng, "Who Is Jillian Robbins?"

26. Mark Parfitt, "Robbins' Case Closed," *Daily Collegian* (Penn State University), June 11, 1998, http://m.collegian.psu.edu/archives/article_a1f69d68-0727-5027-bc38-0ed15a6db836.html?mode=jqm.

27. Cheng, "Who Is Jillian Robbins?"

28. "Who Was Kimveer Gill? (Part 1)," *Gazette (Montreal)*, September 4, 2008, http://www.canada.com/montrealgazette/story.html?id=c7b3f15e-9cdd-4e52-8d86-c1d59e6cff0b&k=40661.

29. "Who Was Kimveer Gill? (Part 2)," *Gazette (Montreal)*, September 4, 2008, http://www.canada.com/montrealgazette/story.html?id=d1933b65-8a0c-454f-bff0-9e072f8918b5&p=1.

30. "Who Was Kimveer Gill? (Part 2)."

31. "A Killer's Dark Mind," *National Post*, September 15, 2006, http://www.nationalpost.com/news/story.html?id=70ca42a5-f979-446f-a9c3-61949f44c737&k=38269.

32. "Who Was Kimveer Gill? (Part 2)."

33. "Who Was Kimveer Gill? (Part 3)," *Gazette (Montreal)*, September 4, 2008, http://www2.canada.com/montrealgazette/news/saturdayextra/story.html?id=a8279d1a-e4a1-43ae-95eb-44281d49c7ef&p=3.

34. "Who Was Kimveer Gill? (Part 3)."

35. "Dawson Shooter's Friend Arrested for Threats," *CTV*, October 21, 2006, http://atlantictest.ctv.ca/servlet/an/plocal/CTVNews/20061021/dawsonshooter_friend_061021/20061021/?hub=WinnipegHome.

36. "Blog Paints Chilling Portrait of 'Angel of Death,'" *CTV*, September 14, 2006, http://ctestp.ctv.ca/servlet/an/local/CTVNews/20060914/gill_profile_060914?hub=WinnipegHome.

37. "Who Was Kimveer Gill? (Part 1)."

38. Kimveer Gill, "Kimveer Gill Online," February 21, 2006, 11–13; and July 28, 2006, 27–28; available online at http://www.schoolshooters.info.

39. Gill, "Kimveer Gill Online," July 28, 2006, 27–28.

40. Gill, "Kimveer Gill Online," July 28, 2006, 27–28.

41. Gill, "Kimveer Gill Online," February 15, 2006, 10–11; February 19, 2006, 11; and September 10, 2006, 45–47.

42. Gill, "Kimveer Gill Online," September 10, 2006, 45–47.

43. "College Shooter Gill Obsessed with Guns," *CBC News*, September 15, 2006, http://www.cbc.ca/news/canada/montreal/college-shooter-gill-obsessed-with-guns-1.589809.

44. Gill, "Kimveer Gill Online," January 18, 2006, 5–6.

45. Gill, "Kimveer Gill Online," March 15, 2006, 14–15.

46. "Who Was Kimveer Gill? (Part 3)."

47. Nelson Kempsky, Gary A. Binkerd, Phil Yee, Allen Benitez, and Richard Yarvis, "A Report to Attorney General John K. Van de Kamp on Patrick Edward Purdy and the Cleveland School Killings" (California: Department of Justice, 1989), available online at http://www.schoolshooters.info. Unless otherwise noted, the information on Purdy in this chapter is from this source.

48. Gary Blonston, "From Quiet, Unhappy Child to Mass Killer," *San Jose Mercury News*, January 19, 1989, 1A.

49. Carl Ingram and Robert A. Jones, "Gunman Had Attended School He Assaulted but Motive Remains Unclear in Attack," *Los Angeles Times*, January 19, 1989, 1, http://articles.latimes.com/1989-01-19/news/mn-1465_1_school-records.

50. Roger Phillips, "Purdy Recalled as Bigot and 'Sick, Sick Man,'" *Record (San Joaquin)*, January 19, 2009, available online at http://www.recordnet.com/apps/pbcs.dll/article?AID=/20090118/A_NEWS/901170304/-1/A_SPECIAL0252.

51. Kempsky et al., "A Report to Attorney General," 50.

52. Kempsky et al., "A Report to Attorney General," 64.

53. Kempsky et al., "A Report to Attorney General," 76.

54. Kempsky et al., "A Report to Attorney General," 76.

55. Kempsky et al., "A Report to Attorney General," 41.

56. Kempsky et al., "A Report to Attorney General," 76.

57. Kempsky et al., "A Report to Attorney General," 75.

58. Kempsky et al., "A Report to Attorney General," 10.

59. Kempsky et al., "A Report to Attorney General," 41.

60. Kempsky et al., "A Report to Attorney General," 10.

61. Catherine Tsai and P. Solomon Banda, "Police: Colorado Gunman Entered the School Earlier," *Associated Press*, February 25, 2010, available online at http://www.timesfreepress.com/news/2010/feb/25/police-colorado-gunman-entered-school-earlier/.

62. Kirk Mitchell, "Suspect's Dad Laments Lack of Mental-Health Care," *Denver Post*, February 28, 2010, http://www.denverpost.com/ci_14485435.

63. Emile Hallez, "Eastwood Reportedly Spoke of Resentments against School," *Columbine Courier*, May 17, 2010, http://www.columbinecourier.com/content/eastwood-reportedly-spoke-resentments-against-school.

64. "Bruco Eastwood, Colorado School Shooter, Has Already Filled Maximum Sentence, Will Not Serve Time in Prison," *Huffington Post*, October 5, 2011, http://www.huffingtonpost.com/2011/10/05/bruco-strong-eagle-eastwo_3_n_996869.html.

65. Michael Roberts, "Bruco Eastwood Found Not Guilty by Reason of Insanity in Deer Creek Middle School Shooting," *Westword*, October 6, 2011, http://blogs.westword.com/latestword/2011/10/bruco_eastwood_insane_deer_creek_middle_school.php.

66. Mike McPhee, Kirk Mitchell, and Karen Auge, "Son Cursed at Imaginary People in Room," *Denver Post*, February 25, 2010, http://www.denverpost.com/crime/ci_14466291?source=pkg.

67. Tsai and Banda, "Police: Colorado Gunman."

68. Adam Chodak, "Shooting Suspect's Father Says Son Sought Help," *9news.com*, February 24, 2010, http://archive.9news.com/news/story.aspx?storyid=133397&catid=222.

69. Hallez, "Eastwood Reportedly Spoke."

70. Roberts, "Bruco Eastwood Found Not Guilty."

71. Tsai and Banda, "Police: Colorado Gunman."

72. McPhee, Mitchell, and Auge, "Son Cursed."

73. Edecio Martinez, "Bruco Strongeagle Eastwood: Colo. Middle School Shooting Suspect Hears Voices, Used My Gun, Dad Says," *CBS News*, February 24, 2010, http://www.cbsnews.com/news/bruco-strongeagle-eastwood-colo-middle-school-shooting-suspect-hears-voices-used-my-gun-dad-says/.

74. Tsai and Banda, "Police: Colorado Gunman."

75. Emile Hallez, "Eastwood Charged with 4 Attempted-Murder Counts in Deer Creek Shootings," *Columbine Courier*, March 15, 2010, http://www.columbinecourier.com/content/eastwood-charged-4-attempted-murder-counts-deer-creek-shootings.

76. "Bruco Eastwood, Colorado School Shooter."

77. Bradley Brooks, "Brazil School Shooting Massacre Opens Up Debate on Bullying," *Associated Press*, April 16, 2011.

78. Marco Sibaja, "Brazilians Bury Children Killed in School Massacre as Calls for Stricter Gun Control Laws Heat Up," *Associated Press*, April 9, 2011, available online at http://www.stalbertgazette.com/article/GB/20110408/CP01/304089910/-1/sag08/children-begged-for-mercy-as-gunman-turned-former-school-into-bloody&template=cpArt.

79. "Brazilian School Shooter Wellington Oliveira Rambled about Plans in Video," *Associated Press*, April 14, 2011, available online at http://www.nydailynews.com/news/world/brazilian-school-shooter-wellington-oliveira-rambled-plans-video-article-1.109857.

80. "In Brazil, from Bullied Student to Cold-Blooded Killer," *Haveeru Daily*, April 9, 2011, http://www.haveeru.com.mv/english/details/35247.

81. Clarissa Monteagudo, Guilherme Amado, and Herculano Barreto Filho, "Realengo: Conheça em Detalhes quem era e como Vivia Wellington Menezes de Oliveira," *Globo*, April 8, 2011, http://extra.globo.com/casos-de-policia/realengo-conheca-em-detalhes-quem-era-como-vivia-wellington-menezes-de-oliveira-1539375.html.

82. "In Brazil, From Bullied Student."

83. Monteagudo, Amado, and Filho, "Realengo."

84. Bruno Rousso, "Autor de Massacre em Escola era Fissuradoem Terrorismo e Conhecido como Al Qaeda, diz Amigo," *noticias.r7.com*, April 7, 2011, http://noticias.r7.com/rio-de-janeiro/noticias/fissurado-em-terrorismo-autor-de-massacre-em-escola-era-conhecido-como-al-qaeda-20110407.html.

85. "Em Nova Carta, Atirador Tenta Usar Bullying para Justificar Crime," *Globo*, April 14, 2011.

86. "In Brazil, From Bullied Student."

87. "In Brazil, From Bullied Student."

88. Monteagudo, Amado, and Filho, "Realengo."

89. "Manuscritos de Atirador Mostram Fixação por Terrorismo," *Globo*, April 10, 2011, http://g1.globo.com/Tragedia-em-Realengo/noticia/2011/04/manuscritos-de-atirador-mostram-fixacao-por-terrorismo.html.

90. Monteagudo, Amado, and Filho, "Realengo."

91. Juliana Barbassa, "Video, Texts of Brazil School Shooter Show Anger," *Associated Press*, April 15, 2011, available online at http://newsinfo.inquirer.net/3409/video-texts-of-brazil-school-shooter-show-anger.

92. "Brazilian School Shooter."

93. Wellington de Oliveira, "Wellington de Oliveira's Suicide Note," trans. unknown, presumed April 7, 2011, available online at http://www.schoolshooters.info.

94. Tom Phillips, "Rio School Shooting: First Three Funerals Held for Victims," *Guardian* (UK), April 8, 2011, http://www.theguardian.com/world/2011/apr/08/rio-school-shooting-funerals.

95. Alaine Griffin and Josh Kovner, "Raising Adam Lanza," *Hartford Courant*, February 17, 2013, http://www.courant.com/news/connecticut/newtown-

sandy-hook-school-shooting/hc-raising-adam-lanza-20130217,0,3344563,print. story.

96. Andrew Solomon, "The Reckoning: The Father of the Sandy Hook Killer Searches for Answers," *New Yorker*, March 17, 2014, http://www. newyorker.com/reporting/2014/03/17/140317fa_fact_solomon?currentPage= all.

97. Kim Murphy, "Hairstylist Remembers Adam Lanza: 'I Thought He Couldn't Speak,'" *Los Angeles Times*, December 20, 2012, http://articles. latimes.com/2012/dec/20/nation/la-na-nn-hairstylist-adam-lanza-20121220.

98. Griffin and Kovner, "Raising Adam Lanza."

99. Barney Henderson, "Connecticut School Massacre: Adam Lanza 'Spent Hours Playing Call of Duty,'" *Telegraph* (UK), December 18, 2012, http:// www.telegraph.co.uk/news/worldnews/northamerica/usa/9752141/ Connecticut-school-massacre-Adam-Lanza-spent-hours-playing-Call-Of-Duty. html.

100. Erik Ortiz, "Newtown Gunman Adam Lanza May Have Wanted to Join Marines or Other Military," *New York Daily News*, December 20, 2012, http:// www.nydailynews.com/news/crime/adam-lanza-wanted-join-marines-article-1. 1224217.

101. Matthew Lysiak, *Newtown: An American Tragedy* (New York: Gallery, 2013), 56.

102. Pete Samson, "Mom Loves Those Kids More than Me: Mother 'Wanted Killer Son Put in Home,'" *Sun* (UK), December 20, 2012, http://www.thesun. co.uk/sol/homepage/news/4706448/adam-lanza-flipped-mum-psychiatric-home-plans.html.

103. Dave Altimari, Edmund H. Mahony, and Jon Lender, "Adam Lanza Researched Mass Murderers, Sources Say," *Hartford Courant*, March 13, 2013, http://articles.courant.com/2013-03-13/news/hc-newtown-lanza-mass-murderers-20130313_1_adam-lanza-nancy-lanza-mary-scherlach.

104. "Adam Lanza Kept Spreadsheet of Murderers for Years before Newtown Shooting: Report," *Huffington Post*, March 18, 2013, http://www. huffingtonpost.com/2013/03/18/adam-lanza-spreadsheet_n_2901377.html.

105. Griffin and Kovner, "Raising Adam Lanza."

106. Murphy, "Hairstylist Remembers."

107. Matthew Lysiak, "Inside the Mind of Newtown Killer Adam Lanza," *New York Daily News*, December 19, 2012, http://www.nydailynews.com/ news/national/exclusive-mind-newtown-killer-article-1.1223612.

108. Stephen J. Sedensky, "Report of the State's Attorney for the Judicial District of Danbury on the Shootings at Sandy Hook Elementary School and 36 Yogananda Street, Newtown, Connecticut on December 14, 2012" (Connecticut: Office of the State's Attorney, Division of Criminal Justice, November 25, 2013), 34, http://www.ct.gov/csao/lib/csao/Sandy_Hook_Final_Report. pdf.

109. Lysiak, *Newtown*, 23.

110. Solomon, "The Reckoning."

111. Lysiak, *Newtown*, 43, 48.

112. David Halbfinger, "A Gunman, Recalled as Intelligent and Shy, Who Left Few Footprints in Life," *New York Times*, December 14, 2012, http://www.nytimes.com/2012/12/15/nyregion/adam-lanza-an-enigma-who-is-now-identified-as-a-mass-killer.html?smid=tw-share&_r=0&pagewanted=all.

113. E. Fuller Torrey, *Surviving Schizophrenia: A Manual for Families, Patients, and Providers, Fifth Edition* (New York: HarperCollins, 2006), 4.

114. Torrey, *Surviving Schizophrenia*, 5.

115. Torrey, *Surviving Schizophrenia*, 7.

116. Torrey, *Surviving Schizophrenia*, 9.

117. Torrey, *Surviving Schizophrenia*, 12.

118. Sedensky, "Report of the State's Attorney," 34.

119. Halbfinger, "A Gunman, Recalled."

120. Sedensky, "Report of the State's Attorney," 33.

121. Lysiak, *Newtown*, 36.

122. Solomon, "The Reckoning."

123. Sedensky, "Report of the State's Attorney," 27.

124. Solomon, "The Reckoning."

125. Joel Kaplan, George Papajohn, and Eric Zorn, *Murder of Innocence: The Tragic Life and Final Rampage of Laurie Dann, "The Schoolhouse Killer"* (New York: Warner Books, 1990). All the information on Dann in this chapter is from this source.

126. Kaplan, Papajohn, and Zorn, *Murder of Innocence*, 9.

127. Kaplan, Papajohn, and Zorn, *Murder of Innocence*, 48–49.

128. Kaplan, Papajohn, and Zorn, *Murder of Innocence*, 13.

129. Kaplan, Papajohn, and Zorn, *Murder of Innocence*, 62, 67.

130. Kaplan, Papajohn, and Zorn, *Murder of Innocence*, 76–77.

131. Kaplan, Papajohn, and Zorn, *Murder of Innocence*, 136.

132. Kaplan, Papajohn, and Zorn, *Murder of Innocence*, 142.

133. Kaplan, Papajohn, and Zorn, *Murder of Innocence*, 200.

134. Kaplan, Papajohn, and Zorn, *Murder of Innocence*, 200.

135. Kaplan, Papajohn, and Zorn, *Murder of Innocence*, 184.

136. Kaplan, Papajohn, and Zorn, *Murder of Innocence*, 186.

137. Kaplan, Papajohn, and Zorn, *Murder of Innocence*, 56.

138. Kaplan, Papajohn, and Zorn, *Murder of Innocence*, 298.

139. Nancy McWilliams, *Psychoanalytic Diagnosis: Understanding Personality Structure in the Clinical Process*, 2nd ed. (New York: Guilford, 2011), 165.

140. Theodore Millon and Roger Davis, "Ten Subtypes of Psychopathy," in *Psychopathy; Antisocial, Criminal, and Violent Behavior*, ed. Theodore Millon et al., 164 (New York: Guilford, 1998).

141. Millon and Davis, "Ten Subtypes," 164.

142. Montgomery Brower, Bonnie Bell, Dennis Breo, Jody Brott, Judy Hevrdejs, Barbara Kleban Mills, Civia Tamarkin, and Justin Greenberg, "Mad Enough to Kill," *People*, June 6, 1988, http://www.people.com/people/archive/article/0,,20099121,00.html.

143. "Second Victim Dies after School Shooting Incident," *New York Times*, September 30, 1988, http://www.nytimes.com/1988/09/30/us/second-victim-dies-after-school-shooting-incident.html.

144. Richard Greer, "Shooting Suspect Kept Thinking of Own Unhappy School Days," *Houston Chronicle*, September 30, 1988, A7.

145. *Wilson v. Ozmint*, United States Court of Appeals, Fourth Circuit, No. 03-3 (CA-02-2030-0-10BD), (2004), 18–19.

146. Emily C. Paavola, "Mental Disability and the Death Penalty: Why South Carolina Should Ban the Execution of the Severely Mentally Disabled," report by the Center for Capital Litigation Columbia, SC: Center for Capital Litigation, 2009), 13.

147. "Second Victim Dies."

148. Greer, "Shooting Suspect," A7.

149. Paavola, "Mental Disability," 13.

150. Olivia Fecteau, "Proving Mental Illness in Legal System Is like 'Trying to Prove the Sun Sets,' Says Blume," *Chronicle Online* (Cornell University), February 25, 2011, http://news.cornell.edu/stories/2011/02/case-sheds-light-due-process-mentally-impaired.

151. International Secretariat Amnesty International, "United States of America: The Execution of Mentally Ill Offenders; Summary Report," (New York: Amnesty International, January 31, 2006), 31.

152. Greer, "Shooting Suspect," A7.

153. *Wilson v. Ozmint*, 19.

154. Greer, "Shooting Suspect," A7.

155. Kara Gormley, "18 Years on Death Row: Background of a Killer," *WISTV.com*, November 14, 2006, http://www.wistv.com/story/5679368/18-years-on-death-row-background-of-a-killer.

156. International Secretariat Amnesty International, "United States of America," 32.

157. International Secretariat Amnesty International, "United States of America," 35.

158. Lord Cullen, "The Public Inquiry into the Shootings at Dunblane Primary School on 13 March 1996" (Scotland: The Stationery Office, October 16, 1996), available online at https://www.ssaa.org.au/research/1996/1996-10-16_public-inquiry-dunblane-lord-cullen.pdf. Unless otherwise noted, the information on Hamilton in this chapter is from this source.

159. Cullen, "The Public Inquiry," 20.

160. Tribunals of Inquiry, "Transcripts of Proceedings at the Public Inquiry into Incident at Dunblane Primary School on 13th March, 1996" (Stirling, Scotland: Tribunals of Inquiry, May 29, 1996), 735 (see note), available online at http://www.scotland.gov.uk/Resource/Doc/158868/0043149.pdf. The pagination of the transcript is erroneous; hence, the page numbers cited here and in subsequent notes for this source refer to the pages of the PDF file itself.

161. Tribunals of Inquiry, "Transcripts of the Proceedings," 855.

162. Tribunals of Inquiry, "Transcripts of the Proceedings," 784.

163. Cullen, "The Public Inquiry," 24.

164. Cullen, "The Public Inquiry," 25.
165. Tribunals of Inquiry, "Transcripts of the Proceedings," 1,118.
166. Tribunals of Inquiry, "Transcripts of the Proceedings," 1,637.
167. Tribunals of Inquiry, "Transcripts of the Proceedings," 449.
168. Cullen, "The Public Inquiry," 55.
169. Tribunals of Inquiry, "Transcripts of the Proceedings," 275.
170. Cullen, "The Public Inquiry," 48.
171. Tribunals of Inquiry, "Transcripts of the Proceedings," 1,208.
172. Cullen, "The Public Inquiry," 47.
173. Cullen, "The Public Inquiry," 54.
174. Tribunals of Inquiry, "Transcripts of the Proceedings," 2,016.
175. Tribunals of Inquiry, "Transcripts of the Proceedings," 2,016.
176. Millon and Davis, "Ten Subtypes," 163.
177. Theodore Millon, *Disorders of Personality: DSM-IV and Beyond*, 2nd ed. (New York: John Wiley & Sons, 1996), 452.
178. Millon, *Disorders of Personality*, 490.
179. Ngoc Huynh, "Jiverly Wong's Father: What Prompted Mass Killing in Binghamton Remains a Mystery," *Post-Standard* (central New York), April 13, 2009, available online at http://www.syracuse.com/news/index.ssf/2009/04/jiverly_wongs_father_our_son_w.html.
180. Manny Fernandez and Nate Schweber, "Binghamton Killer Kept His Fury Private," *New York Times*, April 12, 2009, http://www.nytimes.com/2009/04/12/nyregion/12binghamton.html?scp=1&sq=Until+a+Sudden,+Final+Barrage&st=nyt&_r=0.
181. Fernandez and Schweber, "Binghamton Killer."
182. Fernandez and Schweber, "Binghamton Killer."
183. Ray Rivera and Nate Schweber, "Before Killings, Hints of Plans and Grievance," *New York Times*, April 5, 2009, http://www.nytimes.com/2009/04/05/nyregion/05suspect.html.
184. Joe Kemp, Matthew Lysiak, and Corky Siemaszko, "Who Is Jiverly Voong aka Jiverly Wong? Conflicting Picture of Binghamton Gunman Emerges," *New York Daily News*, April 4, 2009, http://www.nydailynews.com/news/jiverly-voong-aka-jiverly-wong-conflicting-picture-binghamton-gunman-emerges-article-1.359248.
185. Fernandez and Schweber, "Binghamton Killer."
186. Huynh, "Jiverly Wong's Father."
187. Rivera and Schweber, "Before Killings."
188. Kemp, Lysiak, and Siemaszko, "Who Is Jiverly Voong."
189. Kemp, Lysiak, and Siemaszko, "Who Is Jiverly Voong."
190. Huynh, "Jiverly Wong's Father."
191. Huynh, "Jiverly Wong's Father."
192. Jiverly Wong, "Jiverly Wong's Suicide Note," transcription, March 18, 2009, available online at http://www.schoolshooters.info.
193. Huynh, "Jiverly Wong's Father."
194. Wong, "Jiverly Wong's Suicide Note."

8. PATTERNS AMONG SCHOOL SHOOTERS

1. Eric Madfis and Jack Levin, "School Rampage in International Perspective: The Salience of Cumulative Strain Theory," in *School Shootings: International Research, Case Studies, and Concepts for Prevention*, ed. Nils Böckler et al., 82, 85 (New York: Springer, 2013).

2. James Blair, Derek Mitchell, and Karina Blair, *The Psychopath: Emotion and the Brain* (Malden, MA: Blackwell, 2005), 33.

3. Niels Peter Rygaard, "Psychopathic Children: Indicators of Organic Dysfunction," in *Psychopathy: Antisocial, Criminal, and Violent Behavior*," ed. Theodore Millon et al., 254 (New York: Guilford, 1998).

4. American Psychological Association, "Gun Violence: Prediction, Prevention, and Policy," APA panel of experts report (Washington, DC: American Psychological Association, 2013), 8, http://www.apa.org/pubs/info/reports/gun-violence-prevention.aspx.

5. Elliot Rodger, "My Twisted World: The Story of Elliot Rodger," n.d., 15, available online at http://www.nytimes.com/interactive/2014/05/25/us/shooting-document.html?_r=0.

6. Rodger, "My Twisted World," 16.

7. Rodger, "My Twisted World," 16.

8. Samuel Yochelson and Stanton Samenow, *The Criminal Personality: Volume 1; A Profile for Change* (New York: Jason Aronson, 1976), 205.

9. Joel Kaplan, George Papajohn, and Eric Zorn, *Murder of Innocence: The Tragic Life and Final Rampage of Laurie Dann, "The Schoolhouse Killer"* (New York: Warner Books, 1990), 9.

10. Kaplan, Papajohn, and Zorn, *Murder of Innocence*, 12.

11. John Douglas and Mark Olshaker, *Mind Hunter: Inside the FBI's Elite Serial Crime Unit* (New York: Pocket Books, 1996), 106.

12. Janet Warren, Robert R. Hazelwood, and Park Dietz, "The Sexually Sadistic Serial Killer," in *Serial and Mass Murder: Theory, Research, and Practice*, ed. Thomas O'Reilly-Fleming, 82 (Toronto: Canadian Scholars' Press, 1996).

13. Stanton Samenow, *Inside the Criminal Mind*, revised and updated (New York: Crown, 2004), 170.

14. Gary M. Lavergne, *A Sniper in the Tower: The Charles Whitman Murders* (Denton: University of North Texas Press, 1997), 30–33.

15. Chris Cobb and Bob Avery, *The Rape of a Normal Mind* (Markham, Ontario: PaperJacks, 1977), 39.

16. Jane Applegate, "10 Years after Murderous Rampage, Campus Killer Says He Is Now Sane," *Los Angeles Times*, July 6, 1986, http://articles.latimes.com/1986-07-06/local/me-23088_1_murderous-rampage.

17. Nelson Kempsky, Gary A. Binkerd, Phil Yee, Allen Benitez, and Richard Yarvis, "A Report to Attorney General John K. Van de Kamp on Patrick Edward Purdy and the Cleveland School Killings" (California: Department of Justice, 1989), available online at http://www.schoolshooters.info.

18. Marc Lépine, "Marc Lépine's Suicide Note," December 6, 1989 (presumed), available online at http://www.schoolshooters.info.

19. Jonathan Fast, *Ceremonial Violence: A Psychological Explanation of School Shootings* (New York: Overlook, 2008), 26.

20. Vicki Cheng, "Robbins' Mother Struggles to Comprehend HUB Shooting," *Centre Daily Times* (central Pennsylvania), August 24, 1997.

21. Jefferson County Sheriff's Office, "Columbine Documents: 10,001–10,937" (Jefferson County, CO: Jefferson County Sheriff's Office, n.d.), 10,087–88, available online at http://www.schoolshooters.info.

22. Rich Gibson, "Lonely Privilege in Despair: Aiming for Unfeigned Hope," in *The Evolution of Alienation: Trauma, Promise, and the Millennium*, ed. Lauren Langman and Devorah Kalekin-Fishman, 163 (New York: Rowman & Littlefield, 2006).

23. *State of North Carolina v. Alvaro Rafael Castillo*, No. COA10-814 (2010), 11, available online at http://www.schoolshooters.info.

24. "Gill Bought Guns from Club Linked to Fabrikant," *Toronto Star*, September 15, 2006.

25. US Department of Justice, Bureau of Alcohol, Tobacco, Firearms, and Explosives, "Official Report on Duane Morrison," 2006, 53, available online at http://www.schoolshooters.info.

26. Finland Ministry of Justice, "Jokela School Shooting on 7 November 2007: Report of the Investigation Commission," translation of the original Finish report (Helsinki: Ministry of Justice, Finland, 2009), 51, available online at http://www.schoolshooters.info.

27. David Vann, *Last Day on Earth: A Portrait of the NIU School Shooter* (Athens: University of Georgia Press, 2011), 43.

28. Finland Ministry of Justice, "Kauhajoki School Shooting on 23 September 2008: Report of the Investigation Commission," translation of the original Finish report (Vantaa: Ministry of Justice, Finland, 2010), 59, available online at http://www.schoolshooters.info.

29. Petra Von Bornhöft, Klaus Brinkbäumer, Ulrike Demmer, Wiebke Hollersen, Simone Kaiser, Sebastian Knauer, Ansbert Kneip, Sven Röbel, Samiha Shafy, Holger Stark, and Katja Thimm, "113 Kugeln Kalte Wut," *Der Spiegel*, March 16, 2009, http://www.spiegel.de/spiegel/print/d-64628264.html.

30. Ivan Moreno, "Bruco Strong Eagle Eastwood, Deer Creek Middle School Shooter, Tells Authorities He Heard Voices," *Huffington Post*, March 12, 2010, http://www.huffingtonpost.com/2010/03/12/bruco-strong-eagle-eastwo_1_n_496935.html.

31. Matthew Lysiak, *Newtown: An American Tragedy* (New York: Gallery Books, 2013), 70–71.

32. John M. Broder, "Arizona Gunman Chose Victims in Advance," *New York Times*, October 30, 2002, http://www.nytimes.com/2002/10/30/us/arizona-gunman-chose-victims-in-advance.html.

33. Julia Jüttner, "German School Shooter: Armed to the Teeth and Crying for Help," *Der Spiegel*, November 21, 2006, http://www.spiegel.de/

international/german-school-shooting-armed-to-the-teeth-and-crying-for-help-a-449814.html.

34. Katherine Newman, *Rampage: The Social Roots of School Shootings* (New York: Basic, 2004), 269.

35. Lysiak, *Newtown*, 69.

36. Lysiak, *Newtown*, 70.

37. Lysiak, *Newtown*, 71.

38. Matthew Lysiak and Rich Schapiro, "Exclusive: Adam Lanza's Murder Spree at Sandy Hook May Have Been 'Act of Revenge,'" *Daily News*, April 7, 2013, http://www.nydailynews.com/news/national/lanza-article-1.1309766.

39. Vicki Cheng, "Who Is Jillian Robbins?" *Centre Daily Times* (central Pennsylvania), October 13, 1996.

40. "Lad in Ontario Shooting Spree Called Above-Average Student," *Lewiston Daily Sun*, May 29, 1975, 27.

41. Barry Brown, "Ontario Shootings Fuel Call for Gun Control," *Buffalo News*, October 23, 1994, A8.

42. Cheng, "Robbins' Mother Struggles."

43. "Who Was Kimveer Gill? (Part 3)," *Gazette (Montreal)*, September 4, 2008, http://www2.canada.com/montrealgazette/news/saturdayextra/story.html?id=a8279d1a-e4a1-43ae-95eb-44281d49c7ef&p=3.

44. CTV.ca News Staff, "Mother of Marc Lépine Finally Breaks Her Silence," September 25, 2006, available online at http://web.archive.org/web/20090418004957/http://www.ctv.ca/servlet/ArticleNews/print/CTVNews/20060925/lepine_mother_060925/20060925/?hub=Canada&subhub=PrintStory.

45. Kaplan, Papajohn, and Zorn, *Murder of Innocence*, 43.

46. Joseph A. Lieberman, *School Shootings* (New York: Kensington, 2008), 53.

47. Jon Bellini, *Child's Prey* (New York: Kensington, 2001), 16.

48. Bellini, *Child's Prey*, 61.

49. Lavergne, *A Sniper*, 23–24.

50. Lavergne, *A Sniper*, 51.

51. Stephen J. Sedensky, "Report of the State's Attorney for the Judicial District of Danbury on the Shootings at Sandy Hook Elementary School and 36 Yogananda Street, Newtown, Connecticut on December 14, 2012" (Connecticut: Office of the State's Attorney, Division of Criminal Justice, November 25, 2013), 30, http://www.ct.gov/csao/lib/csao/Sandy_Hook_Final_Report.pdf..

52. Pete Samson, "Mom Loves Those Kids More than Me: Mother 'Wanted Killer Son Put in Home,'" *Sun* (UK), December 20, 2012, http://www.thesun.co.uk/sol/homepage/news/4706448/adam-lanza-flipped-mum-psychiatric-home-plans.html.

53. Lysiak, *Newtown*, 50, 62.

54. Beth Karas, "Insanity Defense Takes Center Stage," CNN.com, August 12, 2009, http://insession.blogs.cnn.com/2009/08/12/insanity-defense-takes-center-stage/.

55. Cobb and Avery, *The Rape*, 61.

56. Cobb and Avery, *The Rape*, 60.

57. Cobb and Avery, *The Rape*, 178–79.

58. Lavergne, *A Sniper*, 46–56.

59. Kempsky et al., "A Report to Attorney General."

60. Kaplan, Papajohn, and Zorn, *Murder of Innocence*, 44–45.

61. Vann, *Last Day on Earth*, 30–32.

62. Northern Illinois University, "Report of the February 14, 2008, Shootings at Northern Illinois University" (DeKalb: Northern Illinois University, 2008), 24, available online at http://www.schoolshooters.info.

63. "Transcript of Video Linked to Santa Barbara Mass Shooting," *CNN*, May 24, 2014, http://www.cnn.com/2014/05/24/us/elliot-rodger-video-transcript/.

64. Kaplan, Papajohn, and Zorn, *Murder of Innocence*, 59.

65. Lysiak, *Newtown*, 22.

66. Monique Lépine and Harold Gagné, *Aftermath: The Mother of Marc Lépine Tells the Story of Her Life Before and After the Montreal Massacre*, trans. Diana Halfpenny (Toronto: Viking, 2008), 151–52.

67. Northern Illinois University, "Report of the February 14, 2008, Shootings," 21.

68. Lavergne, *A Sniper*, 26.

69. Ray Rivera and Nate Schweber, "Before Killings, Hints of Plans and Grievance," *New York Times*, April 5, 2009, http://www.nytimes.com/2009/04/05/nyregion/05suspect.html.

70. Richard Meyer, "When the Shooting Stops," *Los Angeles Times*, April 22, 2000, http://articles.latimes.com/2000/apr/22/news/ss-24169.

71. Jefferson County Sheriff's Office, "Columbine Documents: JC-001-025923 through JC-001-026859" (Jefferson County, CO: Jefferson County Sheriff's Office, n.d.), 26,859, available online at http://www.schoolshooters.info.

72. Northern Illinois University, "Report of the February 14, 2008, Shootings," 36.

73. 48 Hours, "The Mind of a School Shooter," *CBS News*, April 14, 2004, http://www.cbsnews.com/news/the-mind-of-a-school-shooter/.

74. "Woodham Testifies He Was Involved in Satanism," *CNN.com*, June 11, 1998.

75. 48 Hours, "The Mind of a School Shooter."

76. *People of the State of California v. Eric Christopher Houston*, S035190, Napa County Superior Court No. 14311 (2008), 86, available online at http://www.schoolshooters.info.

77. Edwin Chen, *Deadly Scholarship: The True Story of Lu Gang and Mass Murder in America's Heartland* (New York: Birch Lane Press, 1995), 151.

78. Vann, *Last Day on Earth*, 99.

79. "Carneal's Signals Went Unnoticed," *Kentucky Post*, September 6, 1999, 1K.

80. Dewey Cornell, *School Violence: Fears Versus Facts* (Mahwah, NJ: Lawrence Erlbaum, 2006), 44.

81. David Harding, Jal Mehta, and Katherine Newman, "No Exit: Mental Illness, Marginality, and School Violence in West Paducah, Kentucky," in *Deadly Lessons: Understanding Lethal School Violence*, edited by the National Research Council, 152 (Washington, DC: National Academies Press, 2003).

82. Jefferson County Sheriff's Office, "Columbine Documents: JC-001-025923 through JC-001-026859," 26,496.

83. Jefferson County Sheriff's Office, "Columbine Documents: JC-001-025923 through JC-001-026859," 26,189.

84. Jefferson County Sheriff's Office, "Columbine Documents: JC-001-025923 through JC-001-026859," 26,012.

85. Lynda V. Mapes, "Bloody Movie, Random Violence Thrilled Loukaitis, Classmates Say," *Spokesman Review* (Spokane, Washington), August 28, 1997, A1.

86. Ronald K. Fitten, "Loukaitis Jurors Hear Parents, See Pearl Jam Video—Mother, Father Testify in Trial of Teen Son," *Seattle Times*, September 9, 1997, B3, http://community.seattletimes.nwsource.com/archive/?date=19970909&slug=2559355.

87. Bonnie Harris, "School Killings All Too Familiar: Moses Lake Horror Parallels Plot of Novel Found in Suspect's Room," *Spokesman-Review* (Spokane, Washington), April 10, 1996, A1, http://www.spokesman.com/stories/1996/apr/10/school-killings-all-too-familiar-moses-lake/.

88. Stephen King, *The Bachman Books: Four Early Novels by Stephen King* (New York: Plume, 1985), 36.

89. Harris, "School Killings."

90. Harris, "School Killings."

91. King, *The Bachman Books*, 27.

92. Lynda V. Mapes, "Loukaitis Delusional, Expert Says Teen Was in a Trance When He Went on Rampage, Says Psychiatrist," *Spokesman-Review*, September 10, 1997, A1, http://www.spokesman.com/stories/1997/sep/10/loukaitis-delusional-expert-says-teen-was-in-a/.

9. PREVENTING SCHOOL SHOOTINGS

1. Matthew Lysiak, *Newtown: An American Tragedy* (New York: Gallery, 2013).

2. Jefferson County Sheriff's Office, "Columbine Documents: JC-001-025923 through JC-001-026859" (Jefferson County, CO: Jefferson County Sheriff's Office, n.d.), 26,317, 26,323, 26,331, 26,325, available online at http://www.schoolshooters.info.

3. Jefferson County Sheriff's Office, "Eric Harris's Diversion Documents," n.d., 55, available online at http://www.schoolshooters.info.

4. Brian Van Brunt, *Ending Campus Violence: New Approaches to Prevention* (New York: Routledge, 2012), xiv.

5. Dewey Cornell and Peter Sheras, *Guidelines for Responding to Student Threats of Violence* (Boston: Sopris West, 2006), 13–15.

6. Van Brunt, *Ending Campus Violence*, 54–55.

7. Mary Ellen O'Toole, "The School Shooter: A Threat Assessment Perspective" (Quantico, VA: FBI Academy, 2000), 32, http://www.fbi.gov/stats-services/publications/school-shooter.

8. James Alan Fox and Harvey Burstein, *Violence and Security on Campus: From Preschool Through College* (Santa Barbara, CA: Praeger, 2010), 68.

9. Jim Adams and James Malone, "Outsider's Destructive Behavior Spiraled into Violence, *Courier-Journal* (Louisville), March 18, 1999, 17A.

10. Katherine Newman, *Rampage: The Social Roots of School Shootings* (New York: Basic Books, 2004), 159.

11. Nadya Labi, "The Hunter and the Choirboy," *Time Magazine*, April 6, 1998, available online at http://content.time.com/time/magazine/article/0,9171,138881,00.html.

12. Joseph A. Lieberman, *School Shootings* (New York: Citadel, 2008), 94–5.

13. Jefferson County Sheriff's Office, "Columbine Documents: 10,001–10,937," 10,468.

14. Newman, *Rampage*, 94.

15. Newman, *Rampage*, 94.

16. Jefferson County Sheriff's Office, "Columbine Documents: 10,001–10,937," 10,415.

17. David Charter, "Finnish Gunman Matti Saari Burnt Bodies after Massacre, *TimesOnline* (UK), September 24, 2008, available online at http://archive.today/KLTAH.

18. John Scott Cowan, "Lessons from the Fabrikant File: A Report to the Board of Governors of Concordia University" (Montreal, Can. January 6, 1994), 5, available online at http://archives.concordia.ca/sites/default/files/uploaded-documents/pages/2011/07/26/Cowan_report.pdf.

19. Morris Wolfe, "Dr. Fabrikant's Solution," *Essays: New and Selected*, n.d., http://www.grubstreetbooks.ca/essays/fabrikant.html.

20. Cowan, "Lessons from the Fabrikant File," 7.

21. Cowan, "Lessons from the Fabrikant File," 5.

22. Van Brunt, *Ending Campus Violence*, 175.

23. Van Brunt, *Ending Campus Violence*, 285.

24. Nelson Kempsky, Gary A. Binkerd, Phil Yee, Allen Benitez, and Richard Yarvis, "A Report to Attorney General John K. Van de Kamp on Patrick Edward Purdy and the Cleveland School Killings" (California: Department of Justice, 1989), 6, available online at http://www.schoolshooters.info.

25. Monique Lépine and Harold Gagné, *Aftermath: The Mother of Marc Lépine Tells the Story of Her Life before and after the Montreal Massacre*, trans. Diana Halfpenny (Toronto: Viking, 2008), 191.

26. "Gill Bought Guns from Club Linked to Fabrikant," *Toronto Star*, September 15, 2006.

27. Catherine Tsai and P. Solomon Banda, "Police: Colorado Gunman Entered the School Earlier," *Associated Press*, February 25, 2010, available online at http://www.timesfreepress.com/news/2010/feb/25/police-colorado-gunman-entered-school-earlier/.

28. Richard Meyer, "When the Shooting Stops," *Los Angeles Times*, April 22, 2000, http://articles.latimes.com/2000/apr/22/news/ss-24169.

10. KEY FINDINGS

1. National Center for Education Statistics, "Student Reports of Bullying and Cyber-Bullying: Results From the 2011 School Crime Supplement to the National Crime Victimization Survey," (N.p.: US Department of Education, August 2013), 5, http://nces.ed.gov/pubs2013/2013329.pdf.

2. Lucile Packard Foundation for Children's Health, "Data from Student Survey Indicate Bullying, Harassment Widespread in California Schools," kidsdata.org, December 6, 2012, http://www.kidsdata.org/advisories/bullying.html.

3. Sandra Graham, "Bullying: A Module for Teachers," *American Psychological Association*, n.d., https://www.apa.org/education/k12/bullying.aspx.

4. James Alan Fox, "The Troubled Student and Campus Violence: New Approaches," *Chronicle of Higher Education*, November 14, 2008.

5. Katherine Newman, *Rampage: The Social Roots of School Shootings* (New York: Basic Books, 2004), 124.

6. Peter Langman, *Why Kids Kill: Inside the Minds of School Shooters* (New York: Palgrave Macmillan, 2009), 138.

7. Alv A. Dahl, "Psychopathy and Psychiatric Comorbidity," in *Psychopathy: Antisocial, Criminal and Violent Behavior*, ed. Theodore Millon, Erik Simonsen, Morten Birket-Smith, and Roger D. Davis, 296–98 (New York: Guilford, 1998).

8. Samuel Yochelson and Stanton Samenow, *The Criminal Personality: Volume 1; A Profile for Change* (New York: Jason Aronson, 1976), 265.

9. Yochelson and Samenow, *The Criminal Personality*, 267.

10. Eric Harris, "Eric Harris's Journal, April 10, 1998–April 3, 1999." Transc. and annot. Peter Langman, 1, available online at http://www.schoolshooters.info.

11. Harris, "Eric Harris's Journal," 3.

12. Harris, "Eric Harris's Journal," 8.

13. Yochelson and Samenow, *The Criminal Personality*, 473.

14. Yochelson and Samenow, *The Criminal Personality*, 285.

15. "Mitchell Johnson Deposition" (Fayetteville, AR: Craighead County, April 2, 2007), 68–69, available online at http://www.schoolshooters.info.

16. Andrew Wolfson, "Michael Carneal Tells His Story," *Courier-Journal* (Louisville, KY), September 12, 2002, 1A.

17. Joseph Lieberman, *School Shootings* (New York: Kensington, 2008), 2.

18. Jon Bellini, *Child's Prey* (New York: Kensington: 2001), 270.

19. John Cloud, "The Troubled Life of Jared Loughner," *Time*, January 15, 2011, http://content.time.com/time/magazine/article/0,9171,2042358,00.html.

20. Cloud, "The Troubled Life."

21. Kate Pickert and John Cloud, "If You Think Someone Is Mentally Ill: Loughner's Six Warning Signs," *Time*, January 11, 2011, http://content.time.com/time/nation/article/0,8599,2041733,00.html.

22. Dan Barry, "A Jigsaw Picture of an Accused Killer," *New York Times*, January 15, 2011, available online at http://www.nytimes.com/2011/01/16/us/16loughner.html?_r=1&pagewanted=all.

23. Erica Goode, Serge F. Kovaleski, Jack Healy, and Dan Frosch, "Before Gunfire, Hints of 'Bad News,'" *New York Times*, August 26, 2012, http://www.nytimes.com/2012/08/27/us/before-gunfire-in-colorado-theater-hints-of-bad-news-about-james-holmes.html?pagewanted=all.

SELECTED BIBLIOGRAPHY

All the sources cited in this book are included in the endnotes. For many shooters, however, there were one or two primary sources that provided most or all of the information I utilized. Those sources are listed here, with the shooters arranged alphabetically. Any of the sources that are in the public domain (such as court cases, official reports, and documents I compiled) are available at http://www. schoolshooters.info. There were no primary sources for Asa Coon, Wellington de Oliveira, Bruco Eastwood, One Goh, Jason Hoffman, Tim Kretschmer, Thomas "T. J." Lane, Barry Loukaitis, Robert Steinhäuser, James Wilson, and Jiverly Wong.

Allaway, Edward

Smith, Nicole. "The Quiet Custodian." *Tusk Magazine*, May 15, 2006. Available online at http://www.hearstfdn.org/hearst_journalism/competitions.php?type=Writing&year=2007&id=1.

Auvinen, Pekka-Eric

Finland Ministry of Justice. "Jokela School Shooting on 7 November 2007: Report of the Investigation Commission." Translation of the original Finish report. Helsinki: Ministry of Justice, Finland, 2009. Available online at http://www.schoolshooters.info.

Bishop, Amy

Wallace, Amy. "What Made This University Scientist Snap?" *Wired*, February 28, 2011. http://www.wired.com/2011/02/ff_bishop/all/.

Carneal, Michael

Harding, David, Jal Mehta, and Katherine Newman. "No Exit: Mental Illness, Marginality, and School Violence in West Paducah, Kentucky." In *Deadly Lessons: Understanding Lethal School Violence*, edited by the National Research Council, 132–62. Washington, DC: National Academies Press, 2003.

Newman, Katherine. *Rampage: The Social Roots of School Shootings*. New York: Basic, 2004.

Castillo, Alvaro

State of North Carolina v. Alvaro Rafael Castillo, No. COA10-814. 2010. Available online at http://www.schoolshooters.info.

Cho, Seung Hui

TriData Division, System Planning Corporation. "Mass Shootings at Virginia Tech: Addendum to the Report of the Review Panel." Arlington, VA: TriData Division, 2009. Available online at http://www.schoolshooters.info.

Dann, Laurie

Kaplan, Joel, George Papajohn, and Eric Zorn. *Murder of Innocence: The Tragic Life and Final Rampage of Laurie Dann, "The Schoolhouse Killer."* New York: Warner Books, 1990.

Fabrikant, Valery

Cowan, John Scott. "Lessons from the Fabrikant File: A Report to the Board of Governors of Concordia University." Montreal, Can. January 6, 1994. Available online at http://archives.concordia.ca/

sites/default/files/uploaded-documents/pages/2011/07/26/
Cowan_report.pdf.

Wolfe, Morris. "Dr. Fabrikant's Solution." *Essays: New and Selected*, n.d. http://www.grubstreetbooks.ca/essays/fabrikant.html.

Flores, Robert

De Haven, Helen Hickey. "The Elephant in the Ivory Tower: Rampages in Higher Education and the Case for Institutional Liability." *Journal of College and University Law* 35 (2009): 503–612.

Gill, Kimveer

Gazette (Montreal). "Who Was Kimveer Gill?" Parts 1–3, September 4, 2008. http://www.canada.com/montrealgazette/story.html?id=c7b3f15e-9cdd-4e52-8d86-c1d59e6cff0b&k=40661.

Golden, Andrew

Fox, Cybelle, Wendy D. Roth, and Katherine Newman. "A Deadly Partnership: Lethal Violence in an Arkansas Middle School." In *Deadly Lessons: Understanding Lethal School Violence*, edited by the National Research Council, 101–31. Washington, DC: National Academies Press, 2003.

Newman, Katherine. *Rampage: The Social Roots of School Shootings*. New York: Basic, 2004.

Hainstock, Eric

Lueders, Bill. "Eric Hainstock: Free at Last." *Isthmus/Daily Page*, July 31, 2008. http://www.thedailypage.com/isthmus/article.php?article=23349.

———. "The Life of Eric Hainstock: A Timeline." *Isthmus/Daily Page*, July 31, 2008. http://www.thedailypage.com/isthmus/article.php?article=23364.

Halder, Biswanath

De Haven, Helen Hickey. "The Elephant in the Ivory Tower: Rampages in Higher Education and the Case for Institutional Liability." *Journal of College and University Law* 35 (2009): 503–612.

Hamilton, Thomas

Cullen, Lord. "The Public Inquiry into the Shootings at Dunblane Primary School on 13 March 1996." Scotland: The Stationery Office, October 16, 1996. Available online at https://www.ssaa. org.au/research/1996/1996-10-16_public-inquiry-dunblane-lord-cullen.pdf.

Tribunals of Inquiry. "Transcripts of Proceedings at the Public Inquiry into Incident at Dunblane Primary School on 13th March, 1996." Stirling, Scotland: Tribunals of Inquiry, May 29, 1996. Available online at http://www.scotland.gov.uk/Resource/Doc/158868/0043149.pdf.

Harris, Eric

Harris, Eric. "Eric Harris's Journal, April 10, 1998–April 3, 1999." Transcribed and annotated by Peter Langman. Available online at http://www.schoolshooters.info.

Houston, Eric

People of the State of California v. Eric Christopher Houston, S035190, Napa County Superior Court No. 14311. Available online at http://www.schoolshooters.info.

Johnson, Mitchell

Fox, Cybelle, Wendy D. Roth, and Katherine Newman. "A Deadly Partnership: Lethal Violence in an Arkansas Middle School." In *Deadly Lessons: Understanding Lethal School Violence*, edited by the National Research Council, 101–31. Washington, DC: National Academies Press, 2003.

Newman, Katherine. *Rampage: The Social Roots of School Shootings*. New York: Basic, 2004.

Kazmierczak, Steven

Northern Illinois University. "Report of the February 14, 2008, Shootings at Northern Illinois University." DeKalb: Northern Illinois University, 2008. Available online at http://www.schoolshooters.info.

Kinkel, Kip

Lieberman, Joseph A. *School Shootings: What Every Parent and Educator Needs to Know to Protect Our Children*. New York: Kensington, 2008.

Klebold, Dylan

Klebold, Dylan. "Dylan Klebold's Journal and Other Writings." Transcribed and annotated by Peter Langman. N.d. Available online at http://www.schoolshooters.info.

Lanza, Adam

Lysiak, Matthew. *Newtown: An American Tragedy*. New York: Gallery, 2013.

Sedensky, Stephen J. "Report of the State's Attorney for the Judicial District of Danbury on the Shootings at Sandy Hook Elementary School and 36 Yogananda Street, Newtown, Connecticut on December 14, 2012." Connecticut: Office of the State's Attorney, Division of Criminal Justice, November 25, 2013. http://www.ct.gov/csao/lib/csao/Sandy_Hook_Final_Report.pdf.

Lépine, Marc

Lépine, Monique, and Harold Gagné. *Aftermath: The Mother of Marc Lépine Tells the Story of Her Life before and after the Montreal Massacre*. Translated by Diana Halfpenny. Toronto: Viking, 2008.

Lo, Wayne

Fast, Jonathan. *Ceremonial Violence: A Psychological Explanation of School Shootings*. New York: Overlook, 2008.

Gibson, Gregory. *Gone Boy: A Walkabout*. New York: Anchor Books, 2000.

Lu, Gang

Chen, Edwin. *Deadly Scholarship: The True Story of Lu Gang and Mass Murder in America's Heartland*. New York: Birch Lane Press, 1995.

Odighizuwa, Peter

De Haven, Helen Hickey. "The Elephant in the Ivory Tower: Rampages in Higher Education and the Case for Institutional Liability." *Journal of College and University Law* 35 (2009): 503–612.

Pennington, Gary Scott

Buckley, Jerry, "The Tragedy in Room 108: An Angry Teen Killed His Teacher and Forever Changed a Kentucky Town." *U.S. News & World Report*, October 31, 1993. http://www.usnews.com/news/articles/1993/10/31/the-tragedy-in-room-108.

Fast, Jonathan. *Ceremonial Violence: A Psychological Explanation of School Shootings*. New York: Overlook, 2008.

Poulin, Robert

Cobb, Chris, and Bob Avery. *The Rape of a Normal Mind*. Markham, Ontario: PaperJacks, 1977.

Purdy, Patrick

Kempsky, Nelson, Gary A. Binkerd, Phil Yee, Allen Benitez, and Richard Yarvis. "A Report to Attorney General John K. Van de Kamp on Patrick Edward Purdy and the Cleveland School Killings." California: Department of Justice, 1989. Available online at http://www.schoolshooters.info.

Ramsey, Evan

Fainaru, Steve. "Alaska School Murders: A Window on Teen Rage." *Boston Globe*, October 18, 1998.

———. "A Tragedy Was Preceded by Many Overlooked Signals." *Boston Globe*, October 19, 1998.

———. "Many Struggle to Put Their World Together." *Boston Globe*, October 20, 1998.

Robbins, Jillian

Cheng, Vicki. "Who Is Jillian Robbins?" *Centre Daily Times* (central Pennsylvania), October 13, 1996.

Rouse, Jamie

Meyer, Richard E. "When the Shooting Stops." *Los Angeles Times*, April 22, 2000. http://articles.latimes.com/2000/apr/22/news/ss-24169.

Saari, Matti

Finland Ministry of Justice. "Kauhajoki School Shooting on 23 September 2008: Report of the Investigation Commission." Translation of the original Finish report. Vantaa: Ministry of Justice, Finland, 2010. Available online at http://www.schoolshooters.info.

Spencer, Brenda

Hart, Eric. *Does Anyone Like Mondays? The Brenda Spencer Murder Case*. N.p.: Hart Publishing, LLC, 2012.

Weise, Jeffrey

Langman, Peter. "Jeffrey Weise: Timeline." N.d. http://www. schoolshooters.info.

Whitman, Charles

Lavergne, Gary M. *A Sniper in the Tower: The Charles Whitman Murders*. Denton: University of North Texas Press, 1997.

Woodham, Luke

Bellini, Jon. *Child's Prey*. New York: Kensington, 2001.

Wurst, Andrew

DeJong, William, Joel Epstein, and Thomas Hart. "Bad Things Happen in Good Communities: The Rampage Shooting in Edinboro, Pennsylvania, and Its Aftermath." In *Deadly Lessons: Understanding Lethal School Violence*, edited by the National Research Council, 70–100. Washington, DC: National Academies Press, 2003.

INDEX

Carter High School, 60–62; École Polytechnique, 127–129; El Cajon, California, 70–72; Frontier Junior High School, 14–15; Granite Hills High School, 70–72; Gutenberg School, 23–25; Heath High School, 34–37; Hubbard Woods Elementary, 143–147; influence of previous, 38–39; Jokela High School, 47–50; Northern Illinois University (NIU), 114–116; Northwestern University, 145; Oakland Elementary, 147–149; Oikos University, 123–125; Oliverhurst, California, 57–60; Orange High School, 44–47; Parker Middle School, 37–39; Pearl High School, 31–34; Pennsylvania State University, 129–131; prevented, 185; preventing, 181–193; primary, 149–153; Red Lake High School, 72–76, 181; reports prior to, 92; Richland High School, 62–64; St. Pius X High School, 7, 10; Sandy Hook Elementary, 140–142, 143; at schools attended in past, 134–143; Seinajoki University, 117–119; settings of, 200; SuccessTech Academy, 79–80; Tasso de Silveira Municipal School, 138–140; threat assessment, 183–184; Thurston High School, 39–42; University of Alabama, Huntsville (UAH), 99–102; University of Arizona, 91–93; University of Iowa, 86–88; University of Texas, 103–107; Virginia Polytechnic Institute and State University, 110–114, 190; warning signs, 118, 184–189; Weston High School, 76–78; Westside Middle School, 16–18, 68–70. *See also* misconceptions

Scotland, 149–153

secondary school shooters: defined, 2; psychopathic, 5–28; psychotic, 29–53; suicide rate among, 204–205; traumatized, 55–83; typology percentages among, 206–207. *See also* psychopathic secondary school shooters; *specific perpetrators*

Seinajoki University, 117–119

sexual abuse, 66; identity and, 57; trauma from, 56

sexual bondage, 7, 28

"The Sexually Sadistic Serial Killer," 160

sexual orientation, 59

Shan, Linhua, 86–88

Shapiro, David, 52

Sheras, Peter, 183–184

shootings. *See* school shootings

sibling rivalry, 173–174

Sigana, Michelle, 75

Simon's Rock College, 107–110

Slobodian, Michael, 162

social class, 200

South Carolina, 147–149

South Korea, 123

Speck, Richard, 106

Spencer, Brenda, 10–13, 21, 131

Spriesterbach Award, 87–88

Springfield, Oregon, 39–42

Steinhäuser, Robert, 23–25

stories, written by school shooters, 186–187

Stout, Martha, 13

Strand, James, 37

stress: financial, 94; PTSD, 55–56; in schizotypal personality disorder, 51

Student Bar Association, 95

students: threat assessment training of, 184; violence in writings of, 186–187

stuttering, 61

substance abuse, 174

subtypes, psychopath: abrasive, 88, 90, 92–93, 96, 99, 110; covetous, 147; disingenuous psychopath, 153; explosive, 22, 96, 107; malevolent, 15, 93; risk-taking, 13, 15; tyrannical, 22; unprincipled, 18, 25, 27, 110. *See also* personality types, psychopath

SuccessTech Academy, 79–80

suicide, schizophrenia and, 30, 204

suicide rates: among aberrant adults, 205–206; by age, 206; among college shooters, 205; comparative, 207; across populations, 204–205, 207; population with highest rate of, 204–205; in random and targeted attacks, 205; among school shooters, 203–206

ABOUT THE AUTHOR

Peter Langman, PhD, is a psychologist whose work on school shooters has received international recognition. His previous book, *Why Kids Kill: Inside the Minds of School Shooters*, was named an outstanding academic title by the American Library Association and was translated into German, Dutch, and Finnish. Dr. Langman's research has been cited in congressional testimony on Capitol Hill. He has been interviewed by the *Today Show*, the *New York Times*, CBS, Fox, CNN, the BBC, and over 150 other news outlets in the United States, Canada, Europe, Asia, Australia, and the Middle East. Dr. Langman served on the Pennsylvania Joint State Government Commission's Advisory Committee on Violence Prevention. After the Sandy Hook attack, his recommendations on school safety were presented by the CEO of the American Psychological Association to President Obama. Dr. Langman has trained thousands of professionals in education, mental health, and law enforcement in identifying potential school shooters. His website, http://www.schoolshooters.info, is the largest online collection of materials relating to school shooters. He is in private practice in Allentown, Pennsylvania. Dr. Langman is also a poet and playwright.